This book is not a manual on church strategy, metrics, or leadership theory. It is pastoral theology at its best. Written from the heart of the Lutheran tradition, *The Care of Souls* draws on the classical sources of Christian wisdom and reaches out to the entire Body of Christ. Every pastor, and everyone who wants to be a pastor, should read this book.

Timothy George
Founding Dean, Beeson Divinity School, Samford University;
General Editor, *Reformation Commentary on Scripture*

During my own seminary days, when there was a nascent but strong interest in classical Christian texts, new books focusing on real *Seelsorge* ("cure of souls") were very rare. Oden and Peterson were beginning to ring the bell. Though there is a genuine and extremely helpful discipline of psychology, psychological fads had supplanted genuine care of souls driven by the Word of God and the Sacraments. Since then, we've been delighted by a plethora of resources old and new. In Lutheran circles we've enjoyed the complete translation of C. F. W. Walther's pastoral theology as well as that of Wilhelm Loehe. Now Rev. Dr. Senkbeil reaches deep into the Scriptures under the influence of the best of the ancient and new experts on soul care, combines it with his rich pastoral experience, and provides us with an instant classic. The office of the ministry is, above all, about shepherding lost sheep into the fold, caring for them and retaining them for eternity. This book's moment has come, and it could hardly have a better author to lay its eternal wisdom before us.

Matthew C. Harrison
President of the Lutheran Church—Missouri Synod

Warm, personal, practical, born of years of experience, this book will provide encouragement and help to many pastors, not only Lutherans, but those of various confessions. Reading this work, one thinks not only of Luther ("experience alone makes a theologian"), but also Johann Gerhard, who understood theology as a "God-given habitus." Hal Senkbeil brings a rich reminder of this truth in its application to pastoral ministry.

Mark Seifrid
Professor of Exegetical Theology, Concordia Seminary, St Louis

Many pastors these days suffer from a crisis of identity. They're not sure of who they are or of what they're supposed to be. Which is perhaps why so many burnout or, worse yet, simply blow-up. That's why I am delighted to see Harold L. Senkbeil's *The Care of Souls: Cultivating a Pastor's Heart*. Distilled from his decades of pastoral experience and theological reflection, Senkbeil offers every confused or weary pastor a compelling invitation to return to the heart of the matter, to what it means to be a pastor—to shepherd God's sheep, to give to others only what we have first received from God, to cultivate a pastoral habitus in reliance upon the Spirit, to engage in the ministry of love. Filled with wisdom yet aflame with passion for the care of souls, this book is substantive without being stodgy, wise without being condescending, and practical without being superficial. I wish I would have read it years ago—and on a yearly basis ever since!

Todd Wilson
President of the Center for Pastor Theologians

Dr. Harold Senkbeil has distilled the wisdom that comes from long service in the church as a pastor, missionary, and seminary professor into this volume. His writing is rich and robust with biblical insight that has sustained pastors through the ages. His is a classical approach to shepherding that is attune to contemporary realities. *The Care of Souls* will be a welcome companion to both novice and veteran pastors who take seriously their Lord's mandate to faithfully tend His flock.

John T. Pless
Assistant Professor of Pastoral Ministry and Mission/Director of Field Education, Concordia Theological Seminary, Fort Wayne, IN

We live in challenging days for pastoral leadership, for many pastors are taking their cues in this vital area of the church's life from models alien to the Scriptures and the good traditions of the church. Hence, the need for solid works like this one from Harold Senkbeil that retrieve and crystallize what Scripture has to say about the ground of all true ministry leadership—the pastor's own spiritual formation. An enormously helpful work.

Michael A. G. Haykin
Professor of Church History and Biblical Spirituality,
The Southern Baptist Theological Seminary

As one who regularly interacts with the rising generation of theologically grounded, joyfully servant-hearted, missions-minded future pastors and church leaders, I can tell you what they need is an abundance of tried and tested mentors who are likewise grounded and focused but who also have a deep well of experience from which to draw from years of faithful ministry. Such are in short supply and this is why I am grateful for Harold L. Senkbeil's *The Care of Souls*. This book and its author give a well-rounded and thoughtful pastoral theology that will serve many."

Jason G. Duesing

Provost and Associate Professor of Historical Theology,
Midwestern Baptist Theological Seminary, Kansas City, Missouri

In *The Care of Souls* Harold Senkbeil draws on decades of hands-on parish ministry to offer a rich handbook for parsons and priests. I say handbook, because it's almost all here: the practice of listening; the attentive diagnostic analysis of the acute suffering, often repressed or displaced, that everyday people live with and deal with; the alternate pitfalls in ministry of giving up or hyper-activity; the inner/psychological side of surviving critics in the parish; and perhaps my favorite imperative, "Pray out loud!"

Pastor Harold also has his eye on contemporary issues such as pornography, the proper Christian resistance to cultural confusion and degeneration, and "the computer age." He comes across as an "old guy" who is wonderfully compassionate, nobody's fool, and absolutely Pauline in discipleship and practice.

In short, I wish Pastor Harold were my local minister. But if he can't be, at least I've got his book!"

Paul F. M. Zahl

Former President and Dean, Trinity Episcopal School for Ministry

Senkbeil combines personal experience in ministering to God's people, recounted in lively recollections, with immersion in God's Word and the presence of Christ it brings to depict the habitus—the character or nature—of the shepherd of God's people as Scripture shapes it. He invites readers to accompany him along his own journey through the church's daily life, and he shares with them the adventures that await the servants whom God calls to pastoral ministry. Here readers find descriptions and models of how listening to God in Scripture and to human conversation partners—and taking both seriously—sets the human stage for the way in which the Holy Spirit makes the gospel of Jesus Christ come alive for his people and brings them the comfort that comes as we stand before His cross and empty tomb.

Robert Kolb
Professor of Systematic Theology, Concordia Seminary,
Saint Louis

A pastor is not primarily a psychologist, an entrepreneur, or a C.E.O. According to classical Christianity, a pastor is a physician of souls. What physicians do for their patients—give them long-term care for their physical health and specific treatments when disease strikes—pastors do for their congregations, offering on-going spiritual care in their relationship with God and curing their souls in times of trial. This book recovers that dimension of the pastoral office, showing how to diagnose spiritual problems and how to treat them.

Drawing on vivid personal examples from his own ministry, Rev. Senkbeil covers the whole range of what pastors are called to do (from evangelism to ministry to the dying, from mundane administration to spiritual warfare) and the problems pastors must struggle with, both in their members and in themselves (sexual sin, spiritual boredom, burnout).

Rev. Senkbeil also takes the pressure off by reminding pastors that their ministry does not rest on their own doing, but that, by virtue of their office, Christ Himself is working through them.

You don't have to be a Lutheran to learn from this Lutheran pastor. And you don't have to be a pastor to find this book inspiring. As a layman, I found that this book opens up what all of my pastors have done for me.

Gene Edward Veith
author of *God at Work: Your Christian Vocation in All of Life*

No one is better equipped than Dr. Harold Senkbeil to write a book on the pastoral office.

It is *not* the usual "Pastoral Theology" handbook (these historically have been guides to Lutheran clergy as to how to tackle 895 confounding situations, counsel as to "how to respond"). Rather, it is a masterful theology of pastoral *Seelsorge* (as sinful healers attempting to always deliver Christ's healing to sinful and troubled souls).

Even with his use of word *habitus*, Senkbeil tries constantly to turn us pastors from wrongfully imagining that we are anything but sinners ourselves—great! But we are, more importantly, ambassadors of a sinless, divine Christ who *can* heal and is the Only One who can. Lord Jesus, be near our pastors!

Rod Rosenbladt
Professor Emeritus, Concordia University Irvine

Excellent for personal reflection and for pastoral study groups, *The Care of Souls* is an invitation to a safe place where we can reflect on our ministries in light of the incarnate Christ and in His caring body, the Church.

Dale A. Meyer
President, Concordia Seminary, St. Louis, MO

Summarizing nearly a half century of pastoral labor is no small task. Distilling such extended service into a useable overview with a compelling narrative is quite remarkable. Making such a volume serviceably practical is truly noteworthy. Pastor Harold Senkbeil's *The Care of Souls* informs and assists those entrusted with care of souls in the church by locating their service in the work of the Great Shepherd of the sheep and by sharing with us the gracious working of our Lord Christ in his own ministry. What a blessing this book is and will be for pastors!

Lawrence R. Rast Jr.
President, Concordia Theological Seminary (Fort Wayne, Indiana)

The Care
of Souls

The Care of Souls

CULTIVATING A PASTOR'S HEART

HAROLD L. SENKBEIL

Foreword by Michael Horton

LEXHAM PRESS

The Care of Souls: Cultivating a Pastor's Heart

Print ISBN 9781683593010
Digital ISBN 9781683593027

Lexham Editorial: Todd Hains, Eric Bosell, Erin Mangum
Cover Design: Kristen Cork
Typesetting: Abigail Stocker

Contents

133883

Foreword

B ooks on preaching, church leadership, vision, and strategy continue to flow from numerous presses. Pastors' conferences abound for those who want to learn how to reach particular niche demographics. And all the while, pastors are dropping out of ministry in droves and parishioners often feel that they must look elsewhere for real spiritual support.

What is going on? Why have so many who entered the ministry precisely in order to cure souls found it an intolerable burden? Why is there so much technique and so little help to aid those who aspire to be, more than anything else, *shepherds* of Christ's flock? Harold Senkbeil offers here not only the best explanation of this problem but the best alternative that I have seen in many years. A friend of many years, Harold has impressed me as one of the few real guides for how the gospel is applied in pastoral ministry. His first book of interest to me personally was *Dying to Live: The Power of Forgiveness* (1994). Sanctification—the theme of that book—is not "our part" in salvation; rather, it is Christ's work by his Spirit (always through the gospel). Driven by forgiveness and justification, the Christian life is true freedom. Growing in the grace, knowledge, and obedience of Christ is the result of being united to Christ himself—his person and his work.

The Care of Souls is of the same spirit, but it is written for pastors and it is a more thorough treatment of what the gospel means not just for others, but for the pastor as well. If the shepherd is not gospel-driven in his own life, it should not be surprising that the sheep experience a disconnect between justification and sanctification. Christ becomes the center of the one, but not of the other.

Yet this book is much more than a pastoral theology deduced from a central dogma. Besides being theologically-informed, anchored in the Reformation heritage, the insights of this volume are the fruit of a half-century of pastoral ministry, including many years of pastoring shepherds as well as sheep. Just as we can lose the joy of our salvation, we as ministers can lose the joy of our vocation.

Among younger evangelicals there has been a great renaissance of interest in the Reformation and its theology. This is very exciting. Yet it is remarkably thin. Justification, election and other truths of God's free grace in Christ are often lifted out of their wider gospel context. When it comes to actual pastoral ministry, however, many "Young, Restless and Reformed" pastors don't know where to turn and simply fall back on seminary courses or resources that are grounded in a quite different orientation. They may have learned a new doctrine. However, Reformation piety is not just a doctrine; it is a new way of conceiving God, humanity, salvation, vocations in the world, and the hope of resurrection. It is a new way of being a pastor, of leading God's people. Just as one cannot patch up an old wineskin, one cannot simply tack on a few Christ-centered doctrines to an essentially human-centered approach to pastoral ministry. The Reformation was not just about doctrinal correctness; it was about salvation, which can only be found in Christ—even for lifelong believers. Consequently, both Lutheran and Reformed traditions produced a large literature on the cure of souls. This legacy is largely unknown today. It is easy to tack on the "Five Points of Calvinism" or "Justification" to approaches to ministry that are fundamentally at odds with the basic insights of the Reformers. Many seem to assume that while the Reformation recovered a few important doctrines, one must turn elsewhere for rich expositions of biblical piety and pastoral ministry. This is to ignore the vast resources that can provide deeply-needed evangelical wisdom in our own day. There are many overlapping emphases between Lutheran and Reformed traditions, but each is a system with its own integrity. Their respective approaches to ministry, pastoral care and discipline are essential links in a broader interpretation of Christian faith and practice.

As a Reformed minister reading this volume, I could not help but think of Martin Bucer's *Concerning the True Care of Souls*. Martin Luther's contemporary and a mentor of John Calvin, Bucer prefaced his remarks with the recognition, "For there are not a few who, as soon as anything is said about church discipline and order, are always crying out that we want to bring back the traditions and bondage of men." The Reformation did not cast off sixteen centuries of pastoral theology; instead, it returned the focus of the ministry to the public and private application of the word to the lives of God's people. Lutheran and Reformed confessions are next of kin, especially in comparison with the trajectories of pietism and revivalism that have infected Anglo-American evangelicalism. Both focus on Christ alone through faith alone as the source of justification, sanctification, and glorification. Both insist that sanctification is driven by the gospel. For both confessions the ministry of word and sacrament is central, the fountain of God's favor to sinners throughout their course in this life.

Nevertheless, the two confessions are different. And it is precisely in this difference that I find encouragement as well as fraternal correction and admonition. Evangelicals rarely encounter confessional Lutheran sources and this is a pity. This book constitutes persuasive evidence of the richness of distinct Lutheran emphases in relation to pastoral ministry. All of us need this wisdom.

Harold Senkbeil does not offer yet another how-to book. But it is also not mere theory. Instead, he focuses on the old theological concept of *habitus*: a disposition to one thing or another. One may have a propensity to become an artist, for example, without ever making an artistic product. The best soul doctors have recognized that their primary concern is less external practices and behaviors than the shape of the soul: its direction, purpose, course, and desires. Perhaps the maxim, "What is old is new again," applies here. Drawing on classic Lutheran sources, Harold's insights are remarkably relevant in our chaotic context today.

How does the formation of the pastor affect that of the sheep? How does joyful, confident ministry in Jesus' name infuse the whole body of Christ with a similar confidence? Can we recover the classic view of the pastor as a physician of the soul, providing diagnosis and treatment of issues that are at their core bound up with sin and grace?

Harold not only provides the needed arguments; drawing on his five decades of pastoring shepherds as well as sheep, he offers candid anecdotes and illustrations. This is a very practical book in the best sense, touching on concrete issues of pastoral ministry.

Readers will not agree with everything in this book. Lutheran and Reformed churches disagree on important matters. However, when it comes to the central concerns raised here, the traditions are at one— in some contrast with many who claim to be recovering Reformation emphases in our day, but with little to no actual connection with the living tradition of Lutheran or Reformed pastoral ministry. Lutherans in particular have a gift to offer to the wider Christian church. Over many decades now, I have come to appreciate the Lutheran elements in my own (Reformed) tradition, including a central commitment to word and sacrament ministry. Yet I have also come to appreciate the distinct voice of Luther and his heirs on many topics. Anyone who thinks that Luther has nothing to say about sanctification, church life and discipline, and pastors and pastoral ministry, will think differently after reading this book.

More important than the historical correction, all of us can only come away from *The Care of Souls* with a remarkably different view of what it means to be called to care for the sheep who belong to the one who cares for the shepherd as well. I hope that this book becomes standard reading now and in generations to come especially wherever thoughtful leaders are seeking a *practice* that truly follows from the good news.

Michael Horton, Ph.D.
J. Gresham Machen Professor of
Systematic Theology and Apologetics
Westminster Seminary California

Preface

"Of making many books, there is no end"
(Eccl 12:12).

Well, here's one more. And now that you've opened the cover, you can be sure I wrote it just for you. You could be a pastor, a student, or someone simply interested in how God forms shepherds of souls. Ideally you're all three. You could be a man or a woman; clergy or lay. But here's the deal: I hope you'll find something useful within the pages of this book no matter who you are. I've done the best I can with what I've been given—and my goal is to pass along to you some of the wisdom and insight I've received from others. I don't claim any unique authority. Frankly, if you run into someone who claims to be an expert at ministry, you should run the other way. That's the first thing you should know about this book: I don't pretend to have all the answers.

It's both foolhardy and dangerous to embark on pastoral work all by yourself. That is why Jesus sent his disciples out two by two, and that's why all the mission imperatives in the New Testament are in the plural. We are not solo entrepreneurs in this business, and it's not a business. It is rather a ministry that finds its source and goal in the eternal mission of the holy Trinity. All that was planned by the Father before the world began was accomplished in time by his only Son, Jesus Christ, our Lord and continues to be delivered day by day by the Holy Spirit who works through the preached word and sacraments administered in his name. A minister acts on behalf of another in a proxy capacity, bringing gifts that are not his own. Pastors are agents of the Lord Jesus, stewards working with him to administer God's gifts. We dare never venture out alone in pastoral work. We must consciously cultivate the company and support of colleagues in office.

Therefore, I dedicate this book to generations of pastors past, present, and future whose hope is in the Word made flesh—those stalwart men who went before us are true fathers without whose example we would be traveling blind. Those intrepid men who currently share our burdens and joys as we forge ahead are indispensable brothers in this quest. Those eager men who come after us are the sons whose paths we are preparing. Fathers, brothers, sons—we're all in this together, and not one of us is worthy of the office we hold. In fact, this office is bigger than any one of us—and all of us put together aren't worthy to tie the sandals of the One who first blazed the trail ahead and now calls us to follow in his steps.

This book was a long time in gestation. In many ways it's been a lifetime in development. In these pages I'll share various vignettes from my childhood on the farm that shaped me early on, together with snapshots of hands-on ministry as a window into what I learned from God's sinner-saints over nearly five decades. My beloved bride, Jane Nesset Senkbeil, has been at my side throughout, and she rightly shows up everywhere in this book. She is the love of my life and I think you'll see in these pages why she is the helper fit for me. I literally would not be who I am today without her.

This book didn't arise out of a vacuum. Many had a hand in its development. The idea for this book first surfaced in conversation with my treasured colleague, Dr. Beverly Yahnke. Bev and I have been involved in that conversation for nigh unto twenty years. Insights from her long experience as a Christian psychologist supporting church workers and their families were of incalculable value in the design and launch of DOXOLOGY: The Lutheran Center for Spiritual Care and Counsel (www.doxology.us). Almost since the very beginning, she has been pushing me to sit down and write a book for pastors. What I've learned from her and with her as founding co-executive directors for DOXOLOGY has profoundly influenced what you are about to read.

The theological and spiritual insights reflected in these pages stem from my study of the classical heritage of the "cure of souls," as it is called in the church's collective tradition. Two twentieth century champions of this classical legacy were especially influential for me. Thomas Oden, late professor of theology and ethics at Drew University, led his fellow "young fogies" in rebellion against fashionable modernist trends in theology to drink from the deeper wells of the pastoral theologians of classic antiquity and enlighten the rest of us. Likewise, Eugene Peterson, for many years parish pastor in suburban Baltimore and then professor of spiritual theology at Regent College in Vancouver, championed this classical approach steadily over the years despite the passing fads of many popular ministry trends. Together, their seminal writings have had tremendous influence on my own thinking as I reflect on all my years as a pastor and teacher of pastoral theology.

But without the pivotal influence of John Kleinig, emeritus Professor of Theology at Luther Campus, Adelaide, Australia, the book you have in your hands could never have taken shape. John's extraordinary exegetical insight and theological depth is combined with an amazing pastoral instinct. These ingredients for faithful ministry impact almost every page you are about to read. John's scholarly erudition and pastoral wisdom are matched only by his genuine warmth and good humor. He was an early advisor in the formation of DOXOLOGY and its training program, and we remain both friends and colleagues. The friendship of a theological giant like "Doctor John," as his former students affectionately call him, is remarkably humbling to this country boy. But when you consider that he too was raised on a small farm "down under," perhaps our parallel paths are not completely happenstance.

The editorial team at Lexham Press shared their remarkable expertise in print and digital media and effectively brought my words to your attention. Special thanks to Todd Hains, my very patient and considerate editor, whose diligent attention to detail made those words worth reading. Likewise, my deep appreciation to Jonathan Mayer of Scapegoat Studios, whose masterful illustrations illuminate the rural life of my childhood along with the core of the church's ministry, God's word and sacraments.

Sprinkled throughout this book you will hear my view on the importance of pastoral friendships; it's my conviction that the art of friendship has fallen on hard times among men—sadly, especially those engaged in ministry. One of the reasons this book is at last seeing the light of day is that I've been blessed with a remarkable friend who can also be a persistent nag. Lucas Woodford got on my case quite a few years ago to get this project going—and he's remained extraordinarily obstinate about it. This book's major themes took shape in the personal and professional give and take that has increasingly marked the deep friendship we've forged over the last decade. Augustine described his close friend Alypius as *frater cordis mei*—"my heart's brother." I thank God daily that Lucas is the Alypius who has greatly enriched my life and enlarged my vision for ministry. I pray God may likewise bless all of you with such friends and brothers in office.

" He said to him the third time, 'Simon, son of John, do you love me?' Peter was grieved because he said to him the third time, 'Do you love me?' and he said to him, 'Lord, you know everything; you know that I love you.' Jesus said to him, 'Feed my sheep' " (John 21:17).

This is the secret for sustainable pastoral work: You need to realize that you've got nothing to give to others that you yourself did not receive. Jesus loves you first, then you love him back by loving his sheep and lambs in his name and stead. If pastoral ministry is anything at all, it's a ministry of love. It's being one more link in the unbroken chain of love that extends all the way back to Calvary one dark Friday outside the city gates of Jerusalem. There they nailed up the Lord of life to die a cruel death he didn't deserve, but willingly— even joyfully—embraced so he could give us his own life to live, risen out of death and into life eternal.

No matter how compassionate and empathetic a pastor is, there's just no way he can come up with what it takes to feed the sheep of Christ effectively, much less tend to their spiritual heartaches, bruises, and injuries. He's going to run dry sooner or later, and most likely sooner. I learned that the hard way. As a young pastor, I thought the best I could do for people was to give them my own love and compassion. That was, of course, wrongheaded, but I didn't know it way back then. In those early years of ministry, I began to learn the lesson I'm still learning every day now nearly fifty years later: The best we pastors have to give Christ's sheep and lambs doesn't come from within; it comes from him. His love is perfected through us; it reaches its goal when we extend the love we've received from him. We love because he first loved us (1 John 4:11, 19).

And Christ's love never runs dry.

F inally, you should know this: I'm Lutheran in conviction and confession. But don't let that scare you. I've written this book expressly with you in mind, whether or not you share my doctrinal convictions. Every Christian confession has its own set of clichés and mantras. I've tried as best I could to avoid "Lutheran-speak" in these pages so you can capture my line of thought without getting bogged down in the lingo. Yet the discerning reader will quickly see my Lutheran garb is showing. The language of Luther's Catechism, for instance, shapes my thinking and articulation of the faith once delivered to the saints—just as your own tradition will color yours. Yet I'm happy to share what I've been given with you so that you can incorporate these insights into your own perspective on pastoral work. After all, Lutheran teaching is not narrowly sectarian, but genuinely ecumenical: "that ancient, united consensus believed in by the universal, orthodox churches of Christ and fought for and reaffirmed against many heresies and errors."[1]

---

1. "Preface to the Book of Concord," in *The Book of Concord: The Confessions of the Evangelical Lutheran Church*, eds. Robert Kolb and Timothy J. Wengert (Minneapolis: Fortress Press, 2000), 5.

I write these introductory lines on the day set apart on the church's liturgical calendar in thanksgiving for John the Baptizer, the forerunner of Jesus. That seems especially appropriate, for though I don't believe in "patron saints," I do think the saints of old have much to teach us by their example—John especially. If pastors had a patron among the saints, it would surely be he. John's testimony to his cousin Jesus is in many ways the subtext of this book—and I pray it will likewise impel you on toward excellence in ministry: "He must increase, but I must decrease." (John 3:30)

Harold L. Senkbeil
The Nativity of St. John the Baptist
June 2018

The Pastoral Craft

One Farm Boy's Story

M y childhood and youth were spent on a farm in western Minnesota—my father's farm and his father's before him. It wasn't much by modern standards, just a tiny patch of ground. But it was my whole world, and what a wonderful world it was. My mom and dad worked hard from earliest dawn until dusk, and sometimes late into the night. But somehow it didn't seem like work; it was life to them, and so it was my life too and my two sisters' lives once they came along.

My earliest childhood memories are bound up in the soil, the sun and rain, bright endless days of summer and the brisk, cold bite of winter winds, the icy crunch of hard-packed snow underfoot. There was the pungent smell of fields newly plowed, the sweet aroma of new-mown hay and, of course, the necessary stench of animal manure (what goes in one end must come out the other, after all). When you tend animals, you feed them. Then you clean up afterwards; it's a package deal.

My real apprenticeship in the ministry was served right there on that modest farm at my father's side. There was always work to be done and lots of it. Though my dad was rather laid back as farmers go, he was a hard worker. There were cows to be fed, hogs to be slopped, eggs to gather, manure to be shoveled, hay to be cut, baled, and stacked, corn first to be planted, then cultivated, later picked, then finally shelled, grain to be drilled and harvested. I learned from dad the invaluable lesson that the best work of all is work done for its own sake.

In my earliest years I watched my dad hitch his team of horses (faithful Pete and Colonel) to our two-row corn planter or the dump rake to heap dried brome grass into mounds to be gathered up, then piled high onto haystacks. Later in the season I would carry his lunch out to him as he labored under the hot July sun to lean bundles of oats or wheat up against each other in tent-like shocks by hand. And my first "big boy" job (at the tender age of six or seven) was driving the tractor as he deftly picked up those same bundles with a three-tined pitchfork and hoisted them up high onto a bundle wagon. Then together we would triumphantly haul the heavily laden wagon to the stationary threshing machine—a big, roaring belt-driven mechanical monster that chewed up the grain bundles in its steely jaws, digested the resulting bits and pieces in its internal system of rapidly shaking racks and sieves, poured out a bountiful stream of grain into a waiting wagon, and then spit out the leftover straw and chaff via a powerful blower-driven spout onto an ever-growing golden stack. Meanwhile, in the kitchen my mother and her helpers labored just as hard as the field hands over a hot oven and steaming kettles, preparing home-made bread and rolls, vast savory heaps of mashed potatoes, meat and gravy, tasty salads and vegetables, delectable pies and cakes to keep the ravenous threshing crew of neighborhood men and boys well-fed all day long.

I didn't know it then, but God was preparing me for pastoral work in that rustic rural setting so long ago. While I observed faithful animal husbandry and careful crop cultivation firsthand, he was laying the foundation for what I have been engaged in now for nearly five decades: the craft of the care and cure of souls.

LEARNING MY CRAFT

I thank God for every teacher I've had over the years, especially those who schooled me in Scripture and theology, the science ("knowledge") that lies at the heart of pastoral work. But equally important to the science of theology is the art of pastoral care. Every body of knowledge is incomplete without its corresponding art—its careful, deliberate application. So too knowledge and craftsmanship (science and art) belong together in pastoral formation; the one is incomplete without the other.

In retrospect, I now know that my pastoral education began quite early. Some of the science of theology I learned from my father and mother, who were my first catechists and teachers, schooling me to know and love the God who made me, redeemed me, and sanctified me. I learned my basic Bible lessons sitting between them in church and at our kitchen table, where each day was punctuated by prayer and my Sunday School lesson was dutifully previewed every Saturday night after the requisite weekly bath. Christian living was not so much taught as caught, for I saw it unfold before my eyes day by day as my parents loved me, corrected me, and forgave me.

I went on to higher things theologically, of course, studying the science of theology intensely first in college, then in seminary and graduate school—coming to grips with the accumulated wisdom of the great teachers of the church over the centuries. I came to a working knowledge of the biblical languages, and to this day I can still work my way through a Hebrew or Greek text (occasionally reverting to exegetical crutches). Over the years I've managed to acquire two earned degrees in theology and one honorary degree bestowed by an institution that considered my work somewhat noteworthy and useful. Yes, the science of theology is vitally important. But you need a lot more than book learning to be a pastor. So here are some extremely useful things about the art of pastoral care that I learned long ago back on the farm.

PATIENCE

On the farm, I learned to wait. One of my earliest memories as a child was walking out into the spring fields with my father to see how the corn was coming along. In my mind's eye I can still see him kneeling there in the dirt in those bib overalls he always wore, using his hardened, calloused farmer hands tenderly to brush the soil away from the swollen seeds he knew lay under that deep black Minnesota loam. Already in those cool May days he was checking for signs of germination, the first tiny sprout of life that would become a tall, vigorous stalk with dark green leaves waving in the bright August sunshine. But in his mind's eye he was looking far beyond tropical August to frosty October, when kernel-laden cobs would tumble out of the corn picker in a rich golden harvest.

In our hurry up world, patience is a short commodity. Especially among pastors, I might add. Now and then I hear from young pastors, recent grads, all of them. Most of them zealous, some of them gifted, but all of them bothered. And what bothers them? Lots of things actually. Sometimes it's something they wished they'd been taught in the seminary. Others, more honest, are bothered by something they wished they'd paid closer attention to in seminary. It's always gratifying to be asked to respond to these questions of either variety.

But the most satisfying questions fall into neither category. These are the questions that arise from the deep recesses of a genuinely pastoral heart: "Why do some people seem to pay no attention to God's word?" "Why is it that God's people often seem bent to self-destruction?" "What do you do when you're aching to tend the sheep, but they keep going off on their own?" Questions like that do my own heart good, for they are the sure sign of a true shepherd's soul.

If we can learn anything from the Scriptures and the ancient heritage of the care of souls, it's this: Impatient shepherds are their own worst enemy. We certainly don't want pastors to be slackers. All the same, souls are not won or kept by hectic activity, but by steady, deliberate work in service of Christ Jesus, who is the real bishop and guardian of souls. Whoever wants to provide real help in Christ's sheep pen had better keep one steady eye on the sheep and the other fixed on the Good Shepherd.

Frenetic busyness undermines careful pastoral work. You dare not rush the harvest. James frames the situation in words that sound quaintly antique to our twenty-first century ears, yet actually they're cutting edge and state of the art: "Be patient, therefore, brothers, until the coming of the Lord. See how the farmer waits for the precious fruit of the earth, being patient about it, until it receives the early and the late rains" (Jas 5:7).

My dad never studied agriculture, but he was a diligent and ardent farmer all his life. Remember him kneeling in that cornfield? Nary a plant could be seen, yet he knew that given enough time—plus the intervention of a very gracious God—that field would produce an abundant harvest. He also knew it couldn't be hurried along. Even the tender sprouted seeds uncovered in his search he carefully patted back in place into the nurturing soil. A good farmer waits. For farmers, patience is not only a virtue; it's a necessity. And that's true for pastors too.

So pastors need to hunker down for the whole growing season. The joy of the harvest awaits. You can't make the crop grow—but you can plant and you can tend while God gives the increase.

THE JOY OF WORK

It seems odd that there was so much joy in the work we did back then on the farm. It was hard, backbreaking labor; mostly done by hand. Haying time is but one example. Picture balancing yourself on a bouncing bale wagon, stabbing each seventy-five pound rectangular bale with a metal hook, then stacking it up on the growing stack behind you in one swift, sure motion. It required manly strength plus a dancer's agility.

Then after a long, hot, itchy day of baling hay came the daily closing ritual of evening chores: calling the cows, feeding them, milking them, and turning them out to pasture again. Then and only then came a refreshing shower, supper, and finally you fell exhausted into bed, only to get up and do it all over again the next day.

But I learned something in those scorching summer days so long ago: Work done for the right reason is its own reward. There were bills to be paid and income to be earned, but that side of farming didn't register much with this teenager. All I knew is that a field of new-mown hay raked into orderly symmetric windrows had a certain haunting beauty in the red glow of the setting sun (and a wondrously sweet fragrance all its own). There was something deeply satisfying that went with working hard all day long in the sweltering heat, knowing that the hay stacked so neatly up there in the haymow would sustain the cows in their stalls below all through the long frosty days of winter ahead.

Of course, we pastors work primarily with mind and heart, not muscles and brawn. Yet pastoral ministry likewise demands long hours of tireless labor in service of the Lord who sends out laborers into his harvest (Luke 10:2). It requires consistent, unbroken persistence to tend and feed the lambs and sheep of Christ who need to hear his voice and gather in the other sheep for whom he died (John 10:16). That work is never done; no sooner is one conversation finished than another beckons. Finish one sermon and there's another to prepare. Welcome one wandering sheep into Christ's flock, and there are hundreds more to evangelize. Baptize one new soul into the kingdom and he or she needs to keep on growing in the nurture and admonition of the Lord. Comfort one anguished, fearful heart and another takes its place. Guide one soul safely through the valley of the shadow of death to fall asleep in peace and someone else is at death's door. Jesus' sheep need his voice to find their way. That's where pastors come in. They are sent to preach and teach his word so Christ's lambs and sheep can hear his voice. Jesus commissions pastors to do his work among his sheep in his name and stead, and that work is never done.

Christ's sheep are not all that easy to tend. They have minds of their own. They tend to wander off in strange directions and get lost in the most dangerous predicaments. There are diseases to diagnose and treat, predators to warn against and fend off. And there is manure to shovel. There's always one mess or another to clean up in the church. There's good reason for that, because every believing soul is also a sinner, and sinners sin. Whether they sin against each other or their pastors, we are called to love them anyway and forgive them just as Jesus has.

And yet "whoever desires the office of bishop (pastor) desires a noble task" (1 Tim 3:1). The nobility of the office resides not in the man who holds the office, but in the Lord who has commissioned and sent him. And just as Jesus finds his delight in continually doing the work of the Father (John 5:17) so pastors continue to extend Jesus' work among his people. And here's the thing: The Lord of the church gives his ministry to pastors for their enjoyment; he gives them a front row seat in the drama of salvation. Pastors get to experience the joy of seeing Jesus at work through what they say and do in his name (John 15:11).

The lesson I learned on the farm has been reinforced for me in the ministry: Work done *for the right reason* is its own reward. Ministry can be a chore. Sometimes it's a pain. But remember my chores on the farm? Simply because they were burdensome and repetitious didn't mean they were without meaning or purpose. There's a strange beauty in the most menial (even distasteful) tasks of the ministry when you realize that they are Christ's tasks and that he works with you and through you for his purpose. Of course, if you're not careful you can burn yourself out in pastoral work. Sadly, thousands of pastors end up spiraling into emotional and spiritual collapse every year.

But when you take care to receive Christ's own love and strength by means of his Spirit through his word, you have something to give to others without yourself being depleted and emptied. Daily and richly the heavenly Father gives his Spirit to those who ask him (Luke 11:13). Empowered by the Spirit, you have the satisfaction of knowing that Christ Jesus works in you both to will and to do what pleases him and benefits his beloved church (Phil 2:13). That's when pastoral work becomes its own reward. Then you can find real satisfaction in a job well done, a foretaste of that joyous scene that awaits when Jesus welcomes all his servants to the eternal kingdom on the last day with the words: "Well done, good and faithful servant; you have been faithful over little; I will set you over much. Enter into your master's joy" (Matt 25:23). Yes, unimaginable joys lie ahead; you can count on that.

But tomorrow is another day. And tomorrow there will be more work to do.

What Is a Pastor?

The Classical Model

O nce you know who you are as a pastor, you'll be much more confident about what you're supposed to be doing as a pastor. And it seems to me that's the most frustrating thing about ministry in the twenty-first century. We've inherited multiple competing models of what a minister supposedly is, each with its corresponding job description. Many seem diametrically opposed. Is a pastor a chaplain or a missionary? Is he to focus on tending people who are already Christians, or on winning more people to a living faith in the Lord Jesus? Is the pastor a coach or care giver? Is he a manager or CEO of an organization or a preacher of God's word and steward of his sacred mysteries?

These various models aren't mutually exclusive. Winning souls and tending souls go together. Likewise management and leadership skills are helpful when it comes to the day-to-day life of the average Christian congregation in our world today. Yet that's just the point. Lots of things may be helpful, but which are necessary? Many things can be beneficial to the life and mission of the church, but which are essential? What should be the primary focus of our daily work as pastors? That's what I want to explore with you in this chapter. Let's take a look at the Scriptures and see what Jesus has to say about his church and her care. Let's discuss how Christ and the apostles understand the office of pastor and the nature of pastoral work. After that we'll consider how the church over the centuries has understood pastoral care.

CHRISTOCENTRIC PASTORAL CARE

"I decided to know nothing among you except Jesus Christ and him crucified," Paul wrote to the Christians in Corinth (1 Cor 2:2). There's a framework for pastoral work that translates well over the centuries; it's both transcultural and timely in that it connects with people groups no matter where or when they live. In our pluralistic and syncretistic era, Paul's words sound hopelessly stilted, narrow, opinionated, and— dare we say it?— downright intolerant. In an age when religious faith has been relegated to the narrow confines of personal experience and preference, language like this sounds off-putting. Nobody loves a hater. When inclusivity and tolerance are the norm and people are falling all over themselves to accommodate the diverse religious feelings of an increasingly eclectic and fragmented population, it's tempting to write Paul off as some kind of religious fanatic or bigot.

Yet the facts of the case are entirely different. Highly educated in both theology and the secular arts and sciences, Paul was thoroughly familiar with all the religious options of his day. During his far-flung missionary journeys he moved easily and comfortably between the radically different subcultures of the sprawling Roman Empire. He related naturally both to the common person and to the elite. For his time and place, he was a thoroughly modern man; fully aware of the intellectual, emotional, and religious sensitivities of a wide swath of diverse ethnicities. He moved confidently through the intricate layers of the social structure of his day, interacting comfortably with common citizens (Acts 16), elite intelligentsia (Acts 17), Roman bureaucrats (Acts 25), and Jewish potentates (Acts 26). Paul was no narrow-minded bigot. Why, then, despite all the diversity he encountered would he insist that his entire ministry be focused exclusively and explicitly on Jesus Christ and, of all things, his cross?

GOD ENFLESHED:
MYSTERY HIDDEN AND REVEALED

The answer lies in the unique identity of Jesus. He's not the Christian equivalent of Siddhartha Gautama, Confucius, Mohammed or, for that matter, Moses or Elijah. It's clear from the original sources that Jesus didn't see himself as one in a long line of religious teachers, but consciously and deliberately identified himself with the unseen and almighty Creator of heaven and earth (e.g., Luke 1:32; John 8:51). He was not just another religious teacher or guru, but he did things only God can do: He created all things (John 1:3), forgave sins (Matt 9:6), and claimed the power of God for the final judgment (Mark 14:62). There's compelling evidence that he was ultimately tried, convicted, and executed not for some capital crime under Roman law, but because he had the audacity to claim he was God's own Son—unspeakable blasphemy in the eyes of his own contemporaries (John 19:7).

That's why Paul the apostle was so intent on the person and work of Jesus. Though he spent the early part of his career ferreting out the first Christian followers for being adherents of what he considered a Jewish heresy (Acts 9:2), Paul had a spectacular change of mind and heart. After his dramatic conversion (9:4–6), he first carefully researched the Scriptures, then finally consulted with men who had been personally taught by Jesus (Gal 1:17–18). From then on Paul was absolutely enthralled and captivated with what he called "God's mystery" (Col 2:2): that the man Jesus, besides being fully human, was at one and the same time God.

"Mystery" means something beyond the reach of human sensory perception and intellect. And that's certainly true when it comes to the true identity of Jesus. No one could tell that Jesus was God just by looking at him. It's just the same today; no one can conclude that Jesus is God using human sensory and reasoning capacity alone; it remains an article of faith. Yet this faith is not a stab in the dark. It's grounded in the tangible reality of Jesus' human flesh and blood: born of his virgin mother, crucified, dead, and buried, but then on the third day raised from the dead—forty days later to ascend into glory. It sounds like a fairy tale, but it's not.

The mystery of Christ isn't the product of an overly creative religious imagination. This mystery didn't happen in some never-never land, but within the time-space reference of the men and women most intimately connected with Jesus. To cite one example: John the apostle was with Jesus the night of his betrayal (John 13:23). He stood at the foot of the cross the day Jesus was executed (19:27). He observed firsthand the open tomb (20:8) and was there one week later when Thomas pressed his incredulous fingers into the living flesh of Jesus (20:27).

Toward the end of his ministry, John testified that the message of the gospel was built around the tangible and audible evidence of his personal firsthand encounter with Jesus: "That which we have seen and heard we proclaim also to you, so that you too may have fellowship with the Father and with his Son Jesus Christ" (1 John 1:3). For John, the gospel was not merely a concept or abstract idea. He believed that the very life and ministry of Jesus and the forgiveness and life he came to bring was actively present and conveyed through his own apostolic ministry.

This is mystery in action: It is enacted and embodied in sensory form even among us still today. Jesus comes audibly and tangibly in human speech and actions, bridging time and space to connect with people in a completely different time and place. What remains hidden to human beings using only their senses and intellect is revealed and enacted in the preaching of the gospel and the administration of the sacraments. Thus in apostolic preaching and sacramental administration history repeats itself; Jesus is again present with his gifts. "That which was from the beginning, which we have heard, which we have seen with our eyes, which we looked upon and have touched with our hands, concerning the word of life" (1 John 1:1). John contended that in his preaching and teaching he was passing along exactly what he had received and heard from Jesus. In the baptizing, teaching, and communion of John and his fellow apostles, those early Christians who had never met Jesus during his earthly ministry themselves received exactly what the apostles did, plus *fellowship*—a real and genuine connection and communion—with God the Father and his beloved Son, Jesus Christ.

How does all this talk about mystery inform pastoral work and ministry in our time, you ask? That's simple—and yet quite profound. Mystery is by very nature both. Mystery remains forever inaccessible to human scrutiny. Yet mystery revealed provides access to the inaccessible. We all have little epiphanies (disclosures) of mystery in our ordinary human lives that give us a bit of insight here. For example, I love my wife more than life itself. Yet for all the 47 years our Lord has given us together, I find there's always something more to learn about Jane; there's no way I can completely plumb the depths of the mystery of our love and life. That's the very nature of mystery. There's always more to learn.

So if you've been worried that you don't quite have it together in ministry or that others are savvier when it comes to theology, lighten up on yourself. If you don't have all the answers, join the crowd. The best pastors among us are the ones who realize how little they actually know and how much more they have to master concerning the art of the care of souls. Soul care, too, is a mystery. The more it dawns on you, the more there's left to grasp.

Christ Jesus is himself God's great mystery "in whom are hidden all the treasures of wisdom and knowledge" (Col 2:3). In this man Jesus the disciples were in contact with the living God; he was their tangible link with eternity. Yet the more the disciples came to know Jesus, the more they realized there was yet to discover. His mystery revealed remains perpetually hidden. Yet in Jesus the almighty Maker of heaven and earth came down from heaven to give his life to the world, and the world has never been the same since.

THE HIDDEN WORK OF GOD

The very night of his "departure," as the gospel writers referred to his sacrificial suffering and death, one of the disciples of Jesus laid before him the nub of the issue: "Show us the Father," Phillip said, "and it is enough for us" (John 14:8). I think we can understand his frustration. Who hasn't ever yearned for incontrovertible proof of God's existence, some tangible evidence that he is actively working on our behalf? Jesus' answer has deep implications for how you and I still do ministry today: "Have I been with you so long, and you still do not know me, Philip? Whoever has seen me has seen the Father. How can you say, 'Show us the Father'? Do you not believe that I am in the Father and the Father is in me? The words that I say to you I do not speak on my own authority, but the Father who dwells in me does his works. Believe me that I am in the Father and the Father is in me, or else believe on account of the works themselves" (John 14:9–11).

Here the mystery is unveiled. Jesus contends that in his words and works God the Father was actively speaking and doing. "My Father is working until now, and I am working" (John 5:17). The word Jesus spoke on earth, he spoke as the divinely authorized Son of God. He exercised the power and authority of the Father in whatever he spoke and did. And it was never depleted. The more power and authority Jesus exercised, the more power and authority he had. When he forgave sins, sins were forgiven before God in heaven. When he healed the sick or raised the dead, God the Father was at work in him. Here is mystery, as simple and profound as it can ever get: Jesus the man is also God at one and the same time. When you met Jesus the only begotten Son of God, you met God himself. Clothed in the physical flesh of Jesus, all the fullness of the godhead was pleased to dwell bodily (Col 2:9). Hidden within him, God had come to take up residence on earth. And his power was inexhaustible. He never ran out of authority. The power and authority of Jesus the Son was the power and authority of God the eternal Father in action. With him it truly was a case of "like Father, like Son." And that's the situation still today. From his exalted throne in glory at the right hand of the Father, Jesus personally continues to forgive sins day by day, healing bruised and hurting souls, bestowing life and every blessing in this dying world by means of his spoken word. And here's the astounding thing: Still today, Jesus calls weak and fallible men like us into the pastoral office. He works through us to carry on the ministry of his profound mystery here on earth in the space and time in which we live.

It would be nice if God had given us a magic wand to erase the effects of sin and death, to undo the tangled web of deceit and corruption that has engulfed planet earth ever since our first parents rebelled against the Creator, making us all insurgents against the God who in the beginning made us holy like himself. But we pastors are not magicians and there is no incantation that can drive away the deathly spell that has fallen like a sullen pall over all the earth. We are not traffic cops and policemen, ferreting out sin and corralling scoundrels and reprobates, strong-arming people into swapping their vices for virtue in a corrupt and decaying world. We are not called to haul out trite and worn bits of "god talk" in a futile attempt to make people feel better. We're not commissioned to go around pasting smiley faces on human hurt and tragedy. We are not charged to throw around mantra-like formulas designed to cheer people up in the midst of bitter suffering and loss. Most certainly not—no magic for us. Nothing less than mystery will do, and that's exactly what we've been given.

Jesus promised: "Truly, truly, I say to you, whoever believes in me will also do the works that I do; and greater works than these will he do, because I am going to the Father" (John 14:12). That's exactly what happens in the pastoral ministry. Just as Jesus did his Father's work on earth so long ago, pastors carry on Jesus' work today. Daily they do and say what Jesus did and taught—and so through their very human work God the Father's will is done on earth as it is in heaven (Acts 1:1–2). Men, women, and children come into contact with Christ Jesus, the great mystery of God, through the work pastors do in his name and stead. Like the apostle John before them, pastors touch and handle things unseen. They speak words given by Jesus to his apostles, the very words that came from Jesus' lips were "spirit and life" (John 6:63). They give and bestow the power of the Holy Spirit, who is both Lord and giver of life eternal.

The wondrous thing is that this Spirit-filled, life-giving word of God comes in more than one way. In baptism the word of God is joined to the water so that it is a "washing of regeneration and renewing of the Holy Spirit" (Titus 3:5). Baptism is thus in effect a "liquid word." Likewise God gives us an edible word. In the sacrament of the altar, God joins his word to the elements of earthly bread and wine so that the sacred cup is a participation in the blood of Christ once shed for the forgiveness of sins, and the bread of the Lord's Supper is a participation in the very body once laid low in death to forever remove the sins of all the world (1 Cor 10:16).

Thus the essence of pastoral work is not just evoking vaguely religious feelings in people or providing them with a few platitudes to brighten their day. Pastors do not teach mere ideas or concepts; by their ministrations they bring Jesus himself into the hearts and lives of people ravaged with guilt, burdened with shame, and struggling under a boatload of pain in all its dimensions: physical, emotional, and spiritual. Into empty, hopeless lives, pastors bring transcendent peace and hope. We comfort others with the comfort with which we ourselves have been comforted by God (2 Cor 1:4). Wherever pastors bring the words and mysteries of Jesus, they bring Jesus himself, and he personally does the comforting. "Come unto me," he invites, "and

I will give you rest." So to every lonely, god-forsaken soul in every age, Jesus comes again by means of the word he gives pastors to speak and the sacraments he places into their hands to distribute.

MYSTERY AND MISSION

Whenever and wherever pastors do this work of Jesus, Jesus himself is present, even though he remains unseen. And where Jesus is present, there is peace once more even in the midst of distress and heartache. This is mystery in motion and mission: in every era actively inviting broken, shattered people from every land and nation into God's eternal kingdom. "And this gospel of the kingdom will be proclaimed throughout the whole world as a testimony to all nations, and then the end will come" (Matt 24:11). People have been scrambling to find some way of carrying out what seems to be an impossible task: making disciples in a world that seems with every passing year less and less inclined to become disciples. All kinds of methods have been borrowed from business, advertising, and the social sciences in service of Christ's commission. Yet the most important ingredient in that mission is often overlooked: the promised personal presence of Jesus by means of his word and sacrament. "Baptizing them in the name of the Father and of the Son and of the Holy Spirit, teaching them to observe all that I have commanded you. And behold, I am with you always, to the end of the age" (Matt 28:19–20).

It's time to call a halt to the false dichotomy between pastors and missionaries, between shepherding and evangelizing. The gospel and the sacraments of Jesus are given to his church to reach the lost, then gather them into his flock and tend them as his sheep and lambs. Wherever these mysteries are proclaimed and administered, Jesus is personally at work. By means of these mysteries Jesus is himself both evangelist and shepherd, both missionary and pastor. Most importantly, by these sacred means Jesus himself remains present with his church until the end of time to rescue, tend, and bless all his own.

WHAT IS A PASTOR?

There's a lot of confusion these days about what in the world pastors are supposed to be doing. To many people they're irrelevant vestiges left over from a simpler, more religious era. For others, pastors are nice to have on call to apply religious bandages to some of the bumps and bruises of life but otherwise not much needed. Even among deeply spiritual and religious people, ministers of the gospel are variously understood as spiritual traffic cops, chief executive officers or religious activity directors hired by churches; back-slappers, hand-holders or conflict managers; motivational speakers, perhaps.

Each of these roles comes with its own job description, of course. No wonder then that we find a lot of churches confused over what to expect from their pastors. No wonder we find pastors and church leaders frequently at loggerheads over conflicting and conflicted understandings of just what pastors should be doing. In fact, it's no wonder that every year promising young (and not so young) clergy are exiting active ministry. Sometimes, sadly, dysfunctional congregations drive them out of the ministry. Many times, though, they've simply given up on the work because they find it not only overwhelming and draining, but also depleting and discouraging. And who wouldn't become depleted and discouraged in this kind of situation? When you hand someone a job description so wide-ranging and complicated that it's unmanageable—or so nebulous and undefined that it can apparently be changed on whim—wouldn't that deplete and discourage the best of men?

The premise of this book is that action flows from being; identity defines activity. Thus a clearer vision of what the pastoral ministry is will lead to a clearer understanding of what a pastor does day by day. I'm going to suggest a radical idea: Let's get back to the root of the matter. "Radical" after all has to do with roots. And here's the root of the matter: When ministry is rooted in Jesus and his gifts, then that ministry will be all the more fruitful.

THE CLASSICAL DEFINITION

This chapter is about the classical model of pastoral care. The very nature of things classical is that they have a timeless quality of both substance and relevance. In all the classical arts there's an essential core of truth that easily connects with the endlessly shifting ebb and flow of passing time and circumstance. Instead of being bound to any one era or people group, classical approaches are adaptable to the vast spectrum of human experience. In a very real way, things truly classical are always contemporary. As important as it is to connect in a meaningful way with your present context, the problem is you can never link up in any substantial way with each succeeding current situation. Like a flowing river, the contemporary picture is forever in motion. No sooner do you grasp one aspect, but it starts to morph before your very eyes. As one wag has put it: "Whoever marries the culture is destined to be an early widower."

So then, effective and faithful pastoral ministry in each succeeding era must remain intimately connected with its essential core—the divinely given presence of Christ Jesus and the truth of his word by which alone we live. The challenge for pastors in every generation is to link the person and work of Jesus to every shifting era by means of his unchanging word—not to contextualize the message, but to textualize people into the text of Scripture, you could say. Thus the only really effective way to prepare for ministry in a meaningful way is to get a good grip on pastoral identity. This is the best way to do pastoral work with both flexibility and integrity. You need to know who you are before you can know what to do. Otherwise you'll forever be reinventing yourself to conform to rapidly shifting circumstances and expectations, and the ministry you carry on will be little more than a weak and pale imitation of the secular culture around you. When that happens, ministry is drawn from human experience rather than the living and abiding Word.

THE PASTORAL *HABITUS*

The classical texts of pastoral care have always called the cure of souls a *habitus*, a pastoral temperament or character worked by the Holy Spirit through his means. The ministry, you see, is never "one size fits all," and it's not "off the rack." You can't acquire all the necessary skills through classroom instruction or even mentoring designed for mass production. Seminaries are not factories churning out men with identical skill sets perfectly suited to the unique complexities of their particular era. While proficiency in biblical languages, church history, dogma, and pastoral skill are all prerequisites for ministry, the cure of souls is more of an art than a science. To make pastors you need the person and power of the Holy Spirit who forms and shapes men inwardly to be fit vessels for the treasures of God's transcendent and transforming gifts in his gospel and sacraments. None of these men are perfect vessels. Like Paul, pastors remain all their lives just "clay pots," inevitably warped and damaged by their own sin and the sins committed against them. Yet God is surpassingly rich in his grace. In the forgiveness and healing the Spirit brings them in Christ Jesus, pastors are given to share these gifts to other shattered souls like themselves "to show that the surpassing power belongs to God and not to us" (2 Cor 4:7).

A pastor's habituation, or character, is what counts most in ministry. This *habitus* can't be instilled merely through pedagogy or acquisition of intellectual knowledge, though instruction and knowledge remain vital and indispensable components in pastoral education. The great nineteenth-century American Lutheran theologian Carl Ferdinand Wilhelm Walther put it this way in his *Pastorale:*

> Pastoral theology is the God-given practical disposition of the soul [*pracktische Habitus der Seele*], acquired by certain means, by which a servant of the church is equipped to perform all the tasks that come to him in that capacity—validly, in a legitimate manner, to the glory of God, and for his own and his hearers' salvation.[1]

Every useful human endeavor is more than just mastering external skills; these flow from an inner attitude or aptitude developed by repetition. By practicing for years a musician grows not only in instrumental proficiency, but the artistic expression that informs reliably fine performances. A chef's expertise isn't merely a matter of external technique, but the internal intuition that results from years of habitually blending the right ingredients, timing, temperature, seasoning, and presentation that makes for consistently fine cuisine. And as you will see by my recurring stories throughout this book, a farmer learns his craft over time and experience as he is shaped by the very animals and crops he tends and harvests. Habit is not something you were born with; it's obtained over long experience.

---

1. C. F. W. Walther, *Pastoral Theology*, trans. Christian C. Tiews (St. Louis: Concordia Publishing House, 2017), 7; C. F. W. Walther, *Amerikanisch-Lutherische Pastoraltheologie* (St. Louis: Druckerei der Synode von Missouri, Ohio u. a. Staaten, 1872), 1.

It's no different when it comes to pastors. A "practical *habitus*" for ministry is never completely mastered. This "practical disposition" is acquired through a lifelong process by which the pastor as Christian goes on receiving what he brings to others. So for as long as he lives the pastor, like other children of God, treads the path of continual repentance and faith on his own personal pilgrimage back home to the Father's house. Daily he confesses his sins and daily he receives the Holy Spirit and everything that Jesus died to bring him: forgiveness of sins, life, and eternal salvation. This daily dying to sin and rising to new life through faith in Christ is the pivotal hinge in every Christian's life, and it's an essential ingredient in faithful and consistent care of souls. No pastor can give to others what he himself has not received. Turn that around and you have the very core of what pastoring is all about: giving out the gifts of God in Christ that you yourself receive by faith. The essence of pastoral work is to bring the gifts of the Good Shepherd to his sheep and lambs. And here's the well from which you can draw inexhaustible grace every day as a pastor: In the church the Holy Spirit daily and richly forgives all your sins along with the sins of all believers.

The pastoral *habitus* is "acquired by certain means," Walther contended. I think he was right. On the one hand it is a *charism*, a gift bestowed by the Holy Spirit when a man is set apart for public ministry on his ordination day by God's word and the prayer of the Christian assembly, consecrated for service in this holy office by the blessing of fellow pastors ("elders," 1 Tim 4:14), bestowed by the laying on of their hands. Yet just as the Holy Spirit is received not just once, but daily by meditation and prayer focused on the word of God, so a pastor is continually a work in progress. Daily his sinful nature is drowned and dies through contrition and repentance and a new man emerges and arises to live in righteousness and innocence through faith in the shed blood of Jesus.

Just so, pastoral skills are not acquired all at once, but honed and developed through deliberate and diligent interaction with the people of God. A genuinely pastoral demeanor and disposition grows within him as a pastor is actively engaged in the work of shepherding the flock in which the Holy Spirit has made him overseer. You learn by doing. Like other useful arts, pastoral work involves more than book learning. There's no substitute for practice when it comes to developing pastoral skills and aptitudes. As a pastor is actively engaged in visiting the sick, consoling the troubled, warning the hardened, and comforting the conscience-stricken, he learns to use the tools of his trade all the more skillfully and intelligently. Like any skilled artisan or craftsman, a pastor learns by both observation and doing. He learns his trade by practicing his craft. He is *habituated*—shaped and formed into a shepherd of souls—by being actively engaged in the work of shepherding. Gradually, almost imperceptibly it may seem, he is being continually shaped and molded into a confident workman that does not need to be ashamed, rightly dividing the word of truth (2 Tim 2:15).

DOWN ON THE FARM

My dad learned the art of farming the same way. He was born in 1915 in the farmhouse his father had built for his mother back in 1906 and lived there himself after he took his own bride in 1943 until health issues forced them off the farm some forty years later. His farming experience spanned the bitter years of the great drought—the "Dirty Thirties"—and the economic squalor of the Great Depression. That double whammy was enough to test the mettle of any farmer. But hardship alone didn't shape what he became. My dad had acquired the *habitus* of farming day by day long before during his boyhood working at his father's side, diligently plying the trade he was to practice for the rest of his life.

My father learned the art of animal husbandry by tending animals: trimming the great hooves of our work horses so they wouldn't impede the sure-footed traction required to pull heavy implements around the fields, helping a young heifer through the difficult delivery of her first calf, then ensuring that it found its way to the nutrient-rich first milk of its mother. Dad learned to keep vigil with every brood sow in our hog pen at the first signs of labor and impending delivery, watching to make sure she wouldn't accidentally roll over on one of her piglets after they came squealing into this world. Occasionally he would bring the scrawniest pig in the litter into our house to be kept warm in a box near the wood stove and bottle-fed; those little "runts" just couldn't compete with their larger littermates all hungrily jostling for a good suckling position.

My father's *habitus* included agronomy skills as well. As a young man in the days before hybrid seed corn he practiced good plant genetics by setting aside the largest ears from the annual corn harvest to be kept for seed the next spring. Late each winter he would test sample kernels from each of those promising cobs to see if it would germinate and sprout. Unpollinated ears couldn't generate any new plants and would be used for animal feed. My dad could gauge the moisture content of hay by its smell, its heft and feel; you couldn't rake moist hay into a stack or store it in bales because it would ferment and spoil. Wet hay stored in haymows was sometimes known to spontaneously combust with disastrous results. So you needed a good nose and practiced hands to detect when hay was dry enough to process.

Likewise dad could tell just by biting a kernel of oats or wheat between his teeth if it was ready for harvest. Before the era of grain dryers every crop was dried naturally by sun and wind; combining or threshing too early could result in fermentation and more spoilage. My father knew the precise conditions of the soil needed for proper tillage. If it contained too much moisture, the plow wouldn't "scour"—turn the topsoil over thoroughly and cleanly—leaving precious compost from the previous season's crops lying uselessly on the soil surface.

CRAFTSMEN AND CRAFTSMANSHIP

I know. I'm reminiscing again. And like any kid, I'm bragging on my father a little in the process. But these personal vignettes from those farming methods of yesteryear support my point: Every constructive field in human endeavor has its corresponding *habitus*. Through his immersion in the farming enterprise and his long involvement in it, my dad acquired the *habitus* of farming. What he did was one piece with who he was; conversely who he was determined what he did. There's a lesson here for faithful and joy-filled ministry, despite the long hours and heavy emotional and spiritual investment. We need a "nose" for pastoral work, you might say, and a practiced hand when it comes to caring for Christ's lambs and sheep. That's what we can learn from skilled pastors who've gone before us. And if you are blessed with an experienced contemporary colleague in ministry who serves as your mentor and confidante, so much the better. But ultimately, there's nothing that takes the place of hands-on work—dedicated, determined effort in service of the Lord who bought the flock with his own blood (Acts 20:28). We learn by doing. That's how we develop our pastoral nose; that's how you and I become habituated into the pastoral calling. And it's a cyclical process. For while we faithfully practice our craft from one day to the next, we acquire a pastoral *habitus* for the long haul and our work comes more and more naturally to us.

When the habits of a *habitus* begin to inhabit a workman, he becomes a craftsman and his work a true craft.

Notice you don't adopt a *habitus*; you acquire it. You might say you don't find a *habitus*, rather the *habitus* finds you. When "occupation" becomes vocation, when calling and work merge as one, it's a happy combination in any line of work. When your work becomes more purposeful and fulfilling, then you know you're well on your way toward acquiring a *habitus*, no matter what you do day by day. Farmers, physicians, dads, moms, computer programmers—or the proverbial butcher, baker, and candlestick maker—there's a *habitus* that informs and shapes every essential enterprise.

There's a lot about pastoral work that still frustrates and pains me after all these years, yet to this day there's a sense of quiet contentment and satisfaction in a sermon well-crafted and delivered, a soul consoled and strengthened, hearts enlightened and inspired through faithful teaching. It's the very same satisfaction and peace I experienced as a youth after a very long day of exhausting manual labor, gazing at a field of new-mown alfalfa neatly windrowed in the waning light of the setting sun, waiting for the harvest. That, I think, is genuine *habitus*: doing all you've been given to do in the full realization that you're only an instrument for the Lord to do his work through you.

There is nothing better for a person than that he should eat and drink and find enjoyment in his toil. This also, I saw, is from the hand of God, for apart from him who can eat or who can have enjoyment? (Eccl 2:24–25)

STEWARDS OF GOD'S MYSTERIES

The core of the pastoral *habitus* revolves around what I've been talking about in the pages above: mystery. If the content and source of ministry is Jesus Christ, the central mystery of God, then pastors are themselves stewards of that mystery. In contrast, if you and I see ourselves merely as peddlers or purveyors of a spiritual "message," we rapidly become salesmen for the gospel instead of true ministers of the gospel. That is, we're always scrambling to persuade reluctant customers to buy our product, rather than serving as emissaries sent by God to issue his perennial joyous invitation toward genuine freedom and release: "Repent and believe the good news" (Mark 1:15).

Paul had a clear understanding of his identity that influenced his life as a pastor: "This is how one should regard us, as servants of Christ and stewards of the mysteries of God" (1 Cor 4:1). A steward is never a salesman, but an agent. He serves in place of another. Pastors are true agents of Jesus, speaking his words and doing his works: forgiving sins, comforting souls, dispensing Christ's own hope and life in a despairing and dying world.

SERVANTS OF JESUS

If you and I as pastors persist in seeing ourselves as servants merely at the beck and call of the people we serve, then we're forever in flux and never really free to serve them well. If we measure our worth by public opinion, we'll always be tempted to give people what they want instead of what they need. As a young pastor I was eager to get people to like me, and I was crushed one day when I discovered a couple who had been my great fans were bitterly disappointed in me over their son's experience in our youth group. For a guy who likes to be liked, that was hard to take. I got over it, but that was the beginning of an important lesson in ministry.

You and I are people persons, and it's never easy to discover we've disappointed someone. Callous disregard for people's feelings isn't the way to go either. Yet measuring our worth by our popularity is deadly. That's been a persistent temptation throughout my years in ministry. In the last parish I served we went through major turmoil over the nature of the church's worship, and the internal strife and personal attacks nearly did me in. In both cases I had mistakenly begun to measure my worth by public opinion rather than faithfulness to what I'd been given to do. Take it from me: That attitude is a killer. It can deplete and deflate your ministry overnight.

On the other hand, if we're truly servants of Christ, we're simply what I like to call "errand boys for Jesus"—giving out his divine gifts for the healing and strengthening of those we serve in his name. This is not an elitist understanding of the ministry that separates us from people. Nor does this view elevate us to a pedestal of prestige. Being a steward of God's mysteries actually binds us closer to people rather than distancing us from them. Remember the scene of Jesus with his disciples at supper in that upper room the night of his betrayal? He made the rounds among them, humbly washing all their feet one after another. The instructions he gave those apostles afterwards serve as the hallmark of faithful ministry to this day: "If I then, your Lord and Teacher, have washed your feet, you also ought to wash one another's feet" (John 13:14). The Lord who wrapped himself in a servant's towel to wash grimy dirty feet that night sends his men out today to do the same. The title "servant of Christ" does not isolate pastors in a sterile bubble, but it connects them all the more intimately with people in all their earthy humanity.

One of my deathbed calls illustrates this pretty well.

LIFE IN THE MIDST OF DEATH

Let's call her Roberta; she was clearly near the end of a very long journey toward death's door. Roberta's cancer was a particularly nasty variety; by now it had eaten its way into most of her vital organs. The scarf that concealed her balding head bore silent testimony to the radical regimen of chemotherapy her body had endured in a vain attempt to stave off death. She extended a weak hand and a wan smile to greet her pastor. Her skin was pasty and cold to the touch, her breaths labored and shallow, exuding the sweetly sour smell of impending death. Though her eyes were losing their luster she gladly, eagerly heard the word of God, clinging to every syllable. "Would you like the Lord's Supper?" I asked. "Oh yes," she whispered in her weak little voice.

We launched into the timeless ritual of all the faithful, Roberta and me. The meal that nourishes every saint throughout earthly pilgrimage all lifelong culminates in the Marriage Supper of the Lamb in his king-dom. So that dreary winter afternoon, from a makeshift bedside table set squarely in the valley of the shadow of death, Roberta received a foretaste of that eternal feast still yet to come. "Our Lord Jesus Christ, on the night when He was betrayed," I began, consecrating the tiny bit of bread I thought she might be able to swallow. Together with a miniature chalice with its little sip of wine, these would be for her the very flesh and blood of Jesus, the sign and seal of her redemption and the promised resurrection of her worn and dying body. In this sacred meal Roberta would obtain not merely forgiveness, but also life in all its fullness already here and now on the very brink of death.

But then a logistical problem: how commune someone who could no longer lift her head? Gingerly slipping onto the edge of her bed, I gently wrapped one arm beneath her frail bony shoulders and lifted her feather-light torso, cradling her like some skeletal baby. With my other hand I placed in her mouth the gifts her Savior died to bring: the bread of heaven here on earth, the cup of salvation poured out for all the world. "Take eat, the body of Christ, given for you," I said. "Take drink, his blood shed for you for the forgiveness of your sins." Then a parting blessing with the sign of the cross traced on her ashen forehead with my thumb: "The body and blood of our Lord Jesus Christ strengthen and preserve you in body and in soul unto life everlasting. Depart in his peace."

And she did. Not right then, but not many days later we gathered to give thanks for all our Lord's many mercies, to celebrate his grace, and then to commit Roberta's body to the ground; earth to earth, dust to dust, ashes to ashes, in the sure and certain hope of the resurrec-tion unto eternal life which God grants all the baptized who die in faith in Christ, the Living One.

But that day there in Roberta's apartment as I packed up my com-munion case and bade farewell to her family and friends keeping vigil with her, one of them said admiringly: "You had death in your hands here today." I'm not sure how I responded then. But here's what I should have said: "Maybe so, but I also had life in my hands to bring."

That's what it means to be a servant of Christ. You get your hands dirty among his earthly–and earthy–people. But you do it because you have life in your hands to give them.

Stewards are like that. They serve; they do what Jesus did among his people; they're foot washers at heart. They carry out Christ's work in each succeeding generation by humbly and repeatedly giving out the mysteries of God in his name and stead. Stewards are not museum caretakers or warehouse managers. Nor are they custodians or guardians of empty, dead traditions; stewards always remain servants actively giving out and distributing the gifts Jesus died and rose again to bring. And those spiritual gifts remain forever the same: Christ's own forgiveness and life flowing out of faithful preaching and sacramental administration. Jesus is actively present in his word proclaimed, in his baptismal washing, and in the eating and drinking of his flesh and blood in the Lord's Supper. And you can be certain that wherever Jesus is present with his gifts, there is life and salvation.

So right up front, let's start with this foundational definition: As a pastor you're above all else a true servant of Christ and steward of God's mysteries. Let that identity—that *habitus*—dictate everything you do and say in ministry. Then you yourself will be well served as you serve others in Jesus' name.

Let's take a more careful look at pastoral work. What exactly is it that pastors have been given to do in the name of Jesus?

MEANS OF THE SPIRIT

You and I are not God. Therefore when Jesus says that his disciples (and their successors in the pastoral office) will do greater works than he (John 14:12), he obviously doesn't mean that they will do divine works under their own power. Rather, as fully authorized servants of Christ, his ministers are endowed and equipped with Christ's own power and authority. And that's exactly what Jesus did to equip the twelve for ministry. Having taught them carefully for three years, having finished his saving work of suffering, dying, and rising, Jesus authorized them to do his own work by bestowing on them his Spirit.

"On the evening of that day, the first day of the week, the doors being locked where the disciples were for fear of the Jews, Jesus came and stood among them and said to them, 'Peace be with you.' When he had said this, he showed them his hands and his side. Then the disciples were glad when they saw the Lord. Jesus said to them again, 'Peace be with you. As the Father has sent me, even so I am sending you.' And when he had said this, he breathed on them and said to them, 'Receive the Holy Spirit. If you forgive the sins of any, they are forgiven them; if you withhold forgiveness from any, it is withheld' " (John 20:19–22).

As the Holy Spirit once hovered over the dark empty chaos of the initial creation to bring light and order into the universe (Gen 1:1–3), as God the Father breathed his divine Spirit into the nostrils of Adam, creating a living soul from inanimate dust (Gen 2:7), so also on that first Easter evening Jesus Christ, the Son of God, fresh from the grave, brought life and immortality to light by breathing out the Spirit upon his chosen disciples to equip them to carry on his work on earth. Until he comes again in glory, it is the intention and will of the Lord Jesus to bring all the straying sheep of humanity into one flock under one shepherd so that they may hear his voice (John 10:1–18).

So abjectly ruined is humankind since the fall into sin that people are unable to come to faith under their own volition. "No one can say Jesus is Lord except by the Holy Spirit" (1 Cor 12:1). Therefore in the work of evangelizing, preaching, teaching, catechizing, comforting, warning, consoling and equipping Christians for life "in the trenches," the presence and power of the Holy Spirit is essential. While you can and should defend the foundation of faith in history and scriptural text using sound reason and argumentation, you can't argue people into the faith, nor can you keep them spiritually strong and morally pure by influence of your personal charisma or charm. Only the Holy Spirit can accomplish the ministry, and he does exactly that through you.

That's not quite correct. The Holy Spirit doesn't work through you as a person, but through the tools you've been given by Jesus for the blessing of his church and for the benefit of all the world: the gospel and sacraments. Through these, God the Father sends his Spirit to work faith whenever and wherever it pleases him. The ministry of Christ's gospel is always a ministry of the Spirit, for the Holy Spirit is at work in the gospel and is given through it (2 Cor 3:8).

By Jesus' own express design he gives out the Spirit by his word. "It is the Spirit who gives life; the flesh is no help at all. The words that I have spoken to you are spirit and life" (John 6:63).

I can guarantee you'll be strung out, tapped out, and burned out in the ministry very quickly if you don't grasp this one central truth: By your own power or strength you can do absolutely nothing as a servant of Christ and steward of his mysteries. I've seen it over and over again: A bright, gifted young pastor is driven to despair and the brink of emotional and spiritual collapse simply because he set out to do ministry relying on his own ingenuity and internal resources. Please get this straight: It's not that you do part of the work and God does the rest; it's not that you do a little bit and God does a whole lot. Rather, in Christ's church the Holy Spirit does everything. Martin Luther put it this way in the Small Catechism (published in 1529), his little handbook on Christian faith and life:

> I believe that I cannot by my own reason or strength believe in Jesus Christ, my Lord, or come to Him; but the Holy Spirit has called me by the Gospel, enlightened me with his gifts, sanctified and kept me in the true faith. In the same way he calls, gathers, enlightens, and sanctifies the whole Christian church on earth, and keeps it with Jesus Christ in the one true faith. In this Christian church he daily and richly forgives all my sins and the sins of all believers. On the Last Day he will raise me and all the dead and give eternal life to me and all believers in Christ.[2]

Notice that from beginning to end, the life of the Christian is a gift of God's Spirit. Since the fall of Adam every human from birth is spiritually blind, dead, and an enemy of God. That's why it always takes the Spirit's power for anyone to come to faith and trust in the Lord Jesus. Not only can I not believe in Christ my Lord by my own reason or strength, I can't even "come to him."

But what I cannot do by my reason or strength, God the Holy Spirit accomplishes. First, he calls me by means of the gospel. Then

---

2. Martin Luther, *Luther's Small Catechism* (St. Louis: Concordia, 1986), 15.

having first enlightened me with his gifts of forgiveness, life, and salvation, he also sanctifies me— he shares his holiness with me—and keeps me in the true faith. What the Spirit does for me he also does for the whole Christian church on earth. Working in parallel fashion, he calls men and women everywhere to faith by means of the gospel, sanctifies them in one holy catholic and apostolic church and keeps them with Jesus Christ in the one true faith.

But having done all that, the Spirit's work is still not complete. Daily and richly in this holy church the Holy Spirit continues forgiving the sins of every Christian all their lives. What you might consider mundane routine is the very heart of your calling: to preach the unsearchable riches of Christ and to administer his life-giving sacraments. Preaching, baptizing, communing may be ordinary and God-ordained—but they are never dull. Through these sacred acts, God gives his Holy Spirit, who works faith when and where it pleases him in those who hear the gospel. Week after week, day after day, these seemingly ordinary tasks of a pastor are extraordinarily rich in their impact: Sinners are forgiven, saints restored, lives enriched and hearts consoled—all by your mouth and hands! The Spirit's work continues through you daily and richly in his holy church. This may be routine, but it's never boring.

And then, to top it all off, the Spirit also raises up all the dead and then gives to all believers in Christ eternal life. Sounds too good to be true, doesn't it? But this is most certainly true, for that's what God himself has decreed.

Now if you're a fair to middling theologian, no doubt you've grasped this sanctifying work of the Spirit pretty well when it comes to how he operates in the life of individual Christians and the church as a whole. But how about in your life as a pastor? Have you come to realize that by your own reason or strength you can accomplish absolutely nothing in the ministry? Or are you still operating under the delusion that some of it is your own doing? Are you by any chance thinking that by your personal ingenuity, intelligence, adrenalin, and exertion you can anticipate every contingency, outsmart the opposition, and accomplish great things for God and his kingdom? It gets ugly very quickly when we try to do things our way rather than God's way.

By our Lord's own mandate, he has so arranged it in his church that we grow, are fed, nourished, guarded, and protected not out of the weakness and ineptitude of our ministers but rather by the tools Christ has entrusted into their hands. The gospel and the sacraments are not static entities—mere object lessons by which we advertise and promote the kingdom of God. Rather, the gospel and sacraments throb with vitality. They are filled to the brim with the energy and life of God's own Spirit. The actual words that originated from the mouth of Jesus are the instruments and tools of the Holy Spirit to create and sustain faith. And just think: Jesus has given those very words to you. He has entrusted into your all too human and very flawed mouth and hands the gospel and the sacraments by which the Holy Spirit continues to call, gather, enlighten and sanctify his church on earth. You might fail; in fact, from my own bitter experience I have to say you most certainly will fail—repeatedly and spectacularly. But we believe in the forgiveness of sins also for pastors! So let me tell you this: Though you will falter and fail, God's Spirit will not. The Lord God never slumbers nor sleeps, Scripture reminds us (Ps 121:4). His word never returns to him void, but always accomplishes the purposes for which he sends it (Isa 55:11). So also the Holy Spirit will never falter nor cease until he has gathered into one flock all Christ's sheep under one shepherd (John 10:16).

THE SPIRIT'S WORK

We've seen how the Holy Spirit is absolutely indispensable when it comes to God's saving mission. Everything God the Father planned from all eternity and everything that God the Son accomplished for our salvation in time is delivered in each succeeding generation by God the Holy Spirit working through the means of word, washing, and meal. This is where pastoral work finds its warp and woof; the pastor serves God's people with his gifts, weaving the rich tapestry of his grace and mercy into their hearts and lives.

That grace and mercy is a sure thing, a done deal—accomplished once for all when Jesus was put to death on his cross after calling out, "It is finished!" (John 19:30). And so it was. The work of our salvation was completed then and there. Christ was put to death for our offenses, then raised again for our justification. There is now therefore no condemnation to those who are in Christ Jesus. He is our righteousness before God in heaven; justification is a once for all reality.

So by definition the pastor is always working in the area of sanctification—the Spirit's work of making holy what has been injured and defiled by sin. As he preaches, baptizes, distributes Communion, counsels, absolves, prays and blesses, the pastor is always working in God's arena as the Holy Spirit calls, gathers, enlightens and sanctifies for himself a holy people called out of darkness to live as lights in this dark world.

Many find the Christian gospel mind-numbing, a complex set of abstract theological axioms. True enough, there are profound mysteries in the Christian faith, but they all revolve around one simple truth: that God was in Christ Jesus reconciling the world unto himself (2 Cor 5:19). Therefore like Paul before him, every pastor is single minded: "I decided to know nothing among you except Jesus Christ and him crucified" (1 Cor 2:2). Christianity is nothing more than the life and truth that God has disclosed and transmitted through the incarnate flesh of Jesus, his eternal Son. But of course that life and truth remains infinitely unfathomable. You can never wrap your brain around it, and mere human flesh and blood is totally incapable of receiving such great wonders. As noted above, we cannot by our own reason or strength believe in Jesus Christ our Lord—or even come to him. But when we could not go to him, he has come to us—in washing, word, and meal—there to be received by faith. Pastoral work by definition is spiritual work.

THINGS OF THE SPIRIT

Pastors are always working in the spiritual realm. Though rooted solidly in this concrete, material world, they teach and preach, they tend and nourish, they pray and bless to connect people with things eternal and non-corporeal yet very real. But not in the generic sense of the "spirituality" of our age. Rather, they bring within the range of the five human senses the gifts of God's own Spirit; in that sense they're actual "errand boys for Jesus." Paradoxically, in pastoral work, what is inherently physical is simultaneously the most spiritual. Pastors are Christ's servants, authorized by him to bring God's people all the benefits of his saving work: forgiveness, life, and salvation.

It's an astonishing vocation, this pastoral task. God the Holy Spirit places his word and sacraments into frail, fallible human mouths and hands so people in every age can taste and see that the Lord is good even amid the broken rubble of a fallen and decaying world. In the midst of sorrow, pain, and loss people can participate already now in the life of that world still yet to come where sorrow turns into joy, where death is no more, and God wipes tears away from every eye with his own hand.

But you and I can't see that yet; that's where faith comes in. And that's why God's Holy Spirit is indispensable in the pastoral enterprise. At every turn, whether comforting the sorrowing, consoling the suffering, or celebrating with the joyful, pastors rely on the power and presence of the Holy Spirit. While we seek the best possible education in the science of theology and the art of pastoral care, ultimately what we do is not of our own doing, but entirely reliant on the Spirit's work. Christian "spirituality" is not spirituality in the usual sense of the word at all. Rather, Christian spirituality revolves around the person and work of the Holy Spirit.

Here's the way Paul put it: "Now we have received not the spirit of the world, but the Spirit who is from God, that we might understand the things freely given us by God. And we impart this in words not taught by human wisdom but taught by the Spirit, interpreting spiritual truths to those who are spiritual" (1 Cor 2:12–13).

A LITTLE GRAMMAR LESSON

Sometimes translations of the New Testament necessarily obscure certain key elements of meaning accessible only through careful study of the original Greek; there just aren't English equivalents that do justice to the original. But in this case the clear thrust of Paul's original intent regarding "Spirit"—or πνεῦμα (*pneuma*) as he wrote it—comes through nicely in translation. "Spiritual" is directly related to "Spirit" in precisely the same way as πνεύματος (*pneumatos*) is related to πνεῦμα (*pneuma*). So we see that the pastoral role is to interpret "spiritual truths" (πνεύματος, teaching) to those who are "spiritual" πνευματικοῖς (*pneumatikois*). Pastors impart teaching that comes from the Holy Spirit of God and they bring that divinely given teaching to people who have received the Holy Spirit by faith. The Spirit of God is the connecting link between humanity and all the gifts of God; he remains forever both Lord and giver of life, just as the church's ancient creed confesses him.

This little grammatical digression demonstrates that from beginning to end, pastoral work is dependent on the presence and power of God's Spirit for both its content and its result. By our own reason or strength we can accomplish nothing. Rather, we're only agents of our Savior, Jesus Christ, who sends out his servants in every age just as he sent his apostles Easter evening: "'As the Father has sent me, even so I am sending you.' And with that, he breathed on them and said: 'Receive the Holy Spirit; whosoever sins you forgive they are forgiven, whosoever sins you retain, they are retained' " (John 20:21–23).

Considerable skills are required of those who serve as pastors. Yet they cannot do their work by their own reason or strength. No amount of the powers of persuasion, personal charisma, charm, leadership and administrative skills will ever bring people to Jesus and his gifts; only the Holy Spirit can do that as he works through the word preached and taught by pastors and day-to-day as he undergirds and empowers ministry in Jesus' name.

SPIRITUAL PHYSICIANS

Since at least the fourth century, pastors have been known in the church as "spiritual physicians." They tend Christ's sheep and lambs much as a shepherd would, guarding them from predators, seeing to their feeding and their care with an eye out for their health and safety. Whenever one sheep falls ill, a good shepherd is all eyes, ears, and hands in order to help it toward recovery. First he carefully examines the animal to diagnose its ailment. He works from symptoms toward diagnosis. It won't do just to treat the symptom; he will have to know how to apply a cure to the disease itself.

In the old days back on the farm, farmers learned the necessity of animal husbandry the hard way. Many of them like my dad were pretty good diagnosticians even though they'd never been to veterinary school. They learned from generations before them and gained significant practical skill by focused observation of the animals they tended, watching carefully for the peculiarities of each animal to learn how they behaved in a variety of different situations. So when they saw something out of the ordinary, they knew they had to act quickly.

Here's one notable example. In springtime when our cows were first let out to pasture, they tended to gorge themselves on succulent new grasses and overeat. Their voluminous bellies could consume quite a quantity of legumes, and on occasion my father needed to take drastic action. When a cow's flanks began to swell abnormally and she began to pant with increasingly shallow breaths, she was experiencing the bovine equivalent of acid indigestion. The results could be fatal if those gases in her stomachs expanded to the point of stopping her respiration. More than once I saw my dad take out a knife and plunge it into a bloated cow's side and let out the accumulated gas to save her life. He needed to know exactly where the knife could be inserted without slicing into an artery and killing her. It was radical treatment, that's for sure, but it was necessary for healing.

Yet dad knew he could no more cure that cow than he could raise a crop. He was simply the agent of the Creator in both arenas. Seedtime and harvest had been preordained by God the Father; all he could do was till, plant, and cultivate, waiting for the harvest. Likewise God the Father opens up his hand and satisfies the desires of all his creatures; my father could only put the cows out to pasture so they could graze on the fodder God provided—and in this case, when they ate too much, all he could do was relieve their bodily distress for their health and safety. All the while it was God himself who tended that herd through the watchful eye of its herdsman.

Remember, then, that you can no more grow Christ's church or tend his people than my dad could grow a crop or feed his cows. The church already has a Savior. What she needs now is the Savior's servant, someone to do his bidding and bring his gifts. That someone is you; always remember you're nothing more than an errand boy for Jesus. That's hard to keep straight. We keep thinking, you and I, that if anything good is going to happen in God's kingdom, it will depend on our persistence, drive, and clever ingenuity.

SAVIOR OR SERVANT?

I've known this temptation myself, and I've seen it over and over again through the years in others. We begin to think we can salve people's wounds and solve their problems if we'd just work a bit harder or longer or smarter. How sick is that? How twisted are we to base the validity and value of our ministry on how busy we are and how hard we work? How arrogant to begin to think we are the Savior rather than his servant?

The opposite extreme is a persistent temptation as well—to use Jesus as a screen for the old Adam, who is an inveterate loafer. I've seen that fallacy in action too: Why work so hard? By my own reason or strength I can accomplish nothing in the kingdom; it's all up to Jesus, so why bother? That, too, is a lie straight from hell. To be an agent and emissary of Jesus energizes and empowers you for active work as his servant. Just think: Christ Jesus, your Savior and your Lord, has called and commissioned you to love and serve the very sheep and lambs for whom he shed his blood and gave his life. How great is that?

Getting this point straight and keeping it straight is the source of vitality and energy in the ministry whenever you're tempted to laziness, and it's the source of sanity and stability when you're tempted to frenetic busyness. You'll be run ragged if you think that by your own reason and strength you can accomplish the myriad of things that need doing. Worse, when you begin to believe that you're the actual source of spiritual help for people rather than a conduit, you're setting yourself up for spectacular failure.

And we're not just talking about being somewhat ineffective as a pastor; we're talking crash and burn.

That's why you'll need an anchor for your soul if you are to continue to be faithful in ministry. And that anchor is at the same time your one sure and certain tool for ministry: the word of God.

CHAPTER TWO

The Word of God

Ministry's Source and Norm

I n our digital age, we're swimming in gigabytes of data, but thirsting for reality. We're drowning in information, but starved for genuine community. Technology links us instantaneously with people all around the globe, yet paradoxically the more information we get and the more virtual connections we acquire, the more isolated and lonely we become. I enjoy all the technology of social media as much as anyone else, yet these virtual communities are poor substitutes for the kind of exchange that happens when I put my arms around my wife, hold my grandchildren on my lap, or sit face to face with a friend for mutual conversation and the consoling flesh and blood interchange of what lies on our hearts.

If that's true in terms of relationships between humans, how much more essential is it when it comes to our relationship with the Lord God, who made heaven and earth? Though we can infer something about God by looking at the world he has made (his power and majesty, for instance) we would know nothing about his true nature if he hadn't revealed himself to us.

The God of the Bible is not a God of human conjecture, but a God who speaks. He reveals himself to humankind in human language. In the opening verses of Genesis he begins his self-revelation by speaking and then he never stops—right through to the closing verses of Revelation. The God who marked the beginning of the universe by speaking into the black and empty void of the initial creation—"Let there be light" (Gen 1:3)—anticipates its culmination at the glorious return of his incarnate Son, who promises: "Surely I am coming soon" (Rev 22:20).

If you want to know something about God, you'll need to get to know him by his word; that's the long and the short of it. There simply is no reliable knowledge of God apart from his word. That makes the word of God the sole source and norm of all teaching in the church and therefore the sole source and norm for all pastoral work. Yet that word is not the kind of information dump we've come to associate with most ordinary human communication—a kind of data transfer. Rather, God's word is the means by which he discloses himself and opens up his heart to us so we can see what kind of God we have, how he may be addressed and accessed here in this world, and how we can receive his gifts for our forgiveness, life, and salvation.

FIRST THINGS FIRST

"In the beginning was the Word" (John 1:1). This means that before there was anything else in this world, there was the Word of God. We read in the very first verses of the very first book of the Bible that God the Creator spoke the creation into existence. Bleak and empty, the created order was topsy-turvy before God began to speak. First came the word "let there be light," then came light, then everything else followed in sequence—the sun, stars and moon, the cattle and all creeping things, the birds of the air, the fish of the sea, even the myriads of swarming insects—the whole complex creation was called into being in six short days by God's decree. Last of all, at the close of God's creative work, there was a consultation among the persons of the holy Trinity. Something was missing; creation was incomplete; it needed a crowning touch—created beings to manage and tend the rest of creation in God's place. "Let us make man in our image, after our likeness. And let them have dominion over the fish of the sea and over the birds of the heavens and over the livestock and over all the earth and over every creeping thing that creeps on the earth," God said. "So God created man in his own image, male and female he created them" (Gen 1:26–27).

You know the rest of the story—how God first shaped a man from dirt, then breathed into his nostrils his own life-giving Spirit, and

Adam became a *"nephesh hayah"*—living soul—an embodied spirit or a spiritual body, depending on how you look at it. He had a body made from the stuff of earth filled with God's own heavenly life. Adam was a body/soul—one being simultaneously existing in both spiritual and material domains. So far, so good.

But Adam was not yet complete. He was inadequate for the job God had in mind. "It is not good that the man should be alone," said the Lord. "I will make a helper fit for him." So he put Adam into a deep sleep, reached into his side and extracted a rib from which he built a woman and then brought her to the man, bone of his bone and flesh of his flesh, to be joined in heart, mind, and body with him in holy matrimony as one flesh. Eve was exactly like Adam in so many ways, yet distinctly different in significant ways that made them sexually and emotionally complementary. Thus to this very day we see creation unfolding around us as in generation after generation a man leaves his father and mother and cleaves to his wife and they two become one flesh. Through their bodily union as husband and wife they engender still more human beings created in the image and likeness of the Lord God Almighty. Thus in a very real way, all humanity has its origin in the Word of God; each generation in turn arising from that initial command flung into the chaotic primordial darkness: "Let there be … " and flowing from that mysterious consultation within the holy Trinity before the dawn of humanity: "Let us make … "

THE EMBODIED WORD

So John is right: In the beginning was the Word. But that's not the half of it. "The Word was with God," he writes, "and the Word was God. He was in the beginning with God. All things were made through him, and without him was not anything made that was made" (John 1:1–3). And here's an even deeper mystery: The Word by which everything was created is none other than the eternally begotten Son of God come down from heaven to take on human flesh in Jesus. "The Word became flesh and dwelt among us, and we have seen his glory; glory as of the only Son from the Father, full of grace and truth" (John 1:14).

But you and I haven't seen the glory of Jesus with our own eyes. We were not with him on the holy mountain when he was transfig-ured before the eyes of his friends and they saw him conversing with

Moses and Elijah and heard the voice of the Father declaring Jesus his beloved Son (Mark 9:2–8). We were not there when they crucified our Lord or when God raised him from the tomb.

The apostles were there, however. Peter was with Jesus on that transfiguration mount (2 Pet 1:16–18). With James and John, he was among the most intimate friends of Jesus within the circle of the disciples. His experience on that holy mountain impacted his life and ministry for the rest of his life. If tradition is correct, he met a miserable and torturous death, impaled upside down on a cross. But what impelled him forward all through his life and what sustained him in his final agonizing hours was what he heard and saw that day in Galilee: the sound of the Father's voice from heaven saying, "This is my beloved Son with whom I am pleased; listen to him." (Matt 17:5)

John was there too that day. His many experiences with Jesus before and after the momentous week of his betrayal, execution, and resurrection sustained him all his long life. Again, if tradition is correct, John is the only one among the disciples who died a natural death, exiled to the isle of Patmos during the Christian persecution under the Roman emperor Domitian. Reliable sources narrate how in his dotage the elderly apostle John, no longer able to ambulate or preach, was carried into Christian assemblies where his exhortation consisted of a mere five words which he simply repeated —the main theme of his first New Testament epistle: "Little children, love one another" (1 John 3:18).

For John, love was the essence of the whole life and ministry of Jesus. Christ Jesus was the very embodiment of the love of God the Father: "God loved the world so that he gave … " (John 3:16). John saw that love in action with his own eyes as Jesus touched frail and contaminated human flesh to make it clean and whole again. He heard the message of God's eternal life as it flowed from the Savior's mouth in his teaching, he stood at the foot of the cross and with his own eyes he saw that eternal life and love flowing down from the Savior's bloodied and tortured body in his death. As his most intimate friend humanly speaking, Jesus entrusted John with the care of Mary his mother there at the cross. Most vividly and memorably, John touched the risen and living flesh of Jesus with his own hands three days after they laid his dead body in a tomb. No wonder then that this "beloved disciple," as he called himself (John 21:2), pointed to his own personal experience with Jesus as the root and ground of his apostolic ministry.

"That which was from the beginning, which we have heard, which we have seen with our eyes, which we looked upon and have touched with our hands, concerning the word of life—the life was made manifest, and we have seen it, and testify to it and proclaim to you the eternal life, which was with the Father and was made manifest to us— that which we have seen and heard we proclaim also to you, so that you too may have fellowship with us; and indeed our fellowship is with the Father and with his Son Jesus Christ" (1 John 1:1–3).

But where do you and I come into contact with the words and deeds of Jesus today? No, we weren't there when they crucified our Lord or when he rose up from the tomb. Nor were we among the chosen few who were with him on the holy mountain to see him transfigured in divine glory, conversing with the prophets of old.

WORD AND SPIRIT

Yet the disciples have nothing over us when it comes to experiencing Jesus. We, too, are given to hear his word and so receive the forgiveness and life that is found in him. You see, there is a continuing link between Jesus as the embodiment of the eternal word of God the Father, the experience Jesus' followers had with him and his teaching, and us today. Jesus hasn't gone away and left us comfortless. His Holy Spirit is "another comforter" (John 14:16–17) whose continuing presence sustains and empowers us just like Jesus. He sends his Spirit by his word. Word and Spirit are inseparably linked. If you want the Spirit of God, you need the word. It is a brightly shining lamp in the darkness of this conflicted world of ours.

If you and I are to be true physicians of souls in these dark and foreboding times, we'll need tools for accurate diagnosis, which I'll get to later. Right now I'd like to focus your attention on the cure, which is always the proper distinction and discerning application of God's living and abiding word.

Please keep in mind that that the Bible is much more than a book of instructions. Whenever you apply the word of God, you have a tiger by the tail. The Bible is the Holy Spirit's book, and it throbs with the life and vitality that is the Spirit's own. It contains much practical information for living the Christian life. Especially in the lawless world we live in, people need instruction on how to live a life that pleases God. And that's exactly what we find in God's word. It provides the boundaries of right and wrong and clear, useful guidelines for living a fulfilling, satisfying life not only pleasing to God but also helpful to our neighbor.

Yet God's word contains both command and promise, judgment and grace, law and gospel. That's where the science of theology comes in; it's important that you and I properly interpret the intent and thrust of any text of Scripture before we begin to apply it in any circumstance of ministry. But we are not merely scientists. We're craftsmen engaged in the art of the cure of souls. And that's where sensitive discernment comes in and faithful application of the word of God. There's an unfortunate tendency, it seems to me, toward a minimalist understanding of God's word, using it as a means to achieve a stated or implied goal. When the living and abiding word of God becomes just another instruction manual to attain a particular desired outcome, we shortchange God's intended use. He is a God who both wounds and heals, who kills and makes alive (Deut 32:39). His word, like the rain and snow that waters the earth, never returns to him void, but accomplishes the goal for which he sends it forth (Isa 55:11).

So, for God's sake please don't use the word of God casually. Your goal is not to create a soothing, calming mood by mouthing spiritual platitudes. You want to do something with God's word; his word really does what it says—in the very saying. This is the living word of the living God. He doesn't speak in platitudes; he speaks realities. He's not providing people with helpful hints or useful strategies to fix their own problems. He both kills and makes alive, he wounds and heals; he metes out death to the old Adam and raises souls made new again in the Savior's love. His word is an efficacious word; it does what it says. Therefore as his servant, when you wield the Spirit's sword, you're delivering real balm and help to hurting, dying souls. You're not just talking about abstract ideas or categories; you are enacting his life-giving word in the hearts and lives of suffering souls.

Faith always comes from hearing the word of Christ, primarily because Christ Jesus is himself the embodied word of the Father. As the Father has life in himself, so, too, has Jesus. Like Father, like Son. All the life and light that was in God the Father from eternity is wrapped up and conveyed in his incarnate Son.

In one famous dialogue with his disciples, Jesus explored the impact and power of his spoken word as an expression of the eternal life originating in his eternal Father and extended into time by means of his incarnation.

"'As the living Father sent me, and I live because of the Father, so whoever feeds on me, he also will live because of me. This is the bread that came down from heaven, not like the bread the fathers ate, and died. Whoever feeds on this bread will live forever.' Jesus said these things in the synagogue, as he taught at Capernaum.

"When many of his disciples heard it, they said, 'This is a hard saying; who can listen to it?' But Jesus, knowing in himself that his disciples were grumbling about this, said to them, 'Do you take offense at this? Then what if you were to see the Son of Man ascending to where he was before? It is the Spirit who gives life; the flesh is no help at all. The words that I have spoken to you are spirit and life' " (John 6:57–63).

Can you see the connection and continuity? There is a chain of life unveiled in these verses. Jesus calls his Father the "living" Father, then ties his own life-giving flesh to its origin in God the Father. So intimately are they joined that whoever eats and drinks his flesh and blood partakes of the divine life that was with the Father from before the creation of the world.

Many of his disciples balked. And who can blame them? It is indeed a hard saying that whoever feeds on Jesus will share in the eternal life yet to come. Yet that's the fact; like Father, like Son, remember? The heavenly Father, full of life, sent his Son into the world as the embodiment of that life. Thus everyone who eats his flesh and drinks his blood has eternal life and will be raised up on the last day (John 6:54). Yet eating and drinking are not the main thing in the sacrament. The word of God remains front and center. Joined to the

The Care of Souls

element, God's word is the source and power of the sacrament, providing forgiveness and life to every believing sinner.

The word is the vehicle of God's power, you see. Jesus said so. The Spirit gives life; the flesh is of no avail (6:63). He continues: "The words that I have spoken to you are spirit and life." The words that Jesus spoke are filled to the brim with life because they originate in Jesus who is the embodiment of the Father's life, and because they are filled with the power of the Holy Spirit, the giver of life.

So whether you're looking for help for yourself or giving it to another broken and wounded sinner, you need to look to the living and abiding Word. Above all else you need Jesus who is the living Word of the living Father. So wherever you are on the pastoral depletion spectrum, this is the remedy and treatment. Whether just confused, becoming desperate or well on your way to capitulation, you'll find your life and light in Christ by means of his life-giving word. Though you cannot see him with your eyes, you can hear his word just as it fell from his lips, chock full of the life and healing of God. His words, he said, are more than merely information; they are both spirit and life. Just ask Peter.

MYSTERY AND LIFE

When others in the broader company of disciples gave up on Jesus, Peter didn't. They couldn't stomach what Jesus was teaching about his flesh and blood being vehicles of divine life. There are people still today who can't wrap their heads around this great mystery that mere bread and wine could possibly be the actual flesh and blood of Jesus given and shed for their forgiveness, life, and salvation. And that's just the point. This sacrament remains forever mystery just as Jesus himself is mystery, the great sacrament of God, our "tangible link with eternity," as I've explored above. You can't get your head around mystery; you can only grasp it with your heart.

So Jesus asked his twelve disciples if they too were going to give up on him. "Do you want to go away as well?" (6:67). "Lord, to whom shall we go?" Peter answered. "You have the words of eternal life."

Jesus still has the words of eternal life. Whether you are merely bummed out in ministry or well on your way toward burn out, you will find eternal life in the words of Jesus. You'll need to do more than merely read those words or study them. You'll need to chew them over verbally, mull over them mentally, and make them your daily bread and butter; you'll need to meditate on them.

Note that the words of Jesus are more than just words on a page. They are the words of Jesus just as he gave them. More than mere data, they are full of the life of Christ just as he is full of the life of God the Father. They are information in the truest sense; they form people from the inside out, bringing them to full maturity in Christ Jesus.

Yet the wondrous paradox is that these verbal life-giving words of Christ are accessed by means of words on a page. You and I have the words of Jesus available to us because they are in fact written down for us to learn—to "read, mark, learn, and inwardly digest," as one liturgical prayer puts it.

These words of the word of the Father were inscripturated— or recorded in a text by means of inspiration—as Paul the apostle explains it to young pastor Timothy. Timothy had been catechized by his mother and grandmother in the writings of the Old Testament prophets, which as Paul put it were "breathed out by God"—a direct reference to the Holy Spirit, the divine breath by which the universe was created and the source and origin of all life.

"But as for you, continue in what you have learned and have firmly believed, knowing from whom you learned it and how from childhood you have been acquainted with the sacred writings, which are able to make you wise for salvation through faith in Christ Jesus. All Scripture is breathed out by God and profitable for teaching, for reproof, for correction, and for training in righteousness, that the man of God may be complete, equipped for every good work" (2 Tim 3:14–17).

From the Father, in the Son, by the Holy Spirit. This is the divine economy of our salvation, which was planned by God the Father from all eternity before the world was made, then accomplished here in time through his incarnate Son Jesus Christ, and finally delivered to people in every age by means of his Spirit working through his word.

And that's the way the word works still today as well. Jesus, the embodied word of the Father, gives out his gifts by means of the words that he spoke to the apostles, his chosen emissaries. Remember? Jesus told his disciples that the words out of his mouth were vehicles and instruments of the life-giving Spirit. "The words that I have spoken to you are spirit and life." Thanks to the same Spirit, we have the written text of the words of Jesus, his apostles and the Old Testament prophets of God. These sacred writings are therefore not only the sole source and norm for all teaching in the church, but they are the living and abiding word of God for all troubled, anxious Christians.

That means these same Scriptures provide the warp and woof of the woven tapestry of the care of souls. The text of sacred Scripture is at the heart of all pastoral work; the core of what we do in the diagnosis and cure of souls revolves around the word of God in written and verbal form because these in turn flow from Christ, who is the word of God made flesh.

THE WRITTEN WORD

Peter helps us grasp the connection between the person and work of Jesus and the text of the Bible as he relates his personal experience on the mountain of transfiguration where he and brothers James and John observed Jesus conversing with Moses and Elijah about the impending saga of his crucifixion, resurrection and ascension. The life and work of Jesus was no fabricated story spun from the imagination of religious zealots, Peter insists: "For we did not follow cleverly devised myths when we made known to you the power and coming of our Lord Jesus Christ, but we were eyewitnesses of his majesty. For when he received honor and glory from God the Father, and the voice was borne to him by the Majestic Glory, 'This is my beloved Son, with whom I am well pleased,' we ourselves heard this very voice borne from heaven, for we were with him on the holy mountain. And we have the prophetic word more fully confirmed, to which you will do well to pay attention as to a lamp shining in a dark place, until the day dawns and the morning star rises in your hearts, knowing this first of all, that no prophecy of Scripture comes from someone's own interpretation. For no prophecy was ever produced by the will of man, but men spoke from God as they were carried along by the Holy Spirit" (2 Pet 1:16–21).

What Peter saw with his own eyes on that Galilean hill and what he heard there with his own ears gave both impetus and urgency to his own ministry and the life of Christian service he urges on others.

Scripture is the "prophetic word more fully confirmed," he insists. The Bible is God's own book, filled with words not originating in human imagination, but in God himself. True enough, the diverse texts of Scripture all have human authors from various times and circumstances. Yet clearly the writing process was directed by God the Holy Spirit. The writers were not recording their "own interpretation," but were "carried along"—moved and directed—by the Holy Spirit in their writing. Therefore in the sacred text of the written word we have the force and power of the very word of the Father, "full of grace and truth," as John wrote (1:14).

As one who has a number of books in print, I know the power of a written text. It's humbling for me and somewhat mystifying that now for more than 30 years any number of people have had instant access to thoughts I inscribed in print way back when. Books are a veritable time and space travel machine. By means of words on the printed page, I can speak directly across decades and continents that divide me from my readers temporally and geographically. Written words are not mere "signs" or "signifiers" denoting some abstract meaning behind a text. Rather, meaning is linked to the written text. When I write, I often wrestle with a paragraph, looking for the precise language that expresses my intended meaning. It's gratifying now when I run into readers and continue a conversation I started (in some cases, decades ago) by means of the printed page. I've come to see that language is not a tool we use, but in very real way language in fact uses us. We don't communicate as humans in pure thought or by means of mental telepathy. The only meaning we know is conveyed through language; the only reality we have is enacted with words, just as I've been doing in my conversation with you throughout this book.

That's the way it is with the inscripturated word of God as well. We don't stand over the text to judge it using our own subjective criteria, but rather we stand beneath the text and it acts upon us. It resurrects us from the spiritual death in which we live, and then it keeps on shaping and forming us in the image of Christ as our old sinful nature is daily put to death and we rise again with Jesus to live with him in newness of life. Though the Bible originated in multiple ancient cultures spread over thousands of years in widely diverse languages, one central thrust is woven through all its genres and literary forms:

"God was in Christ reconciling the world unto himself, not counting their sins against them" (2 Cor 5:19).

Thus the Bible is not a collection of ancient culture-specific documents that need to be adjusted to fit our cultural context; instead, every consecutive, shifting cultural context must be brought into the perspective of these established biblical texts. Evolving cultural trends must not position the Bible; rather, the Bible positions each changing culture in turn. No prophecy is a matter of private interpretation. The prophets wrote down for our learning by divine inspiration exactly what God wants us to know and believe. Never underestimate the power of the written word—particularly when it is the word of God!

JESUS AND THE BIBLE

Our Lord Jesus—himself the embodied word of God—turned repeatedly to the writings of the prophets as the word of authority, most notably in his battle with Satan. "It is written," he said not once but three times, quoting the written word to silence the devil's sadistic temptations.

> Then Jesus was led up by the Spirit into the wilderness to be tempted by the devil. And after fasting forty days and forty nights, he was hungry. And the tempter came and said to him, "If you are the Son of God, command these stones to become loaves of bread." But he answered, "It is written, 'Man shall not live by bread alone, but by every word that comes from the mouth of God.' "
>
> Then the devil took him to the holy city and set him on the pinnacle of the temple and said to him, "If you are the Son of God, throw yourself down, for it is written, 'He will command his angels concerning you,' and 'On their hands they will bear you up, lest you strike your foot against a stone.' "
>
> Jesus said to him, "Again it is written, 'You shall not put the Lord your God to the test.' " Again, the devil took him to a very high mountain and showed him all the kingdoms of the world and their glory. And he said to him, "All these I will give you, if you will fall down and worship me." Then Jesus said to him, "Be gone, Satan! For it is written, 'You shall worship

the Lord your God and him only shall you serve.' " Then the devil left him, and behold, angels came and were ministering to him. (Matt 4:1–11)

Here you have it: the incarnate word of God quoting the written word against the devil's scheming lies and half-truths. It's an excellent picture of the seamless and intimate connection between the text of the Bible and Jesus, who is the incarnate word of the Father. These three are inseparable. You can't drive a wedge between the word of God, written down by inspiration of God's Spirit, and the Son of God himself. This is a great comfort to pastors who seek to console, to comfort, to forgive, and to cleanse sorrowing, wounded sinners as well as in the important task of exhorting, rebuking, and warning proud and impenitent sinners of their dangerous predicament.

Remember, God's word always does what it says. When you pronounce absolution to a broken man, his sins are forgiven by the power and authority of the word you speak in Jesus' stead. When you comfort dying believers with the promises of God who raises the dead, they find hope and peace in Christ, who is the resurrection and the life. When you employ God's word to sanctify and cleanse a woman who has been abused and defiled by another's sin, she is cleansed, renewed, and purified with a holiness not her own—wrapped in the purity and sanctity of Jesus himself.

God's word is performative speech. Just as God first created something out of nothing, then called forth light from the empty darkness of the initial creation by his declaration: "Let there be light," so he continues to create new realities by the force of his sheer word. When you say, "The Lord bless you and keep you," you are not expressing an empty wish or fervent prayer. All the power of God's own name and word enacts that blessing by which he bestows His enlivening power. When you declare that a man and woman, having pledged themselves together in lifelong matrimony are now husband and wife in the name of the Holy Trinity, they are no longer two but one flesh. When you as the called and ordained servant of Christ and by his authority forgive sins in the name of the Father, Son, and Spirit, those sins are actually forgiven before God in heaven. That's the power of God's word for you. Never just static information, it is the tool and instrument of the Holy Spirit to do what it says, to accomplish what it speaks of, to deliver what it promises. "For the word of God is living and active, sharper than any two-edged sword, piercing to the division of soul and of spirit, of joints and of marrow, and discerning the thoughts and intentions of the heart" (Heb 4:12).

No wonder, then, that Scripture is at the center of the care of souls. God's word delivers the goods. Whether we're dealing with a hurting soul, wounded and broken because of circumstances in life and the spiteful actions of uncaring people or whether we care for a soul burdened and broken by its own sin, the sensitive and attentive delivery of the word of God in either spoken or sacramental form (and it's usually both) is at the heart of the pastoral craft.

THROUGH THE VALLEY
OF THE SHADOW

There are multiple scenes that come to mind when I think of the impact of God's word over the more than four decades I've been privileged to serve as a pastor. Here's one example.

Let's call her Sarah. She's a woman in her forties. Now cancer-ridden, she had once been vibrant and full of life, a bundle of energy as she went about her daily duties. She was all woman: a loving and devoted wife to her husband, a doting mom to her two teenage sons, besides all the tender care she lavished on the patients she tended as a nurse.

I'll never forget the day I called on her in the hospital after she received her diagnosis: an aggressive variety of lymphoma, treatable but not curable. It was the news no one's ever prepared to hear, least of all someone so full of life and with so much to live for. But from Sarah I heard no "Why me?" or "What now?" Her overwhelming concern was not for herself but for her husband and especially her boys: How would they cope? Who would tend to their needs and see them into manhood?

We prayed about those concerns. But not before hearing the promises of God's sure word in the midst of this devastating news: "Thus says the Lord: ... Fear not, for I have redeemed you; I have called you by name, you are mine. When you pass through the waters, I will be with you; and through the rivers, they shall not overwhelm you;

when you walk through fire you shall not be burned, and the flame shall not consume you" (Isa 43:1–2).

Sometimes death comes quickly and unexpectedly; in this case it came in drips and drabs—first in tiny little increments almost undetectable, then later with increasing ferocity. It was terrible to watch. It was hard on her husband and boys to see their wife/mom slowly but inexorably losing strength, then vigor, then capacity. It was hard on me too. No true shepherd of souls enjoys walking through the valley of the shadow of death with his sheep, even though he knows full well the consolation and presence of the Good Shepherd in the encroaching darkness.

I don't remember how long that journey took, but certainly too long by any measure. But for Sarah and her family every month, every week, every day counted. They snatched moments of joy out of what others would call a hellish journey—spending a day or two at a resort hotel whenever they could, seeing family, enjoying friends. My wife, Jane, became Sarah's confidant and friend. When things got overwhelming she knew that loving care and prayerful support was only a phone call way, and many late night conversations ensued, laced with sympathetic tears.

Throughout those long months I tended Sarah and her family with the only tools I had been given: the firm sure promises of the word of God and his precious sacraments. In public worship together with the congregation they regularly received forgiveness, life, and eternal salvation even though death was casting a longer and ever-darkening shadow every day.

When she could no longer attend the services of God's house, it was my honor to visit Sarah and her household with these same gifts: to pray with them, to laugh with them and weep with them—as is the privilege of all God's saints, simultaneously bearing each other's joys and sorrows at one and the same time. But above all I held out the promise of the God who had promised in his sure and certain word: "Thus says the Lord: ... Fear not, for I have redeemed you, I have called you by name; you are mine."

Then one day it happened. On a Sunday morning, just before the bell rang for the late service, I was standing in the doorway of the chancel ready to enter the sanctuary when the message came: "Sarah's dying. She asked if you could come." Quickly filling in my associate pastor, I rushed to her house, only minutes away.

There's something peculiarly tangible about entering a believer's house as death draws near. Any pastor who's been there knows what I mean. It assails your nostrils. It hits you in the face. The finality. The impending grief. But above all, reverence and a holy awe. When saints depart this life for the world to come, you're on holy ground. Though death approaches, immeasurable glories await. When Christ shall come to judge the living and dead death itself shall die; every tear shall be wiped away by God's own hand.

A medical professional, Sarah had carefully prepared her family for this day. They knew what to expect physiologically. But thanks to her living faith, they also knew what to expect spiritually. Another sinner/saint was about to depart in peace, just as Simeon sang so long ago. Sarah's eyes, like his, had seen her Savior. Simeon held him in his arms, but Sarah knew him just as intimately. By his sure word, and in the tangible bread of life she received in his holy supper.

Yet one more time I had the privilege of providing her that precious gift. Wrapped in a warm blanket to ward off death's advancing chill, her extremities were already growing cold to the touch. There were no earthly medications that could help her any more. My nostrils were assailed with that all-too-familiar aroma that lingers in the air around a dying person—the sweet yet pungent stench of impending death. But there on the very brink of eternity it was my privilege yet once more to administer to her the medicine of immortality. There in her basement family room while her life was slipping slowly away, she received the life that endures to all eternity: "Take eat, this is my body; take drink, this is my blood, shed for you for the forgiveness of sins." And then this blessing: "The body and blood of our Lord Jesus Christ preserve you in body and soul unto eternal life. Amen." "Amen," she faintly echoed in return.

"What hymn shall I sing?" I asked. "The Lord's My Shepherd," she whispered, "but the old version." And so I sang:

> The Lord's my shepherd, I'll not want
> He makes me down to lie
> In pastures green He leadeth me

The quiet waters by.
Yea, though I walk in death's dark vale,
Yet will I fear no ill;
For Thou art with me, and Thy rod
and staff me comfort still.
My table Thou hast furnished
In presence of my foes;
My head Thou dost with oil anoint,
And my cup overflows.

It wasn't the finest rendition of that dearly beloved text from the Scottish psalter, but I sang as best I could, knowing that Sarah's journey would soon lead her from this world to the next. And sure enough, just as I finished the last line, she breathed her last: "And in God's house forevermore my dwelling place shall be."

I think that's what the saints of old would call in poignant, poetic terms "a blessed end." These are the sorts of things you get involved in as a pastor; it goes with the territory. I grant you that most people wouldn't sign up for a job that involves tending people during their last hours on earth. But this, too, belongs to the cure of souls; it's part of the pastoral *habitus* into which you grow and it becomes second nature to you.

It's like that in other professions too; I imagine that many things that came naturally to my dad as a farmer would be intimidating to most folks. I've already spoken of the long hours and back-breaking labor, but there were also midnight vigils with farrowing hogs and calving heifers. The outcomes of those vigils were mixed. Joy most often, but occasional stillbirths too. It all went with the territory, part of the *habitus* of farming.

But as you tend Christ's lambs and sheep in the harrowing hours when life hangs in the balance, you're well equipped. You've been given something lasting and eternal to bring into these dark and foreboding situations. The heaviest burdens, the most intense sorrows, the most heart-rending losses—all of these meet their match in the life-giving word of God and his sacraments. They're not magic; these sacred tools don't make the heartache vanish overnight. But they do bring lasting and eternal healing over time, despite the hurdles.

Sarah's situation is a case in point. There were immense difficulties ahead for her husband and sons—a boatload of grief at first and then tons of complications adjusting to the loss of someone so central to their hearts and lives. I'm thankful to tell you the prayers I prayed with this woman all those long years ago have been answered: By God's grace Sarah's boys have grown into fine upstanding, gifted Christian gentlemen. But what impresses me beyond measure is that whole long journey with all its convoluted twists and turns rested securely on the sure foundation of the word of God—our only consolation and hope for this world and the next.

THE WORDS OF GOD

Do you see why I love the care of souls so much? To be able to bring them the one thing needful when all other things fade away, there's nothing quite like it. To have something to give when everyone else stands by helplessly, to be able to say something of eternal significance when all other speech, however well-intended, rings hollow on the ear—this is an experience that humbles every pastor. But there too we have nothing to bring, you and I, that we ourselves have not first received. We are only errand boys for Jesus, emissaries of the one who bled and died to give his life that everyone in this dying world might find their life in him.

When the sincerest human sentiments fall empty and hollow, we pastors have something solid and lasting to give. We are the sweet aroma of life amid the stench of death, for we speak a sure and lasting word when all other human speech falters and fails. "Thus says the Lord"—what comfort for fear-ridden hearts, for anxious, sorrowing souls! Here is something to rest in amid the rush of anxious thoughts, a sure footing amid the shifting sands of human experience.

Sarah's story is only one of hundreds and hundreds of other instances when I've been privileged to speak a word of promise as people's lives have come unraveled and when their futures have grown dark with foreboding. In those situations human compassion can go just so far; when life caves in, broken and shattered souls need more than human kindness. They need God himself.

The astonishing wonderment is that God condescends to place his consoling, comforting word on human lips like ours. And so we, like the prophets of old, open up our mouths to speak that word with the confidence and trust that it does what it says. We have an incredible front row seat seeing God at work as his word has its full effect, creating order out of chaos and bringing solace in the midst of horrific hurt and bitter pain.

And you as pastor are his authorized agent to bring his presence and healing by means of the word and sacraments you bring his sheep and lambs in every circumstance of life, not just in those moments when life itself hangs in the balance, but also in those mundane, routine, ordinary ups and downs of life. You're not a counselor or therapist, of course, but you are Christ's sheepdog to do his bidding. You're an errand boy for Jesus, sent to disseminate hope and peace in the most mundane circumstances of life. A fearful, anxious teen, a worried mother or harried father will find stability in your ministry. Not in you, but in God himself, who has chosen to do his consoling work through the word he's given you to speak. The wondrous reality is that God himself is present by means of his word to settle anxious hearts and quiet fear. "Thus says the Lord." Now that's a mouthful of certainty in an uncertain world!

WORDS OF LIFE

I began this chapter with the words of the apostle John, the "beloved apostle," the one who recorded his personal experience with Jesus—his intimate friend, but at one and the same time his Lord and his God—one with the Father from all eternity, the word of God the Father made flesh for us and for our salvation. He was with Jesus from the beginning of his public ministry until its culmination some three years later. In the Gospel that bears his name, John recorded for posterity by inspiration of the Spirit the signs that Jesus did—his miracles of healing and demonic cleansing—as well as the gracious words of life that fell from his lips during John's three year apostolic internship.

Most significantly, John was there when they crucified his Lord. He stood by the cross with Jesus' mother and the two other Marys (John 19:25). He personally saw with his own eyes all that transpired there at the place of the skull that day when God visited his wrath against a sinful world on his own sinless Son—the Lamb of God who, bearing in his own body all sin and shame, bore the full brunt of his Father's judgment not merely in his excruciating physical agony but in his inscrutable spiritual anguish. What John saw there during those three bitter hours transfixed his life and ministry, observing how sorrow and love flowed mingled down from the Savior's wounds as he poured out his life's blood in his death. With gut-wrenching sorrow he watched the soldiers take Jesus' mangled body down from the cross and he observed how it was placed in a borrowed tomb.

But John also saw everything that transpired three days later with his own eyes; from an empty tomb on Easter morning to the living Jesus standing among his disciples Easter evening, John also had personal life-altering experience of the resurrection. A week later he was among the disciples when an incredulous Thomas touched the living flesh of Jesus and exclaimed "My Lord and my God!"

No wonder, then, that in his first letter John would emphasize his firsthand experience with Jesus from Cana's wedding feast to Easter morning as the basis of his apostolic ministry: "That which was from the beginning, which we have heard, which we have seen with our eyes, which we looked upon and have touched with our hands, concerning the word of life—the life was made manifest, and we have seen it, and testify to it and proclaim to you the eternal life, which was with the Father and was made manifest to us—that which we have seen and heard we proclaim also to you, so that you too may have fellowship with us; and indeed our fellowship is with the Father and with his Son Jesus Christ" (1 John 1:1–3).

The words of Jesus are spirit and life, remember? He is the word of the Father made flesh for us and our salvation. And we have the prophetic word made more certain. What was uttered by the prophets long ago has been confirmed in history and time, then written down so that we too can share in the never-ending life which Jesus came to bring.

Incarnate word—oral word—written word—different forms of the one word of our salvation. What the ancient prophets in the time of Israel heard and were given to say aloud to God's people they then wrote down as they were "carried along" by the Spirit of God. One and the same Spirit inspired the writers of the New Testament as well; they wrote down what they heard and saw of the word made flesh. The apostles had "the prophetic word more fully confirmed," as Peter wrote (1 Pet 1:19).

THE MINISTRY OF THE WORD

One divine word—incarnate, spoken, written—this is the word that you and I bring to God's people yet today as we go about the care of souls. And in that word there is life—the life of Christ for all humanity. That's why everything we do as pastors we do by means of the word of God: We listen to aching souls, we treat their wounds and ease their sorrows and anxieties—all by means of the word. We pray by means of the word; we bless by means of the word. God's word is the golden thread woven through the tapestry of all pastoral life and work. And the goal of this living and abiding word is always one and the same, aptly summarized by John the beloved apostle at the end of his Gospel: "Now Jesus did many other signs in the presence of the disciples, which are not written in this book; but these are written so that you may believe that Jesus is the Christ, the Son of God, and that by believing you may have life in his name" (John 20:30–31).

All ministry with the written word is ultimately the ministry of the one word of the Father made flesh for us and for our salvation. In him there is light in the darkness, for he is the light no darkness can overcome. Ultimately, in him there is life in the midst of death. For though he once was dead, he lives now forevermore, and shares his never-ending life with all the believing baptized.

Christ Jesus is, in fact, our one and only life. He is simultaneously our righteousness and our holiness (1 Cor 1:30). Both are essential in the care of souls. The pastoral *habitus* is not merely a science mastered by the study of theology, but an art refined in the school of experience. As in the practice of medicine, physicians of souls first begin with attentive diagnosis and then move toward intentional treatment using the healing God the Father provides through his incarnate Son in the power of the Holy Spirit. Since Christ Jesus alone is our life, the art of pastoral care always involves the deliberate and discerning application of both his holiness and his righteousness not as mere categorical ideas, but blessed realities. You don't gain that level of skill overnight.

We remain spiritual physicians in training throughout our ministry. As much as we all need competent and knowledgeable mentors to learn our craft, we also need faithful and diligent colleagues to polish those skills.

And that's where you come in.

CHAPTER THREE

The Cure of Souls

Attentive Diagnosis

In the first chapter I called the classical understanding of
pastoral work a *habitus*, or disposition of the pastor's soul
by which he acquires the skills of a spiritual physician, to
discern accurately and then sensitively treat the ailments of
Christ's sheep and lambs. I'll use my own childhood experiences on the farm long ago to illustrate how that works.

My words in these next two chapters may sound like
a foreign language to pastors who want to be cutting edge
and follow current best practices in pastoral leadership. The
latest models of pastoral work lean heavily on technology
and methods borrowed from the social sciences, sales, and
business leadership theory, and you'll find precious little if
any of that in this chapter. No modern farmer would think
of setting up a first-rate farming operation these days with a
team of horses or relying on manual labor like my dad did
eighty years ago. It's possible my readers might think I'm not
only on a nostalgia kick regarding farming in the 1950s, but
that I'm also hopelessly stuck in reverse when it comes to
pastoral care today. This is the twenty-first century, after all,
and no pastor should expect to operate day by day like an
eighteenth-century English country parson.

I'll agree with you there. Technological advances have
given us many tools to use in service of the care of souls.
And the people we work among today face a far more complex world than those of previous centuries—a world that's
becoming more difficult to navigate in, spiritually speaking,
with every passing decade. It's foolhardy to try and turn back

the clock and revert to a simpler era for models of excellence in pastoral care. We surely can't expect to do things exactly the same from one era to the next, nor for that matter from one generation to the next. The stream of life and experience flows steadily onward; we all have to address what is around us now, not what has passed us by.

Like the current of a mighty river, there's no fighting against the cultural stream that flows relentlessly on. We have two choices in addressing our shifting circumstances: We can jump in and go with the flow, morphing our approaches to conform to that river as it rolls steadily onward. Or we can stand on solid ground to bring something to people caught in all the flotsam and jetsam. If we jump in and go with the flow we'll constantly be recalibrating and reconfiguring our approaches—and inevitably the relentless tug of the current will begin to shape what we say and do.

That's where the classical model of pastoral care becomes contemporary and cutting edge. It helps us maintain equilibrium in the rapidly shifting currents of succeeding cultural trends, and yet it gives us ground to stand on so we can accurately and effectively address the genuine needs of God's people floundering amid those very currents. We have something to say no matter what the circumstances, for we speak regarding things eternal and lasting in the midst of things not just constantly in flux, but ultimately fleeting and fast fading away. We find ourselves being able to speak confidently and joyfully about the solid and lasting things of God's eternal kingdom among the strident voices competing to be heard in the cacophony and chaos that inevitably result when people drift helplessly along with whatever is happening around them.

CONTEMPORARY VS. TRADITIONAL

There's a lot of unfortunate banter about "contemporary" and "traditional" in church circles these days. To make matters worse, there's confusion about the meaning of those two terms. *Contemporary* ("with the time") literally means what is happening in real time as it's currently experienced—not whatever fits the latest fads of pop-oriented commercial entertainment. And *traditional* literally means what is "handed on"—not relics of the past, tucked away in the attic of antiquity.

The task of the church—and therefore the challenge before every pastor—is to address what's going on now not with the flimsy fads of pop culture but with the solid truth of the word of God, rooted in Christ and extending throughout all time and space. The church's tradition is the way she delivers to her own contemporaries what she has received from faithful generations past.

The church has her unique transcendent culture into which she invites refugees from every tribe, nation, people, and language to find their refuge and life in Christ and his saving work. There they take their places with saints living and departed—Abraham, Isaac, and Jacob; Moses, Miriam, and Joseph; Matthew, Mark, and Luke; Lydia, Paul, and Timothy—and people of every era and place who with one voice extol the praises of him who called them out of darkness and into his marvelous light. Each generation has its own time and place, its own unique language and indigenous culture. Yet there remains only one Lord, one faith, and one baptism (Eph 4:5). Every generation and people group finds a place in God's eternal kingdom, there to embrace and hold fast the teaching of the church catholic (universal) faithfully handed down from one generation to the next. So faithful tradition ("handed down") takes central place in what is genuinely contemporary ("current") in every succeeding generation. We live as confessing Christians forever in the now, yet what we confess is of one piece with all confessing Christians who have gone before us.

THE CURE AND CARE OF SOULS

I would contend that the classical approach to the care of souls is not only the best approach for our conflicted and confused era, but it's the single best way to address the actual needs of real people in whatever location or generation pastors find themselves. I mentioned that since the fourth century pastors have been called spiritual physicians, or physicians of the soul. So let's start with a review of the underlying terminology for those who aren't acquainted. Bear with me here; if we're going to get our arms around the classic model, we'll have to wrap our heads around its vocabulary. Every craft has its own language, and there are a few concepts we'll need to wrestle with before we begin to apply them. Think of them as hallmarks of our profession.

Cura animarum literally means the care/cure of souls. This is the foundational description of pastoral ministry. From there it passes into the parlance of most Christian churches by transliteration. In my own German Lutheran tradition it was carried over as *Seelsorge*, a combination of *Seele* (soul) and *Sorge* (care/cure). From there it was a short step to refer to the pastor as a *Seelsorger*, or a person who provides care for the soul, a physician for souls. There's good evidence that spiritual care and cure long preceded medical care as we know it today. The classic Greek philosophers of antiquity considered themselves spiritual physicians, but they focused primarily on matters of the mind and cognition. Fourth-century church father Gregory of Nazianzus famously referred to spiritual care as the "art of arts and science of sciences," stressing the complexity of the curative arts addressing matters of the soul in comparison to treating bodily disease and injury.[1] So to speak of spiritual diagnosis and care/cure is not to borrow an analogy from the medical community. If anything, you might say that practitioners of bodily healing arts have commandeered the church's language regarding the nature of pastoral care: the soul's physician.

In my early days in the ministry, I remember silver-haired veterans of the cross being introduced in pastoral conferences as "a real *Seelsorger*." I knew just enough German to realize that this meant someone who cared. And I was perceptive enough to see that these men genuinely did *care*. But now, having developed my own mane of hoary hair in this last stage of my ministry, I've come to realize there's a lot more involved in being a physician of the soul than being a man of compassion and empathy—though these are both critical starting points in ministry.

"Souls" is a tricky word, since most everyone has a general idea of what it means. But that's just the problem; the word has a way of floating off into generic abstracts. "Soul" in popular usage tends to

1. "For the guiding of man, the most variable and manifold of creatures, seems to me in very deed to be the art of arts and science of sciences. Any one may recognize this, by comparing the work of the physician of souls with the treatment of the body; and noticing that, laborious as the latter is, ours is more laborious, and of more consequence, from the nature of its subject matter, the power of its science, and the object of its exercise." Gregory Nazianzus, "In Defense of His Flight to Pontus," *Oration* 2.16.

mean a disembodied spirit, the quintessential spiritual component in a human being. In many people's imagination, the "soul" is that nebulous weightless, odorless, incorporeal substance that resides somewhere just above the hypothalamus, the essential spiritual component in every human being.

WHAT'S A "SOUL?"

My definition for soul won't please everyone. I don't pretend to have mastered the complexity of how the Scriptures use the word nor how it has been used throughout the church's history. However, what I've found works best is to begin simply with this: Biblically speaking, humans don't *have* souls; they *are* souls. When the Lord God created Adam in Eden from the dust of the ground he breathed into his nostrils his own breath (Heb. *Ruach, spirit*) of life, and the man became a *nephesh hayah*, or "living soul" (Gen 2:7). He was alive with God's own life. Part of what that meant was that he was a breathing creature. He was *soul* because he was one totality: a divinely created physical body plus divinely given breath.

While the Scriptures elsewhere distinguish between body and soul, or in some places body, soul, and spirit, nowhere do they teach that human beings can be sliced and diced into two or three components. We are in our totality *souls*. Yes, we are physical creatures with bodies like other animals. But we are also spiritual creatures like the angelic spirits who have no bodies. The Scriptures portray us holistically. We are embodied spirits, or conversely, spiritual bodies. We humans share in many of the aspects of all animal life. But we are unique in that humans stand at the pinnacle of all creation, endowed with God's own breath and life. We were created as his vice-regents, to tend and care for all of creation, both animate and inanimate.

This book's thrust regarding the care of *souls* means to care for *people*, realizing they are not disembodied spirits, but God's own creatures with both fleshly and spiritual features. The terminology of *soul care/cure* (*cura animarum/seelsorge*) is merely the way the church has historically recalled pastors to their essential role—tending people created by God, redeemed by his Son, who need to be sanctified by his Spirit for both time and eternity.

CARE V. CURE

To come to grips with the care and cure aspects of soul care you need to know something about the medical arts. In medical terminology, care and cure are two sides of the same coin. Care is the ongoing treatment you receive for chronic conditions; cure is what you seek when you have an acute need. If someone asks me, "Are you under a doctor's care?" I respond, "You're kidding me, right?" At my stage of life I'm under a doctor's care regularly—getting my annual health check ups, seeing my cardiologist once a year as well to monitor my post-bypass surgery recovery. Yet at times I need and seek medical intervention for an acute need that develops—a fever, perhaps, or some other symptom of disease. For my physical health I need both cure and care.

So also the church through the centuries has seen the vitality and well-being of souls through the duality of both care and cure. In that they are chronic sinners, all of God's people need the ordinary care they receive in the divine service (public worship) where the word of God is preached and the sacrament is administered and where they in turn respond with prayer and praise. But in instances of acute need, these same people need the extraordinary care that provides a cure applied to their most pressing needs. Pastors offer both: care in public worship and cure in private pastoral care as needed. In my experience there's more than enough need to go around among the people of God, and increasingly so with every passing year. Thank God, you and I don't have to meet that expanding need out of our limited inner resources, but from the unlimited reservoir of God's grace and mercy in Christ Jesus.

A soul is a person in relation to God (*coram Deo*). When I use the word "soul," I don't mean the exclusively spiritual dimension of a human being. I mean rather the whole person (body and soul)— and specifically in terms of that person's relationship to God. *Coram Deo* ("in the presence of/before the face of God") is the technical theological terminology the church has used through the centuries to express what I have in mind. People live in relationship—to their families, to other human beings, to their work, to the world around them. But when I speak of a person as "soul," I mean that person in their relationship to God—*coram Deo*. It is this person, divinely created to live in relationship with their Creator for all eternity, to whom we as pastors are to give our full attention.

While there are multiple dimensions to every person's life—bodily, social, emotional and psychological—as a pastor I'm especially attentive to that person's relationship to God. Therefore the soul's spiritual life is my ultimate, though not exclusive, concern. As symptoms arise in that person's life—be they fear, anxiety, distrust, misery, joy or sorrow—I'm always keen on interpreting them in terms of what they disclose about the soul's relationship with God. I'll be misled in my diagnosis and treatment of this soul if I limit my attention to social, emotional or environmental symptoms. Worse, I'll be derailed if I focus on treating a person's emotions rather than the person as a whole. To my way of thinking, that's where pastoral care has taken a left turn; for much of the twentieth century pastors reinvented themselves as activity directors, corporate executives or psychotherapists (poorly trained, unlicensed, and rather inept therapists at that). At best, the results have been spotty. At worst, they've been harmful to people and detrimental to the life and mission of the church.

The complexities of the twenty-first century compel us to re-examine the church's longer heritage of the care/cure of souls as a useful template for contemporary pastoral work. As social structures—notably the family and consequently other institutions—come unraveled and lives fall apart, we can use all the help we can get from good business practices, quality social scientists, and qualified and competent therapists. But faithful pastors will be increasingly forced to direct their attention to the heart of the matter: a person's relationship with God and the healing and renewal that can come only from him through the means he has appointed in his church. What is old is new again. What has always sustained the church's life through good times and bad, growth and shrinkage, popularity and persecution has been this classic approach of the faithful and attentive care of souls. This might seem backward at first glance, like antiquated thinking. But in our conflicted times nothing could be more cutting-edge, more practical, and more important for mission and ministry. We pastors must

The Care of Souls

redouble our efforts to recover and refine once more our competencies and skills as spiritual physicians for our contemporary era. I'm hoping you'll fall in love with this approach; my goal is that you will be as infatuated as I am with the cure of souls.

THE ATTENTIVE/INTENTIONAL MODEL

I'd like to lay out for you a pastoral approach consistent with the church's longer heritage of the cure of souls. Essentially, it's similar to the approach used in recent centuries of medical practice: Good diagnosis leads to accurate treatment. Like any competent physician, the pastor doesn't know what interventions to provide for a distressed soul until he first listens to that soul. He needs an accurate diagnosis, so he begins with the symptoms. But like any good medical doctor, he doesn't treat the symptoms; he treats the illness. Once the illness is remedied, the symptoms diminish or disappear.

So the process of the cure of souls has two phases: attentive diagnosis followed by intentional treatment. Attention and intention are equally important. Misdiagnosis and hasty cure are the pitfalls to be avoided. Accurate diagnosis leads to effective treatment. In the diagnostic phase, the pastor needs to be all ears, paying full attention to the person in every dimension: physically, emotionally, socially, and spiritually. Once he arrives at a working diagnosis, the pastor can provide pastoral care, providing the spiritual cure that's needed in that unique situation. But then in the treatment phase, the pastor needs to be intentional. Prescribing the wrong medication or regimen can be harmful to a medical patient; sometimes it can be lethal. So also the spiritual physician approaches his treatment of the spiritual health of an individual with utmost care, aware that his ministry has eternal implications for the soul.

Remember how my dad took drastic measures when he detected signs of bloating in our cows? One misstep with his knife could be fatal. Yet he couldn't leave a cow in mortal danger; decisive action was his only option. When life hangs in the balance you don't dawdle. Pastoral care is never a casual matter; the souls you are called to serve are always in jeopardy. That's why accurate diagnosis is always important for spiritual physicians; it informs intentional treatment.

THE DIAGNOSTIC PROCESS

When I was teaching this classical model of the cure of souls to seminarians I had an excellent physician whom I saw on a regular basis. At one of my visits I commented on the parallels between physical care and spiritual care, lamenting that we pastors didn't have at our disposal technological tools to analyze spiritual complexities that remain hidden to our human senses. Internally I was jealous; wouldn't it be wonderful if there were x-ray or imaging machines to tell us what was impeding the soul's spiritual health? "It's a common fallacy that we doctors rely on tests like that for our diagnosis," my physician replied. "They're wonderful to give you an accurate picture of exactly what's going on physically right now," he continued. "But they don't reveal the actual cause of the body's distress or disease." He went on to explain that such scans provide only about ten or fifteen percent of the information he needed for a diagnosis. "For that I rely mostly on a patient's oral history."

It amazes me that the medical profession depends on something that we pastors in recent generations have tended to dismiss: quiet, probing conversation accompanied by a great deal of attentive listening. In my experience, the listening itself provides an immensely therapeutic benefit. Most people in our time are frenetically occupied with so many things that they don't take the time to sit down and unburden their hearts. And if ever they are inclined to do so, there's no one to listen. So simply by giving someone your undivided attention for sixty or so clock ticks, you've given them an immense gift.

And so we give the troubled soul our undivided attention for a span of time. You know, I hope, some active listening skills: how eye contact, body posture and facial expression signal your rapt attention and how those conversations should proceed. First listen, then respond, ask, listen, clarify, respond, then ask some more, etc. After pleasantries, begin in a simple conversational style, e.g. "I'm so glad you came in; how can I help you today?" Then the listening begins. Keep your eyes open for any external nervous mannerisms or signs of outward distress or concern. Listen carefully to comprehend the nature of the trouble, but don't use only your ears; listen with your whole being. As much as possible, get inside this person's head and heart to grasp the visceral nature of their distress and the effects of that difficulty emotionally and spiritually. Imagine with your whole heart and mind what this soul is experiencing—all the while remembering that the cure is not found in your empathy or comprehension, but in Christ's compassion and solace.

John Chrysostom warns every would-be shepherd against haste or dictatorial methods in dealing with God's sheep. "The decision to receive treatment does not lie with the man who administers the medicine but actually with the patient."[2] He calls for tact and patience among pastors, lest in rushing ahead with uninvited spiritual care they jeopardize the health and life of the soul. "The shepherd needs great wisdom and a thousand eyes, to examine the soul's condition from every angle," he writes.[3] Proper diagnosis is of the utmost importance for faithful physicians of the soul. To rush in uninvited or with the wrong medication courts spiritual disaster. To use language common to the Lutheran context: "God's word is not rightly divided when the law is preached to those who are already terrified because of their sins, or when the gospel is preached to those who are secure in their sins."[4]

What makes for good public preaching makes for effective individual teaching. The pastor must first listen to the soul before he can minister to the soul. Since the condition of the soul is disclosed primarily by the heart, effective physicians of the soul need to polish their listening skills, opening up not merely their ears, but their hearts to the suffering of the soul as well. As much as humanly possible and as the Spirit leads your understanding, read their emotions. Get inside their skin, as it were, so you can comprehend not merely with your mind but your whole being the complexities of the soul's distress. Faithful pastoral care of the soul starts when one heart discloses itself to another heart—then the healing ministrations of God's word and sacraments may be most effectively applied.

---

2. John Chrysostom, *On the Priesthood*, Popular Patristics Series 1 (Crestwood, New York: Vladimir's Seminary Press, 1964), 56.

3. Chrysostom, *On the Priesthood*, 58.

4. C. F. W. Walther, *Law and Gospel* (St. Louis: Concordia, 1981), 64.

Remember, you have no healing you can personally provide a distressed soul, but our gracious God supplies his gifts in effusive abundance. He's the real healer; you are only his healing agent. As a spiritual physician you will need not only an accurate diagnosis, but a faithful and effective cure. As I indicated in chapter two above, all pastoral ministry is an application of God's word. So it's important that when you speak, you speak with words that are "taught by the Holy Spirit" (1 Cor 2:13). That means you'll need to use both your ears. With one ear you need to be absolutely tuned in with the heart and soul of the person you're tending to. The other ear must be tuned to God's own word.

HOW TO LISTEN

I used to panic when someone began confiding in me. I was all too aware that after that person stopped speaking it would be up to me to talk—and when I did, I was expected to have something significant to say. Not only was that intimidating, it wrecked the listening process. As you can imagine, when my attention was focused on what I was going to say next, I wasn't paying attention to what I was hearing. If I spent all my time flipping through my mental catalogue of Bible texts, I couldn't possibly focus on the person in front of me. Here's where Chrysostom's maxim comes in: Remember you are a shepherd of souls. This is not just a job or a vocation; this is a *habitus*. Remember that what you do flows from who you are. And as you develop the character and identity of a shepherd it colors the way you look at the sheep and interact with them. Rather than a two-stage thinking/doing process, your pastoral response becomes increasingly reflexive and instinctive. You develop a sixth sense—a spiritual outlook, a "thousand eyes" to examine the soul's condition from every angle. You'll need to keep your eyes peeled in more ways than one.

In my teen years I helped my dad take care of our dairy herd. But I dare say he looked at those cows far differently than I did. I saw only a collective bunch of big bovines that demanded a lot of work. But my dad knew them each separately. Some of them had been born on the farm and he had watched them mature; he helped many deliver their first calf and then take their place within the herd. So while I knew them collectively he knew them individually:

their unique habits (yes, cows have individual personalities), their peculiarities and which diseases each was prone to develop. Farmer/dairyman was his *habitus*. So whenever a problem came up, he knew almost instinctively how to handle it. Because of his interaction with them and long attention to cows he was able to tailor his care to the specialized needs of each animal individually. It's the same way in pastoral work too. When you develop the *habitus* of spiritual shepherd, it colors and impacts your care of the sheep. A good share of this comes with practice, shaped and formed by your personal life of meditation and prayer.

The word of God will obviously be the source of the treatment you will provide for the distressed soul, but it's also essential for accurate diagnosis. As you listen you filter what is said (and what you observe) through God's word. Physicians of the soul are operating in the dark; you and I cannot see into the recesses of the human heart or examine the soul's condition with our human senses. Though a person's emotions, external appearance and behavior provide important clues, they remain only clues; we cannot be certain of the actual cause of the distress using only what we see and hear. Therefore in the diagnostic phase God's word and the guidance of the Holy Spirit remain indispensable. It's just as the psalmist puts it: "The unfolding of your words gives light; it imparts understanding to the simple" (Ps 119:130).

There's a range of valid approaches to each situation. It all depends on what you are given to bring the person or persons enmeshed in that particular predicament. And you won't know what to bring them until you know what the problem is. Remember, faithful treatment always hinges around accurate diagnosis. And I suspect the diagnostic process works differently for different spiritual physicians. In medical practice there are acceptable standards for medical care, but the medical art is practiced somewhat differently from doctor to doctor. So also in the care and cure of souls each spiritual physician needs to find his own way. Thus I can't tell you exactly how to function as a faithful "doctor of souls." I can only describe that art to you; you'll have to put it into practice yourself. However, I can share a bit of my own approach with you just in case it would be helpful for you to look over my shoulder.

SPIRITUAL TRUTHS FOR
SPIRITUAL PEOPLE

In my own practice here's the way it works: Whenever someone is asking for my help I give them my rapt and undivided attention. I try to imagine what it took for them to work up enough intestinal fortitude to bring out into the open what in many cases has been kept bottled up and hidden within them for a very long time. I am at once humbled and honored that this child of God has taken the time and invested the emotional capital it takes to lay out its distress. But all that aside, pastoral care is not purely an emotional or relational transaction. Ultimately this is a spiritual exchange. And so at one and the same time as I give my undivided cognitive and sensory attention to what a person is telling me, I simultaneously intercede silently for the Spirit's help and guidance. Specifically, I pray that this soul may speak the truth of what lies heavy on their heart and also that I might accurately discern how best to provide the help and healing that God intends by means of his word and sacraments. While faithful pastoral care demands the highest standards of excellence in training in every discipline of theology (dogmatic, historical, exegetical, pastoral) and the very best skills we can muster intellectually and emotionally, the essential core of what we do as shepherds of souls is always spiritual. By definition, that means our work has to do with the Holy Spirit.

The whole process of the care of souls, as I mentioned in chapter one, revolves around the operation of the Holy Spirit. You and I as spiritual physicians are not interested in generic "spirituality." According to Scripture, what is truly "spiritual" flows from the person and work of the Holy Spirit. Our insight into a person's condition—an accurate diagnosis—and our treatment of that condition both hinge around the revelation of God's Spirit in his word. To properly grasp the whole circumstance we need more than a perceptive mind or emotional intelligence, we need accurate discernment by means of that word. And when we speak, we need more than human wisdom; we need instruction from God's own Spirit by means of his word. Likewise what we bring to people by the power of God's Spirit they are able to receive only because they are "spiritual," meaning they themselves have received the Spirit by baptism into Christ. Just as a transmitter and receiver must be on the same frequency so signals can accurately connect, so the entire process of spiritual care occurs on the "wave length" of the Holy Spirit.

"Now we have received not the spirit of the world, but the Spirit who is from God, that we might understand the things freely given us by God. And we impart this in words not taught by human wisdom but taught by the Spirit, interpreting spiritual truths to those who are spiritual" (1 Cor 2:12–13).

But as I've stressed, physicians really can't proceed with treatment unless they know the ailment they're trying to cure. It simply won't do to treat the symptoms; you only prolong the morbidity in that case. Rather, physicians of integrity know how best to examine the patient, carefully considering all the symptoms to be sure, but using those symptoms to lead them to a more accurate diagnosis of the underlying disease.

Let's call him Dan. A middle-aged father of two sons in their late twenties. One, a very troubled young man named Robert, had given his mom and dad much cause for frustration and worry ever since adolescence. Taking up a position in the family business, Robert was putting out a good faith effort to clean up his checkered past and seemed to be making good progress overcoming some poor life choices. Dan and his wife, Nancy, were beginning to hope that Robert had turned his life around, although his steady girlfriend had recently broken up with him. Robert came in to see me about all of this, and I was able to point him to the promise of healing in Christ; he left my study in apparent peace.

But that night around two in the morning, the shrill ring of my phone shocked me out of deep slumber to instant alert mode. Even in my stupor I recognized Nancy's voice immediately. "It's Robert," she blurted out woodenly. "We've found him in our backyard. He's shot himself." The rest of the night was of course a blur; I threw on some clothes and dashed to their home. Flashing squad car and emergency vehicle lights lit up the driveway and façade of the house in eerie red and blue. Dan and Nancy were in shock; I was in shock too as I prayed and ministered to them, internally going through my own "could have/should have/would have" list about my visit with this young man not twelve hours before he took his own life. You go on autopilot in situations like that; you comfort those who mourn and you weep with those who weep. But mostly you listen in order to try to comprehend the incomprehensible so you can pray God's consoling healing for the inconsolable empty black hole of such a violent, horrific tragedy when everyone is left searching their hearts and finding no answers.

And that's exactly the focus of the sermon I preached to a roomful of hurting friends and family some three days later:

"What shall we say to these things?"

You can say that again. What *can* we say? That's a question we all asked ourselves when we first heard about the tragedy. That's a question we asked ourselves when we came here tonight; that's a question we might go on asking ourselves for a very long time. *What can we say?*

It would be nice to have all the answers; to be able to sit here and put all of the pieces together, to be able to come up with some judgment in this case. But, as we all know, God is the judge, not we.

What can we say, then?

The only thing I can tell you is what I told Robert. He heard this message. He heard it, and it gave him hope. That much I know. What happened that night I don't know, but tonight I want to tell you what I told Robert. It is the one thing I know for sure. And for that reason it is the one thing I have to say to you: "If God is for us, who can be against us? He who did not spare his own Son but gave him up for us all, how will he not also with him graciously give us all things?" (Rom 8:31–32)

God did not spare Jesus, you know, but gave him up for us all. What he gave him up to was the cross. It wasn't a pretty picture, that cross; much more horrible than any Sunday School leaflet would ever dream of printing. There the unthinkable was happening. The eternal, immortal God was taking into himself all of our sin together with all of its consequences. The sinless Son of God was drinking to its last bitter drop the agony of our guilt. Here the Lord of all life lowered himself to death—the ordinary death of a common criminal, which was a subordinary death ... but God did not spare him being beaten to a bloody pulp, then hung up to die an excruciating death. It was the only way he could love us, you see. All of the misery of our life had to be removed. And so he did not spare his own Son, but gave him up for us all.

But I'm here to tell you tonight that since Jesus was abandoned by the Father, you will never be abandoned. No matter how dark the night, no matter how bitter the pain, no matter how deep the loss, you will never be abandoned. God is on your side, for Jesus' sake. He brings light and life and hope into this dark and scary world.

There are lots of questions here tonight. And I don't know all the answers. But let's stick with the one thing we do know: No matter how tough the road, no matter how deep the agony, no matter how sharp the pain, no matter how bitter the grief, no matter how desperate the loneliness, one thing remains forever true: GOD IS FOR US. God is on your side.

Who shall separate us from the love of Christ? Shall tribulation, or distress, or persecution, or famine, or nakedness, or danger, or sword? ... No, in all these things we are more than conquerors through him who loved us. For I am sure that neither death nor life, nor angels nor rulers, nor things present nor things to come, nor powers, nor height nor depth, nor anything else in all creation, will be able to separate us from the love of God in Christ Jesus our Lord. (Rom 8:35–39)

Some days after the funeral Dan called me late one night. "Can I see you tonight, Pastor?" he asked. "Of course," I replied. "I'll meet you in my study in thirty minutes."

The agony was palpable as Dan joined me at my conference table and began. We talked and talked well into the wee hours while Dan relived the misery, pouring out his anguished heart. I heard loss and grief, of course, but I sensed there was more in there. Silently I prayed that the Spirit would give him words to speak and me the ears to hear so this abscess could be lanced. Finally the picture emerged;

Dan was fixated on the argument that he and Robert had the night he took his life. Harsh words had been exchanged between them—bitter words and hateful. Dan's remorse was almost too much to bear. Finally, reached the horrid, ugly core of the matter. "It was my hunting rifle he used," Dan told me through wrenching sobs. "Why didn't I lock it up?"

There's no arguing with regret. There's no use explaining the hard cruel facts: that suicide has many victims besides the one who pulls the trigger, that irrational thoughts lead to irrational actions, that those intent on taking their own lives will find a way no matter what. Being attentive in mind and heart, I diagnosed Dan's core hurt as guilt. Now it was time to be intentional in cure.

"Did you know, Dan, that Christians can be absolved personally and privately for sin just as we do publicly in the Divine Service?" I asked. "Let's take this mess to Jesus where it can be resolved." And so we knelt together, Dan and I, at the prie-dieu in my study. There in the quiet of that night before the image of the Crucified One Dan gave voice to his remorse and guilt—not just to me but to the Lord who by his blood has blotted out every sin. And there that night Dan heard with his own ears not just me, but the Savior who commissioned me to forgive all sins in his name and stead. By my earthly absolution Dan stood forgiven before God himself in heaven.

Dan went home that night freed to live again in hope. But it would not have happened had I listened to him only with my ears or used only my intellect to speculate about his grief. Interceding for the Spirit's guidance, I uncovered the guilt that lay beneath his deep and profound loss. And by the same Spirit I spoke the only word that could free him from his solitary prison: "I forgive you all your sins in the name of the Father and of the Son and of the Holy Spirit." The word of God does what it says. That dark night Dan found new courage in Christ Jesus his Lord.

DISTRESS

Many is the time I've had a person stop by my study—or more likely, inject an "aside" into what seemed like an ordinary conversation, saying something like: "Pastor, I know you're busy and I hate to bother you, but ... " Because people are often unsure of the real problem, they may launch some trial balloons with obvious discomfort and reluctance. Quite often they're looking for advice regarding a decision or quandary facing them. Hardly ever is the person seeing things from a spiritual point of view; more often it seems to them to be an ethical or behavioral question: What shall I do with my problem child? How should I respond to a cranky boss or a complaining spouse? How can I best address a perplexing problem I'm facing?

Other times to be sure there are issues more explicitly and obviously spiritual: How do I handle the simmering rage that seems to percolate within me? How can I live with myself after what I've done? I'm powerless over alcohol or other drugs, porn, sexual temptations and aberrations ... you fill in the blank. The pastor doesn't get to pick his cases; every soul put under his charge is daily faced with a boatload of sin and temptation of every sort that puts people into some pretty seriously compromised situations. Jesus bled and died to purchase every one of those people as his own, and he has placed them into your care and keeping to tend them in his name and stead. He knows full well you have no resources whatsoever to give them; that's why he puts his own word into your mouth to speak and gives you his sacraments to administer to make the wounded whole, to bring hope and healing to despairing and broken souls.

HOW TO BEGIN?

How do you work your way from symptom to accurate diagnosis and then faithful treatment? Some of that comes from practice. Besides that, if you're smart you'll consult regularly with a trusted colleague in ministry to learn from his pastoral experience, taking care to protect confidentiality. Two heads (and hearts) are better than one; you can often see things more clearly by looking at them from more than one angle and by combining a brother's perception with your own. You will certainly learn also from generations past, immersing yourself regularly in the study of classic texts on the cure of souls from antiquity on to more recent times, checking to ensure that they are in accord with Scripture, of course.

Probably the most important skill to acquire is the art of listening to the conscience—listening accurately and spiritually, beneath the surface. In the care of souls one heart must be tuned to the frequency of another. If you listen carefully in this way you'll save yourself a lot of grief stemming from misdiagnosis or hasty cure, the twin perils in the cure of souls. But don't interrogate your sheep; listen to them.

NOT AN INTERROGATION

That's the first thing. Though pastoral work is detective work, it's not an inquisition. Never interrogate your parishioners or other distressed souls. You are not an inquisitor; you're a shepherd tenderly caring for Christ's sheep and lambs. You are interested in the manifold dimensions of their relationship with him. Yet you're not a spiritual voyeur; you never pry into private matter nor go digging for deep dark secrets. In the course of your spiritual care, people may disclose rather personal and intimate aspects of their lives. But your interest in these things is never personal; you are there on errand and commission. You're an ambassador and minister of Christ; Jesus intends to do his work through you. Sometimes situations long hidden are revealed in the course of your pastoral care. Whenever they arise, you deal with those things appropriately with the tools entrusted to you, but you never go digging for dirt. That's Satan's work; he is the accuser. Christ on the other hand is the Redeemer; he has appeared in time to undo Satan's work, to abolish sin and death and bring life and immortality to light through the gospel (2 Tim 1:10). Now you've been sent to do Christ's work, you've been made a minister of his gospel, to set free people long captive to sin and give them a good conscience before God.

So then proceed in your ministry in Jesus' name not as an inquisitor, but just as any good physician would; exploring the symptoms. "Where does it hurt?" your doctor might ask you. In reply you'd attempt an accurate description of the discomfort as best you're able, together with all the pertinent information you can offer. It's your body, after all; the physician's not privy to what's going on inside you. It's the doctor's job, starting by exploring various symptoms, to rule out counter indications systematically until he arrives at a working diagnosis of what might be causing the problem. Then— and only then—does he prescribe a course of treatment. It's just as my doctor told me; most of a good medical diagnosis comes from an oral history.

How do you and I conduct a spiritual examination? As I said, we are not to pry directly into private matters and become the accuser; we don't want to do Satan's work, but Christ's work. So it would be good to take a cue from Jesus himself. When he engaged the woman at the well in Samaria he simply asked her for a drink of water, then went on from there. Yet before the day was over that woman was well on her way toward healing from a life of immorality (John 4:7–29). When someone approached Jesus to serve as an arbiter in an inheritance dispute, Jesus ended up delineating the proper relationship between earthly goods and spiritual riches (Luke 12:13–21). Notice that Jesus didn't undertake an interrogation in either case. He just proceeded conversationally, listening for cues in what the person was saying and then responding accordingly. On other occasions Jesus preached and taught; in these situations he began with insightful listening, then spoke out of the abundance of his heart.

A CONVERSATION

That's the second thing to remember: Let's interact conversationally, responding to questions naturally and then asking our own questions appropriately. When we get answers, we make note of them—not on a flipchart or checklist, obviously, but noting them mentally and internally. We file them away in our heart for future reference. We're paying attention, remember? But we're paying attention in Jesus' name. As much as I'm able under the direction of the Holy Spirit, I want to be the ears of Jesus at this stage, so that eventually I can speak his word and provide his healing during the course of the conversation.

What am I listening for? I've found it useful to be listening simultaneously on four different levels. These are the touchstones for a careful spiritual diagnosis. Think of these four areas as road signs or guideposts for extended conversation. Rarely do I touch on all four in the first conversation; it may take multiple conversations to begin to piece together an accurate picture of what's going on spiritually with a person. Ideally, like the proverbial "family doctor," a pastorate of some length will enable you to get to know your people over a period of years and be in a better position to serve them spiritually. Let's explore these four guideposts for pastoral conversation one by one, noting what to listen for in each area.

F aith. This one is so obvious it seems hardly worth mentioning. But in this era of fading Christian influence when statistically Christian faith is less and less evident in our part of the world, this is the place to begin.

Too often pastoral care and missional activity are treated as polar opposites, as though missionaries do one thing and pastors another. That misconception is unfortunate, for the truth is that all pastors are missionaries. They are forever evangelizing people with the gospel of a Savior who came to seek and to save the lost and to give himself as a ransom for sinners locked in the spiritual prison of sin and death. Likewise, every conscientious missionary needs to be concerned that converts are pastored. People need not only to trust in Christ as Savior, but also to receive from him all good things pertaining to their salvation. Especially as our culture implodes ethically and morally, we will find new converts to Jesus desperately in need of continual pastoral care as they seek to recover from the lingering spiritual damage wreaked by their own and others' sins. They will need cleansing from the pollution of their own sin and healing from the hurts of sins committed against them.

So then the first thing I'm listening for as a physician of souls is faith; does this soul believe on the name of the Lord Jesus? If so, I know how to proceed. If not, I know where to start.

Then there's the question of baptism. Has this soul been washed in the name of the Father, the Son, and the Holy Spirit? Until Jesus comes again in glory, he has commissioned his church to baptize people into the powerful name of the Holy Trinity. By this washing people find forgiveness, spiritual renewal, and the beginning of a whole lifetime of repentance and renewal in Jesus' name.

Heinrich was by his own admission a religious skeptic. Growing up in war-torn Germany, he was trained as a scientist. For him, by definition, that meant he was an agnostic; he viewed all religion as legend and the Bible as mythology. He was curious when his wife and family joined the new church plant I served as missionary pastor. He came, as the saying goes, to scoff, but he remained to pray. No one can say Jesus is Lord except by the Holy Spirit (1 Cor 2:3). But the Holy Spirit works through his word. And the Holy Spirit certainly went to work on Heinrich. For the first time in his life he began to take the Scriptures seriously. Much to his surprise he discovered the biblical narratives were rooted in real history; they had the "ring of truth." God's word and Spirit had its way with Heinrich. One day after about a year of attendance at worship and Bible study he asked me if he could be baptized. It was a joyous day when he received the washing of water with the word, which cemented his union with Jesus' death and resurrection. "I believe in God the Father Almighty ... and in Jesus Christ his only Son our Lord ... I believe in the Holy Spirit, the holy Christian church, the communion of saints." He went on to become a witness to the faith within his scientific profession and an elder in his congregation.

Faith was central for Heinrich as it is pivotal for us all. But baptism is the hinge for daily death and burial of the old Adam and resurrection of the new man for the rest of our lives.

Yet even if we are speaking with a baptized believer, we know the devil is working overtime to thwart God's designs. Martin Luther often said, "Where Christ builds his church, the devil builds a chapel." Besides possessing a living faith in the triune God, believing souls may have also embraced a false god. A good working definition for a god is that to which we look for all good and in which we find refuge in every time of need. And by that definition you know from your own experience that even the most devout Christians can and do have idolatrous beliefs.

So it will be extremely helpful to me as a spiritual physician to know what I'm up against. Which are the other gods this soul worships besides the true God, the Maker of heaven and earth? If I know these idolatrous temptations I can appropriately call the soul to repentance, to turn from idolatry to live once more out of a living faith in the living God.

Better yet, if the soul can name its own idols, he or she is well on the way toward spiritual health. In that case when the person is burdened with sin and guilt I have the privilege of announcing the forgiveness of sins in Jesus' name, acting on his behalf just as he said: "If you forgive the sins of any, they are forgiven them." Then I can gently and lovingly guide this sheep to be alert to habitual temptations, helping them to guard against situations when that false god tantalizingly offers safe refuge or a compelling source for comfort and strength.

I can provide guidance in fending off such idolatrous temptations by prayer and God's word.

P rovidence. The second area I'm listening for is a kind of barometer for faith. How well does this soul handle the reversals of life? Can he or she move steadily on through adversity when it arises, or is this person shaken to the point of wondering whether God has abandoned him? The pastoral care of those in the midst of difficulty depends on where they are on that spectrum ranging from confidence to despair.

As we walk through life we are surrounded on every side by dangers of both body and soul. It's a frightening prospect for even the hardiest of souls. There are days that are sunny and bright, when we're at the top of our game and life seems to fall together in all the right ways—the epitome of the proverbial "God's in his heaven and all's right with the world." Yet ever since Eden life has been lived graveside; in a moment's notice we can have the rug of happiness pulled out from under us. In the very midst of life we can be in death; contentment and serenity can turn to gloom and foreboding overnight.

The Lord Jesus teaches us to rely on his Father in heaven for all we need in every circumstance. "Look at the birds of the air: they neither sow nor reap nor gather into barns, and yet your heavenly Father feeds them. Are you not of more value than they?" (Matt 6:26). No, God has not promised us a rose garden, but he has promised to give us each day our daily bread—those things we need to support this body and life. He makes provision for our genuine needs. Since he gave up his only Son as the sacrifice for our sins, he will most surely along with him graciously supply all our needs (see Rom 8:32).

Indeed, "if God is for us, who can be against us?" (Rom 8:31). Yet when life caves in, faith is often shaken. It's normal for people to seek out their pastors in times of physical or emotional distress. But when they don't, we go looking for them to provide the consolation of Christ. In the course of conversation with a troubled soul I want to be listening for the telltale signs of uncertainty. Does this soul believe that all things work together for good to those who love God (Rom 8:28) or has this person begun to doubt that God is good after all?

Believing Christians have a hard time believing God is good when they are experiencing so many bad things. Physical illness, family dysfunction, emotional distress, natural disaster, acts of terrorism—any number of tragedies can shake the hardiest of faiths.

The natural temptation for caring pastors in these situations is to attempt to explain the hardship or tragedy. We try to figure out what God is up to; often we even try to defend God's reputation in the face of his apparent disregard or inaction. Worse, we sometimes try and decipher the meaning of the tragedy as though we were privy to the mind of God.

A true physician of souls is not a soothsayer or medium. We never attempt to read the tea leaves of tragedy and mayhem here in this world to discover the hidden meaning behind them. The fact is that we human beings, pastors included, are unable to discern God's disposition by decoding the events in a person's life. Our pastoral role in hardship or tragedy is not to venture into an area for which we are neither licensed or authorized, but rather to be a partner in that individual's suffering. We weep with those who weep just as we rejoice with those who rejoice. But there is no healing in our empathetic listening—or our sympathetic tears either. Rather, we point the suffering person to the one place that God has opened up his heart to the world and disclosed his true attitude toward suffering humanity: the cross. Sometimes the only comfort we have to bring is this: We have a suffering God.

Kate was a young mom with a year-old son. She and her husband Tim were on the cusp of new beginnings: a new marriage, a new child, a new home, new jobs—Tim took a position as foreman in a large dairy operation and was working his way into upper management; farming was in his blood and his future looked bright. Kate, a city girl, had willingly followed Tim in his chosen vocation and threw herself into making a home for the three of them in an idyllic country setting, balancing her administrative assistant position with the busy duties of wife and mother.

Tim recently completed a local marathon after long and rigorous training and usually biked to his job on a farmstead about two miles away. One night he didn't come home for supper at the end of his shift. Kate waited a bit, then texted him, expecting some unruly livestock had delayed him. But there was no reply. Finally she put the baby in his car seat and drove over to the work site. The feed truck was parked midway down the pole barn where Tim had been feeding the yearling stock. The motor was running, and she expected to see him pop up behind the truck to greet her with his usual wide grin, apologizing for being late.

But he didn't appear. Slowly she approached the truck, its powerful engine still churning the auger that emptied feed into cattle troughs. Then to her great horror she saw Tim, his body caught in the auger, being torn to bits. She managed somehow to summon someone who turned off the truck and called the EMTs. It was of course too late. The coroner later speculated that Tim died instantly after falling into the truck bed, apparently in an attempt to dislodge some feed stuck in the auger mechanism.

That experience for Kate is something permanently etched into her brain. A therapist later described the trauma of what she saw and heard and smelled that day as similar to what a person without any military training would experience if dropped suddenly into a fierce and bloody battle. She of course needed a lot of help just to recover some measure of emotional stability and functionality. What happened that day has forever altered her life and the lives of those who love her. And it shook her faith, as you can well imagine. "Why doesn't God want me to be happy?" was her burning question.

And, to be honest, that's a question that resonated with her mother and me. You see, Kate is our daughter. What happened there that day in that cattle shed rocked us to the core. It fell to me to phone Tim's parents with the incomprehensibly horrible news that their only son, so bright with promise and so full of life, was dead. Jane and I went on autopilot; a friend flew us north to get to our daughter as quickly as we could. Jane and I wrapped her in our arms. In the middle of a long three-way hug she said: "Would you pray with me? I don't have the words." Tim's parents arrived shortly afterward, utterly wracked with grief. Numbly we began to lay out short and long term plans. The grandmas went into the baby's bedroom; there was comfort watching him peacefully asleep.

Sleep eluded the grownups, though. I remember several consecutive nights of trying to wrap my brain around the incomprehensible. I tried as best I could to do this in silence, but Jane told me the bed shook with my wrenching sobs—it was my body's way of processing this devastating loss to Kate and their son, little Elijah John.

But Tim's death was my loss too. In a few short years he had become my third son. Grief is the other side of love. When someone you love is taken from you, it hurts. And I was hurting, no doubt about it. For our daughter, to be sure; but also for myself. Several sleepless nights later, in the middle of my unspoken prayers—mostly variations on the question "Why?"—I remember a sense that God was telling me: "Trust me on this one." My conscious response was "Okay ... but I don't like it."

Yes, indeed—the will of God is always good; but the fact is, his will remains always inscrutable to us mere mortals. There's no explaining the inexplicable. Rather, the proper response of God's people in the face of death is to weep. Even though we do not weep as those who have no hope (1 Thess 4:13), we weep nonetheless. Love and grief go hand in hand. It's God's own way, this side of the resurrection.

The funeral service, as you can imagine, was a blur of consolation mixed with pain. As Jane and I escorted Kate into the church, I distinctly remember thinking that it hadn't been all that long since I walked her down the aisle to meet her groom. And now here we were, following his casket. Our pastor, sensing our deep pain, reached over and said quietly to Kate just before the procession began: "This is hard, but Jesus tells us that those who mourn will be comforted."

He was right, of course. Grieving was our holy calling. It belonged to all of us who knew and loved Tim to mourn his death. Even though we were convinced of the repose of heaven and the promise of the resurrection for all who die in Christ, it was our God-given job to weep and mourn—not to figure out the unfathomable.

It was tempting for Kate's pastor and us as her family to try and defend God in the face of this horrific tragedy, to explain his hidden will in a way that made some sense in the face of what looked like meaningless catastrophe. But such is not the way of the cross. Rather, in the face of immense pain the best response is just to lament and cry out like Jesus did: "My God, why?" And so sometimes the most effective thing we can do is simply to acknowledge the pain: We weep with those who weep and we mourn with those who grieve. We do not attempt to anesthetize the agony with trite references to God's "hidden plan." When people can't find meaning in tragic events in their lives, they need to be gently guided to another tragic, apparently meaningless event, where God revealed his loving heart to a suffering world—at a place so full of death and agony they called it Golgotha, "the place of the skull."

Only in the cross of God enfleshed for us and for our salvation can we find a gracious God to whom we can go with our heartaches, doubts, and fears. Jesus knows all that ugliness full well, for in his own suffering he, too, cried out in anguish: "My God, my God, why have you abandoned me?" (Matt 27:46). Because he was abandoned in our place, no child of God will ever be.

Our joyous privilege, then, as pastors is to bring the consolations of our suffering Savior to all who are weary and heavy laden. "Come unto me and I will give you rest," he invites. "My yoke is easy and my burden is light" (Matt 11:28, 30). He knows what He's talking about. In his own body he bore the sins of the whole world and shouldered every sorrow.

As much as we'd like to alleviate suffering and pain, it will not be totally obliterated until Jesus comes in glory. While we can and do plead God's mercy and intercede for suffering souls, the very best you and I as pastors can do is to lead sorrowing souls and hurting hearts to unload their sorrows and hurts on the One who cares for them. There are many things about the ways of God we cannot understand. And we dare not speak concerning things we do not know. However, we do know this much: We have a God who is at his best when times are at their worst. As he revealed his love wrapped in the bitter pain and anguish of the cross, so he cloaks himself in human pain to disclose his love intimately and personally under cover of the opposite, as it were. To know Christ is to know not only the power of his resurrection but also the fellowship of his sufferings (Phil 3:10).

H oliness. Holiness is the third area, and it's a perplexing one. Holiness is often confused with morality. True, holy people lead holy lives. But their holiness is a borrowed holiness. Only God is holy in himself. The wonderfully astonishing thing is that in Jesus,

God shares his own holiness with all his children. So this is a fruitful area to explore as a physician of souls. Just as pastoral conversation is always tuned to topics of faith and providence, it's also eager to pick up echoes of holiness—or conversely, defilement. Does this soul even have a category for the sacred, for example? What does he or she consider sacred? Is there a respect and awe for God as separate and distinct from the daily routines of life; does this person regard God as holy?

We live in a highly secularized culture and our collective mindset views everything and everyone—including God—in egalitarian terms. In this worldview everything exists on a common and utilitarian plane. The natural mind just can't conceive of God as holy since it sees everything in terms of its usefulness. I'm never surprised when I meet people who claim to be seeking God but have no fear of him. They think of God pretty much as an entity whose sole purpose is to make them happy.

It's useful, then, to listen carefully for indications of how this person sees the holy things of God. Are they a threat or a comfort? Is there an awareness that God in himself is holy and that he both demands and gives holiness? Does this soul know that by faith in Jesus, God shares his own holiness with believers so they are holy in the same way he himself is holy?

Samantha was a graduate student at the University of Arkansas, where I spent my seminary internship nearly fifty years ago. Her field was psychology, and—like many in her profession—she was a person with a high degree of emotional sensitivity and awareness. Her dream was to spend her career in treatment of the mentally ill.

During that year I formed several study groups for undergrad and graduate students, one of which was an overview of biblical teaching and Christian doctrine. Samantha joined the study, eager to expand her rather rudimentary grasp of Christian teaching.

In the middle of a discussion of the person and work of Christ Samantha became visibly agitated. I couldn't quite read what was going on with her, but as I proceeded to lead the group in exploring the key scriptural texts that unpacked the human and divine natures in the one person of Christ, she gave me rapt attention.

But when we proceeded to review the vicarious satisfaction—the "great exchange" by which Jesus took on himself all human sin and shame and bestows in turn his own righteousness and holiness to all believers, Samantha's restlessness ramped up a notch. Finally she pushed back her chair and began pacing around the room. "Don't mind me," she announced to the group, "I just have to think this through. Do you realize that if what you're saying about guilt and forgiveness is all true, we could empty many of the beds in our mental hospitals?"

Samantha was beginning to grasp the immense implications of what it means for people to participate by God's grace in a holiness that is not their own, to receive not only forgiveness for their sins, but cleansing and renewal within and without.

That dramatic renewal and cleansing is what you and I are privileged to bring and bestow to people wounded by their own and others' sins.

Just as faith or the lack thereof will inform the way I proceed to provide care for the soul, a person's fear or consolation in regard to holiness will inform my approach. Where there's no fear of God and utter disregard for his holiness I will need to apply the judgment and correction of the law; where a person is threatened by God's holiness I will apply the cure of the forgiveness of sins and the sanctification of the sinner in Jesus' name.

Repentance. The final dimension of spiritual diagnosis is in the realm of repentance. Many people view repentance as a threat, but in actuality "repent" is a word of gracious renewal. It's the first recorded word in the preaching of both John, the forerunner of Jesus, and Jesus himself in the New Testament Gospels. Literally translated, it means "change your mind." Like every word of God, it does what it says. It not only commands renewal, but brings renewal by its inherent power. It carries the thrust of a dramatic reversal, turning around, a turning away from sin and a turning toward God as he comes to forgive all sin and usher in his reign of righteousness.

Repentance, then, is one of most elemental factors in spiritual diagnosis. Does this soul even believe that it is a sinner? It's not unusual to run into people who conceive of sin as an antiquated topic. The relentless, obsessive focus of our culture on the hedonistic pursuit of pleasure effectively sets aside sin as a category. So in my initial conversations with any troubled soul I'm going to be listening to detect whether the person I'm talking to acknowledges sin and accountability toward God. If this soul can name its sins, so much the better. If that's the case, I know the Holy Spirit has been working in this person's life by means of the law, leading them to sorrow over sin.

Here's where the faith filter comes into play. If I'm dealing with a baptized believer and there's a sense of guilt before a just and holy God, I can guide that person toward daily repentance. Being baptized into Christ's death and resurrection, he or she has put on Christ (Rom 6:3–4). Each day the old sinful nature is being put to death by contrition and repentance and daily a new man arises by faith in Christ.

A new and clean conscience is the daily gift of God to every repentant sinner in Jesus' name, and I can pronounce an absolution to that end in his name and stead. That absolution brings a whole new mind and new heart in Jesus' name. For such a person there is the ongoing consolation of the forgiveness of sins now each day and the resurrection of the body and the life everlasting yet to come.

David was a complex man. In his mid-thirties, he was the father of a young daughter and a gifted craftsman in landscape construction. His artistic eye and dedicated work ethic combined to earn him the respect of all his clients. Whether he was building a deck or installing trees and shrubbery and plants, his work was always impeccable.

But I learned his industrious nature had a dark side to it. David had a very painful childhood, suffering physical and verbal abuse from a very controlling father. He described to me what it was like as a boy to lay helplessly in his bed as he heard loud arguments between his parents that often ended with his father beating up his mom. David wished he was big enough and strong enough to defend her, but had learned the hard way not to ever try and intervene, often being beaten himself for his efforts.

David grew up a very angry man. His kind and gentle exterior masked a cauldron of seething anger inside, and he turned to alcohol to dull his pain. By the time I met him his alcoholism was in remission, but those addictions never really go away; recovery always remains a lifelong process.

For David that meant that spiritually he was a wreck. Periodically his flashbacks would push him to the brink, and he would seek my help and counsel. Remorse over sins he had committed would plague him, and the resentments he wore like a suit of armor to mask his wounds from injuries received would become unbearable.

Part of what I learned as a physician of souls I learned from David. He once said to me: "Sanctification is such good news." What he meant was this: Having been so badly battered, bruised and defiled by all he had suffered and done, the inner cleansing and blessing he received in Christ Jesus came as freeing and renewing.

But like all recovering addicts, David needed to receive that cleansing over and over again. One day in a particularly low point for him, after attentively listening to the depths of his distress I determined to use all the means at my disposal to provide intentional healing for his soul. We went into the empty church, and there at the altar rail before the emblem of Christ's cross, he unburdened his heart of a load of sin and filth and I forgave him in Jesus' name and stead. Then, taking bread and wine consecrated as his body and blood, I fed David the bread of immortality. "Take eat," I said, "this is the true body of our Lord and Savior, Jesus Christ, given for you. Take drink; this is the blood which he shed for you for the remission of your sins."

And then the dismissal: "The true body and blood of our Lord Jesus Christ strengthen and preserve you in body and in soul unto life everlasting. Depart in peace."

And he did. Like Simeon, David departed in peace. But like all of us recovering sinners, he needed to receive that peace over and over again. And it was my joy—like yours—to provide it again and again as Christ's servant.

So all four of these landmarks or guideposts serve us well. As physicians of souls, we first must listen before we know how to speak. The art of diagnosis and cure calls for careful listening simultaneously on all four planes, accurately discerning and then carefully responding to these four areas through our conversation, prayer, and blessing: faith, providence, holiness, and repentance.[5]

A THOUSAND EYES

Perhaps by now you're beginning to get the picture of the many multifaceted dimensions of the cure of souls. Not only does a physician of souls need a thousand eyes in terms of spiritual discernment, as John Chrysostom put it, but he needs to be well practiced in the art of faithful and effective cure, applying the word and sacrament to the underlying ailments of the soul in a manner intentionally tailored to bring optimal health and healing in Jesus. These four touch points regarding pastoral conversation will give you a running start on the diagnostic phase of the care of souls. You need to be all eyes and ears; you need to pay attention in Jesus' name to the soul before you. The only way you'll know how to proceed is if you attentively discern not just the symptoms of spiritual distress, but their underlying causes.

This is just the first phase of the cure of souls. The second is equally essential: intentional treatment.

---

5. For more on these four categories, see Paul Pruyser, *The Minister as Diagnostician: Personal Problems in Pastoral Perspective* (Philadelphia, Westminster Press, 1976).

CHAPTER FOUR

The Cure of Souls

Intentional Treatment

Over the years I've developed, in good Lutheran fashion, ten theses on spiritual cure, the care of souls. A thesis is an informed opinion intended to invite discussion. Think of these theses as street signs or road markers along the way to faithful ministry in the troubled days ahead. I invite your conversation as we plot our collective journey toward faithful pastoral care in these times.[1]

Thesis One: All spiritual care is provided by God the Holy Trinity through his word in spoken and visible form.

You and I as pastors are not the healers; only God himself can heal sin-sick people and provide consolation and comfort to war-weary, battle-scarred and wounded souls. We've been charged with the responsibility to preach publicly the life-giving word of God and dispense and administer the sacraments, which, to quote an honored tradition in the church, are "a kind of visible word."[2]

The word of God effects or performs what it speaks. It does not merely describe things but creates things. So while

---

1. Review the many resources at www.doxology.us. Use the "contact us" feature to get in touch with me personally.

2. "For just as the Word enters through the ear in order to strike the heart, so also the rite enters through the eye in order to move the heart. The word and the rite have the same effect. Augustine put it well when he said that the sacrament is a "visible word," because the rite is received by the eyes and is, as it were, a picture of the Word, signifying the same thing as the Word. Therefore both have the same effect." Philipp Melanchthon, Article XIII, *Apology to the Augsburg Confession*, in *The Book of Concord: The Confessions of the Evangelical Lutheran Church*, eds. Robert Kolb and Timothy J. Wengert (Minneapolis: Fortress, 2000), 219–20.

you and I as pastors can—and should—express our personal care and concern to suffering souls sympathetically and compassionately, there is only a temporary measure of relief in our concern and compassion. Genuine and lasting healing comes from God, not from us.

It took me quite a while to learn that lesson in the ministry. I was under the false impression that my personal empathy was the main help I could bring to sorrowing or hurting people. Not only was I wrong, but I quickly ran out of empathy. I don't know about you, but I have a limited capacity for compassion. And when I'm running on empty, I've got nothing left to give.

The very first funeral I ever conducted was about eight months out of seminary. A middle-aged farmer died suddenly and unexpectedly. I had just visited him in the hospital that very morning; we thought he was on the mend. I went ice fishing with my father-in-law that afternoon, confident that all was well. But just after we dug a hole in the ice, his brother-in-law pulled up on a snowmobile. "Albert died," he blurted out. My trip back to town was a whirl of emotions as I tried to remember the little I had been taught about funerals and the care of the grieving.

First up, of course, was a visit to Albert's widow. In recent years they had already lost two grown sons tragically: One died from cancer and the other was a casualty of the Vietnam War. So I poured out my heart and soul in a valiant attempt to console Albert's poor widow and their younger children still at home. The days following were a blur of uninterrupted emotional pain and anxiety for me as I tried to fill the family's great gaping hole of grief and loss as best I could out of my own emotional empathy. Foolishly I tried to draw the caring and comfort out of my internal reservoir, which was rapidly running dry. Somehow I managed to hold it together during those draining days.

Albert was a well-respected citizen in our little community. We had to borrow the biggest church in town to accommodate all the mourners, and that sanctuary was jammed to the rafters. I managed to get through the service and my first funeral sermon intact, although it was extremely difficult for me, since I kept trying desperately to lend that whole family my own emotional reserve, which by that time was almost nil.

In my mind's eye I can still see the anguish on the faces of Albert's grieving family as they sat in the front row of the church before the pulpit. When the funeral finally came to a close, as the funeral director shut the door on the hearse, I collapsed into the arms of one of my elders standing by. I was an emotional wreck, the victim of a very common misbelief among us pastors: that people will feel better if we can somehow wrap them up in our personal strength.

Over the years, I've found this first thesis absolutely essential in preserving my own emotional equilibrium in traumatic cases like these. I find I can enter into some pretty dicey situations without experiencing lingering stress myself so long as I am consciously aware that the help I seek to bring is quite beyond my own capacity to give. As the psalmist writes: "My help comes from the Lord, the maker of heaven and earth" (Ps 121:2).

A pastor who grasps the immense power of the word of God and who stands in quiet awe of his still, small voice need not fear tending the sheep and lambs of Christ even when they are in dire circumstances emotionally, physically, or spiritually. While he deals compassionately and lovingly with them he is also fully aware that no amount of his own love or compassion can soothe the sorrowing heart or free the burdened, tortured soul.

So when helping traumatized sheep deal with tragedy, grief, or emotional and spiritual pain, I consciously seek to tend my own soul as well by reminding myself I'm only a messenger—a messenger for Jesus. My motto becomes that of John the Baptizer: "He must increase, I must decrease." (John 3:30) As much as possible, I want to back out of the scene and let Jesus do the heavy lifting. Armed with his word and sacraments, I can be sure that he will do the healing while I do the tending. I am the attending physician with sworn duties and responsibilities to perform. But God himself is the healer, and He— Father, Son, and Spirit—provides the healing through his word and gracious sacrament.

Thesis Two: This care is received by faith. Human beings are created in God's own image. In their bodies, minds, and spirits, they reflect the imprint of God's likeness. They are creatures with intellect, emotion, and creativity, so also pastors—and we need to intelligently harness all our creaturely gifts for the care of souls. Spiritual physicians need to get to know the souls they tend just as medical physicians do their patients. Remember, my doctor told me as much when he stressed how important oral history was for the care of his patients' bodies. So also the conscientious pastor needs to know all he can about the person he is dealing with. No two individuals are alike, and I'm not talking only about the obvious here. Not only does each person have a different body and personality, but he or she has had a raft of unique experiences that comprise their identity.

Longevity in the care of souls is ideal; the more time I have invested in getting to know a person, the more accurately can I discern what's going on with them spiritually and the more precisely I'm able to address their ailments in a way that they find helpful. Clearly I need to speak their language, not just linguistically but emotionally. I need to get inside their skin as much as possible so as to understand them. Their life experiences and culture will certainly affect how well they receive what I have to tell them. And my communication is not merely with my mouth, but obviously includes facial expression, appearance, and my whole being.

But again, ultimately there's nothing in me that brings help and healing to the suffering soul. As I minister in this situation I'm only an instrument who serves at the beck and call of God on this errand of mercy. God, the holy Trinity, is the active agent of healing in this interchange by means of his word spoken or administered, as in the case of sacramental ministry.

Since the power for the spiritual healing comes from God's word, it is received by faith. No one can believe in Jesus Christ as Lord by human reason or strength; faith is not an exercise in rational deduction. God speaks forth his word and human hearts believe it; that's the long and the short of it. While human reason is used in the process of communication and deduction, I can't argue anyone out of guilt, shame, or despair. Only the efficacious word of God that provides absolution and cleansing can heal the sin-sick soul. And that word is always received by faith.

The question is: Where does that faith come from?

Thesis Three: Faith comes by hearing. Paul the apostle wrote: "Faith comes by hearing, and hearing by the word of Christ" (Rom 10:17). This is consistent with what Jesus told his disciples about the words that came out of his mouth: "The words that I have spoken to you are spirit and life" (John 6:63). Only the Spirit of God can create faith within the human heart, blind and deadened by sin. As God's Spirit once created the entire physical universe out of nothing, so he creates a living faith in sinful human hearts, bringing people out of spiritual death to life.

But he accomplishes this new creation by means of the word just as he did the initial creation. In the beginning God said, "Let there be ... " and there was. All animate and inanimate creation was generated by means of his word. So too when Christ Jesus converts souls from death to life he does it by means of his word, then goes on tending and nurturing them by the very same word. As he put it, the words that he speaks "are spirit and life" (John 6:63). They are not mere words like yours and mine, but they are filled with the Holy Spirit and the life he alone can bring.

Pastoral care is always a ministry of the word of God, whether spoken or visible (spoken or sacramental). While taking great care to be as winsome and accessible to people as we can be, the care we bring does not hinge on our personal charisma or likeability, but rather God's living and abiding word. By means of this word God the Spirit creates and sustains faith in the hearts and lives of his people.

If the Spirit of God worked directly in peoples' lives, there would be no interference with his gracious plan. However, in his wisdom he has chosen to work mediately, that is, through the means of the gospel preached and the sacraments administered. That's where you and I come in as servants of Christ and stewards of God's mysteries. The heart of the attentive care of souls is the appropriate use of God's word and sacraments. Yet because the Spirit works not directly but through these means, the whole process is vulnerable to attack.

That is why a pastor's work is so precarious.

Thesis Four: Devil, world, and flesh conspire against faith. From moment to moment, pastoral work is vulnerable to attack. The concerted efforts of Satan, the ungodly world and the sinful nature conspire to undermine the whole enterprise. I'm going to devote a whole chapter in this book to spiritual warfare (chapter nine), so I won't frighten you with all the gory details right now.

Suffice it to say that you can't expect a rose garden when you take up the office of the public ministry of word and sacrament. No matter where you serve, you can expect tough sledding. It goes with the territory. Overt attack and covert resistance can be expected along the way. Satan and his legion are aligned against God and his kingdom. And he has multiple allies: The ungodly world and the sinful human heart refuse to hallow God's name or let his kingdom come among us. You will notice this warfare going on everywhere you go in your work as a servant of the word. Whether you're preaching on the Lord's Day or sitting in someone's living room or visiting a patient in a hospital, multiple roadblocks will be put in the way of the faithful reception of God's word.

True, sometimes roadblocks to faith are very obvious: compulsive or obsessive sin, immorality, vices of all kinds. But in my experience the more dangerous obstacles are the more subtle variety. This happens when a person is unable to hear or believe the word because he or she has embraced some misbelief or fallen into despair. When that happens, faith is undermined. Though the person hears the word, he or she does not believe it and so the wonderful gifts of forgiveness, life, and salvation offered in that word are not received. In a way, Dan with his conflicted conscience and Kate in the trauma she experienced at the violent accidental death of her husband both suffered from spiritual assault—and the only path toward lasting healing for them both was in the ministry of the Spirit through his word.

Therefore, the faithful pastor always invokes the presence and power of the Holy Spirit to attend his ministry and to break and hinder every evil purpose and will so that the word may be received with faith.

Thesis Five: Pastoral care focuses on enabling the soul to hear the word it needs in the context of its distress. You may have run across the word "pastoral discretion" somewhere along the way during seminary training or during your tenure as a pastor. In my estimation, too often that's code language for "suit yourself" or "do as you please." When a man adopts that approach to ministry he's not being faithful to the Lord in whose name he serves. Our task, yours and mine, is not to do our own work but Christ's work. We are not freelancers; we don't make the ministry up as we go along according to personal whim. We stick with what Jesus has given us to do for his flock. It is his intention in every age to continue dispensing the gifts he bled and died to give to his beloved sheep and lambs. And we are duty bound to dispense them in accord with his dominical command.

Remember that scene in the upper room on Easter evening? "As the Father has sent me," Jesus told his disciples, "I am sending you." (John 20:21) We have no authorization to do ministry apart from our Lord Jesus. That means we care for the souls entrusted to us according to his express purpose and will. Thankfully we don't have to make up our ministry as we go along, guided by intuition. That would be the equivalent of a medical doctor prescribing treatment and medication by whim rather than in accord with sound anatomical science and accepted medical practice. Not only would such a doctor lose his license; he could easily end up harming his patients rather than helping them. Likewise, intentional pastoral care for Dan and Kate had to be informed and guided by accurate assessment and attentive diagnosis. "A word fitly spoken is like apples of gold in a setting of silver" (Prov 25:11). The right word at the right time lies at the heart of faithful soul cure, and we won't know what word to speak unless we have both prayerfully mediated on God's word and attentively listened to the soul.

As shepherds of souls, you and I are charged by our Lord to carry on his work faithfully and diligently, applying his word and sacraments in accordance with his will and purpose. What every soul needs is to hear the voice of the Good Shepherd speak through his word and to be nourished with his holy sacrament. Our job as pastors is to see to it that each person hears the word they need for their unique circumstance. Impenitent sinners need his word of correction and judgment lest they continue in their sin and end up enduring God's wrath forever in hell. Broken and contrite souls need to hear that Christ Jesus has borne their sin in his own body to remove their guilt and bestow his own innocence on them instead. Souls wounded and hurt by the sins of others need to hear that in his redeeming love

Jesus also soothes their hurts and heals their wounds, putting every impact of sin into full remission.

So the "discretion" pastors need to exercise is governed by accurate discernment of what to bring each soul under their care. There is a two-fold process involved in that determination.

Thesis Six: Pastors attentively discern what threatens faith; then intentionally address that threat with the word of God. No doctor worth his salt treats his patients without a thorough examination. He needs to know what's going on medically, listening to the body via stethoscope, manually palpitating injured tissue, sometimes testing blood and urine, perhaps obtaining corroborating evidence via electronic scans of the body. But there's no substitute for knowing your patient from long experience, an oral history, or both. Then and only then can a physician determine a course of medical treatment.

It works the same way for physicians of souls. We need to know something about the person we're seeking to serve in Jesus' name. Every person is different, each with a unique personality and temperament—both of which will dramatically affect their response to different circumstances in life. What appears to be nervous fear may actually be joy in disguise. What presents as sullen indifference may instead be the emotional norm for any given person.

But note that we pastors aren't treating emotions; we're treating *souls*—people made in the image and likeness of God and living in relationship to him. Emotions are important in that they reflect the inner condition of the soul. Yet our concern for people is more than skin deep. We strive to get beyond emotional discernment to accurate assessment of the soul's condition before God—or *coram Deo*, in the church's mother tongue.

Two things are indispensable, then, when it comes to serving as a spiritual physician: being *attentive* and being *intentional*. Faithful diagnosis and cure includes both. First we pay attention in Jesus' name, accurately assessing what threatens faith. Then we speak in Jesus' name, intentionally treating the underlying ailment with his healing word.

When God's word is hidden in your heart through your practice of personal meditation and prayer, you have something to bring each troubled soul. You bring something far beyond your own compassion and empathy that—though essential—is a finite commodity. When your heart is filled with the word of God, which is the Holy Spirit's sword, you will be able to speak not only in words of human wisdom, but also in words taught by God's Spirit. The word of God is an inexhaustible reservoir of help and healing from which you can endlessly draw without ever depleting it.

So the more you are practiced in prayer and meditation, the more able you will be as a physician of souls. If you take the time to fill up the reservoir of your heart with the word of God, you can be sure that when the need arises you will have something to give. Then your care and cure will not be confined to the meager resources you can dredge up from your own heart and mind, but will flow from the lavish bounty of God's own grace and truth. So during pastoral care while one ear is focused intently on the distress of the soul, the other listens for the voice of Christ Jesus, the true Shepherd and physician of souls, as he speaks from the bountiful reservoir of his life-giving word.

So too both components are essential for effective cure of souls: *attentive diagnosis* and *intentional treatment*. The first informs the second. Attentively listening to the complaints of the soul, the spiritual physician can then rightly discern the appropriate treatment, intentionally addressing the underlying spiritual ailment with God's word appropriately and compassionately applied.

That healing word of God comes not only in verbal but also physical form.

Thesis Seven: Pastors baptize people into the death and resurrection of Christ for the forgiveness of sins. Baptism is not just water, but the water included in Christ's dominical command and ordered discipleship: "Baptizing them in the name of the Father and of the Son and of the Holy Spirit" (Matt 28:19). Thus you could say that baptism is a kind of visible word, a "watered word" in this case. God's word always does what it says. And sure enough, mighty things are accomplished by the application of water with the word—or to be more precise, by application of God's word in that baptismal water. In baptism sinners are buried with Jesus into his death and joined with him in his resurrection. "Do you not know that all of us who have been baptized into Christ Jesus were baptized into his death?

We were buried therefore with him by baptism into death, in order that, just as Christ was raised from the dead by the glory of the Father, we too might walk in newness of life" (Rom 6:3–4). Thus baptism constitutes the inauguration of the soul's life with God. In a very real way it is the dawning day of eternity for every soul born into this world in captivity to sin; blind, dead and an enemy of God spiritually speaking. Baptized into Christ, the soul is reborn to life eternal. That's the rebirth by water and the spirit that Heinrich experienced when he was plunged into the death and resurrection of Jesus by the washing of water with the word.

Being washed in the powerful name of the Father, Son, and Holy Spirit, a person is cleansed of all sin and given a whole new life to live. All sin inherited from Adam and committed by that person himself is drowned and dies in that water. In a very real way Jesus takes the sinner, sins and all, along with him into his death and buries those sins in a watery grave, never to rise again. Yet from that very water a new man emerges, created in the image and likeness of the Lord who by his sacred blood has ransomed every soul and cleansed it from all impurity.

Baptism thus is an indispensable instrument in the soul's healing and an essential tool for every physician of souls. Pastors baptize a person only once, but the significance of this watery grave for sin continues every day. For the rest of that person's earthly life he or she daily returns to that washing by contrition and repentance so the old Adam continually dies each day and a new person regularly emerges and arises to live before God in Christ's own righteousness and true holiness. So by faithful, patient teaching, by his own example, and through his prayer and blessing a pastor teaches the baptized faithful to "remember their baptism" by daily repentance and baptismal living.

Baptism thus forms the hinge of the new life in Christ. In many ways, the cure of souls is always ongoing baptismal therapy; the pastor applies one aspect or another of Christ's magnificent baptismal gifts to souls burdened with guilt or broken by hurt and shame. At the heart and center of baptism lies the remission of all sins in the shed blood of Jesus: remission for sins we've committed against God and sins others have committed against us.

Though baptism is a one-time event, such remission meets our collective ongoing need for spiritual health and healing. The forgiveness of sins is the daily bread and butter of every baptized soul.

That's why physicians of the soul remain ever alert and eager to forgive sins in Jesus' name.

Thesis Eight: Pastors forgive the sins of penitent sinners and retain the sins of the impenitent so long as they do not repent. On the night of his resurrection, the risen Lord appeared suddenly among his disciples to commission them as his apostles, or "sent ones" and to send them out to continue the mission for which he was sent by his Father in heaven. Breathing on them, he said: "Receive the Holy Spirit. If you forgive the sins of any, they are forgiven them; if you withhold forgiveness from any, it is withheld" (John 20:22–23). In this remarkable text, Jesus gives his church the gift of his continuing absolution. In every age, until he comes again in glory, our Lord intends that broken, wounded sinners receive the forgiveness he died and rose to bring them.

The church refers to this wonderful gift as "holy absolution." And indeed it is holy. After all, it was divinely instituted and given by Christ Jesus himself. This means that when the called ministers of Christ deal with souls by his divine command, whether binding impenitent sinners to their sins until they repent or whether loosing broken sinners from the sins that bind them, this action is valid and certain even in heaven as if spoken by Christ himself.

This spiritual "power of attorney," as I call it, is effective. I've seen the binding key bring souls to their senses and lead them back home again to their Father's house by repentance. But even more impressively, the loosing key has dramatic power to heal and comfort wounded sin-sick souls. Multiple times over the years I've been privileged to speak the freeing word of forgiveness in Jesus' name and see that word at work. Whether in the general absolution spoken in the countless Divine Services I've led or under the sacred seal of private confession, it's a miracle to see what the word of Christ's forgiveness accomplishes. I've seen broken souls find hope and take heart again. I've witnessed people freed from the chains of sins they had begun to believe were so grievous they could never be forgiven. Dan, Samantha, and David are only three examples of the countless people I've been privileged to serve in this way in Jesus' name and stead.

One would think that such unearthly power would go to one's head. But there is nothing more awe-inspiring than to deliver souls from bondage and free them from the oppression of sins they know and feel in their heart—to live once more in the freedom and joy that comes from a clean conscience, confident that by my absolution their sins were removed from them as far as the east is from the west. Of course though I was speaking the absolution, the forgiveness was not my own. That's the whole point of the sacrament of holy absolution—that Jesus forgives sins through the mouth of his called servants, putting his life-giving word on human lips to speak into the ears of another human soul so that soul can find comfort and solace not in the pastor, but in Christ.

But our God is so rich in his grace that forgiveness comes in more than one way.

T hesis Nine: Pastors distribute the body and blood of Christ for the forgiveness of sins and to strengthen and preserve baptized believers in both body and soul. On the night of his betrayal, our Lord Jesus Christ took the bread and cup of the Passover meal and instituted the sacrament of the altar. "Take eat," he said. "This is my body given for you." "Take drink; this cup is the new testament in my blood shed for you for the forgiveness of sins." Though the Hebrew people celebrated their ancient deliverance from bondage in Egypt only once a year, Jesus bestowed this sacred meal on his church as a weekly remembrance and celebration of their deliverance not merely from an earthly tyrant—as at the Passover—but from sin, death, and hell itself.

In the eating and drinking of this bread and cup Christians are given to eat the body of their Savior as evidence that their guilt is fully atoned for and their sins forgiven. They are given his blood to drink as a sign and seal of the entire remission of both sins committed and sins suffered. In this eating and drinking Christians get as close as humanly possible to Jesus this side of heaven. In this Supper he binds himself to them and them to him. It is the Communion of Jesus Christ the heavenly bridegroom with his earthly bride.

But there's another horizontal communion going on in this meal. In Christ's Holy Supper Christians are joined not just to him but to each other as well in intimate union and Communion, confessing together one Lord, one faith, one baptism (Eph 5:4). In this eating and drinking they become what they eat; dining on the body of Christ they are one body in him. Collectively they live as Christ's body before a watching world, bearing testimony in word and deed to the love of God in Christ.

The Lord's Supper is a great antidote to the toxic individualism of our age. Sharing in this sacramental mystery these many individuals become one body, bearing each other's burdens and heartaches and multiplying each other's joys. Further, they join in this sacred meal in intimate communion with the saints who from their labors rest in heaven's glory, gathered there around the throne of God to celebrate the marriage feast of the Lamb in his kingdom ever and forevermore.

It's hard to extol the gifts of the Lord's Supper enough. You and I as shepherds of souls and spiritual physicians do well to instruct and exhort broken sinners and bruised and wounded souls to find their healing regularly at the altar in this sacred meal. It is an inexhaustible source of healing and strength for all the people of God. Ancient physicians of souls called this sacrament "the medicine of heaven." And so it is. The Divine Physician himself continually gives wounded suffering souls the very body and blood first incarnate in the womb of Mary, once nailed to the cross for us and our salvation, and then risen mightily from the dead as victor over death and hell. Now he reigns in glory, never to die again. But in this sacrament he comes each Lord's Day in intimate union and communion to console and heal sin-sick souls. In this meal Jesus gives his own risen flesh and blood as real food and real drink, strengthening, preserving, and enlivening the faithful not just in soul, but in body as well.

The sacrament of the altar lies at the heart of the church's life. Together with the preaching of the word, this "edible word" is the hub of our life together with Christ Jesus. The Lord's Supper remains an essential feature of the cure of souls. In one way or another every aspect of the ongoing care of the souls for whom Jesus died invites them to take possession of the gifts previously given them at the altar.

And then we physicians of souls continually beckon them on to yet another communion until their earthly pilgrimage is done. Then in glory they will join in the ongoing feast with all the faithful who have preceded them in death and together enjoy eternal union and communion in soul and body with their heavenly bridegroom.

But not yet. In the meantime we continually pray, "Come, Lord Jesus, quickly come."

T hesis Ten: Pastors teach souls to pray for what God promises in his word and bless them in the name of the Holy Trinity, applying the promises of his word individually and specifically. As pastors we are always talking. We talk to people on behalf of God, speaking the living and abiding word by which they find their help and solace in every time of need. But we also talk to God on behalf of people. We pray.

Contrary to popular opinion, prayer doesn't come naturally. The "Lord's Prayer," as we call it, was given in response to the request from a disciple, "Lord, teach us to pray as John taught his disciples" (Luke 11:1). Jesus replied: "When you pray, say Our Father … " Three things stand out here: First, prayer must be taught. Second, the most natural way to pray is out loud. Third, when we pray, we pray together with Jesus. For when he instructed his disciples to pray to *our* Father, he implied that his Father was their Father too.

All prayer of the children of God is therefore prayer in and through the one and only beloved Son of God, our Lord Jesus Christ. Baptized into him, we have put on Christ (Gal 3:27). Therefore in union with Jesus we can pray boldly and confidently to God, the maker of heaven and earth, knowing that in Christ he is our true Father and we are his true children so we can ask him anything as beloved children ask their beloved father.

Prayer is indispensable in our ongoing work as physicians of the soul. As I mentioned above, while listening to a soul's complaints we pray silently for the guidance of the Holy Spirit in discerning an accurate diagnosis of the spiritual ailment(s) causing the distress. But we also listen to the anguish or confusion of the soul in order to know what to pray on their behalf. You could say that all one-on-one ministry is ministry by word and prayer. First, we deliver healing and help by means of the word we speak, then we intercede for the needs of the person as we have heard them both at the close of our pastoral visit and also in our private intercessions.

Remember, you and I have nothing to bring these hurting souls that comes from us. Our help is always in the name of the Lord, who made heaven and earth (Ps 124:8). Our personal compassion and empathy is important, but that quickly runs dry. And there is no lasting healing in human empathy. It might relieve the symptoms for a while, but genuine healing comes from God by means of his word. That's why we pastors do everything by means of the word of God. By means of that word he gives his Spirit, who works faith when and where it pleases him.

We even pray by means of the word. That is, the texts of Scripture that form the basis of the consolation and help we apply to the suffering soul we also weave into our prayer on the soul's behalf. All prayer is essentially answering speech; we as the children of God repeat back to him the word he has spoken to us. The first step in such word-based prayer is simply to echo what he has told us, repeating back to him what he has promised or commanded in that word. Then we thank him for that same promise or command, confess our sins against that word, and finally ask him to give or bless whatever he speaks of in that word.

Physicians of souls are men of prayer, always praying and interceding for the souls under their care. Remember what I stressed in the very first thesis above? You and I are not the healers; God the holy Trinity is. He alone provides the help by means of his word and sacraments. You and I are only emissaries—errand boys sent to bring those healing means by which God himself provides the cure.

HOW TO PRAY

But we can't always be with every sheep and lamb in their time of need, though they are continually vulnerable to attack and prone to spiritual disease and distress. Therefore we do well as spiritual physicians to teach each person to tend their own soul by means of prayerful meditation on God's word. One of the most effective things we can do for each soul's ongoing health and recovery is to teach that person how

The Care of Souls

to pray confidently and regularly as a beloved child of the Father in heaven through faith in the Lord Jesus. While we need to be men of prayer ourselves (more on that later), we need also to patiently teach our people the art of spoken prayer rooted in God's word. Over the years I've taught many people Martin Luther's simple approach to such spoken meditative prayer in his "prayer wreath" outlined below. It's simple, ingenious, yet profound all at once. Choose one concise text of Scripture, then pray that text to God, weaving a prayer rosary of four strands from that one word: (1) precept; (2) thanksgiving; (3) confession; (4) supplication.

For example: "Hallowed be thy name."

1. Here, Father, you teach me that your name is holy. As you yourself are holy and reveal yourself to us by your name, so your name is to be revered above all things as holy. In the waters of baptism you have placed your name upon me and claimed me as your own. Now I belong to you, and I am holy as you are holy.

2. I thank you, Father, that you have washed me in the cleansing flood of Jesus' blood and sanctified me to be his own and live under him in his kingdom.

3. I confess that by the things I have done and left undone I have profaned your holy name and defiled the holiness you have so graciously shared with me. Please forgive me for Jesus' sake.

4. Help me, dear Father, to believe your holy word and lead a godly life in thought, word, and deed, so that your name may indeed be holy in my life and others may see my good works and glorify you for your great grace.

What I've observed in the care of other people I've also discovered for myself. Namely, all things can indeed be sanctified by word and prayer (1 Tim 4:5)—even souls as distressed as mine, continually tempted to misbelief and despair. And they can find healing and strength by means of a personalized blessing, as I myself have received many a time.

BLESSING

Let's admit it; most Christians—for that matter, a lot of us pastors—don't know what to do with blessing. It's obviously scriptural, but we can't quite get our arms around it. The biblical languages have extra dimensions to their verbs that we lack in the English language. Just what does "The Lord bless you" or "The Lord be with you" mean, anyway? In every day conversation we describe, we give commands, we express a directive in the first or second person, but not the third. For example I can say, "Be at peace" but nothing really happens as a result. So when I say, "peace be with you," most people would interpret that to mean that I'm hoping that you would be at peace. But when Paul concluded his second letter to the Thessalonians with the following, he wasn't expressing his personal prayer or wish: "Now the Lord of peace himself give you peace always by all means. The Lord be with you all" (2 Thess 3:16 KJV).

Likewise the apostle extends the following blessing as a greeting: "The grace of our Lord Jesus Christ, the love of God, and the fellowship of the Holy Spirit be with you all" (2 Cor 13:14). Many Christians have heard this phrase most of their lives in public worship. They recognize it as churchly language, but they have no idea what's happening in this apostolic blessing. Sadly, many of us pastors don't either; too often a telltale, tentative "may" precedes the blessings we hear in church.

It's important for you as a servant of Christ and steward of God's mysteries to better comprehend the theology and practice of blessing so you can properly apply it in the care of souls as part of your ministry of the word to individuals. The heart of the matter is that God's word is always efficacious; it does not merely describe reality, but creates it. So when you apply the promises of God's word by way of blessing for a troubled soul, you are enacting God's word upon that person.[3]

This divine empowerment is perhaps most clearly evident in the instruction given through Moses to the Aaronic priesthood in the Old Testament.

---

3. For a more comprehensive discussion of the theology and practice of pastoral use of blessings, see the excellent essay by John Kleinig, "Pastoring by Blessing," http://www.doxology.us/wp-content/uploads/2015/03/28_blessing.pdf.

The Lord spoke to Moses, saying, "Speak to Aaron and his sons, saying, Thus you shall bless the people of Israel: you shall say to them,

> The LORD bless you and keep you;
> the LORD make his face to shine upon you and be
>   gracious to you;
> the LORD lift up his countenance upon you and give
>   you peace.

"So shall they put my name upon the people of Israel, and I will bless them." (Num 6:22–27)

Again, the powerful force of the Hebrew original is awkward to people accustomed only to English. This blessing rings in many ears like a mere wish or prayer. But it's clear that God intended to extend his divine presence by means of his holy name. When God's divine name was placed on the people, he promised his active blessing. Note that God's blessing does not merely convey his approval, but actively enacts and bestows his vivifying and enlivening power: his divine protection; his unmerited favor, and his lasting peace in body and soul.

HOW TO BLESS

As a servant of Christ you're authorized to bestow by means of a blessing any promise God makes in his word. Each blessing begins with God because he is always the actor, and the suffering soul the recipient. For example: "The Lord God, who has (insert his creative, redeeming and sanctifying power here) give you his blessing that you may (find required help, comfort, strength, etc.) for (purpose)—and the blessing of God Almighty: the Father, the Son and the Holy Spirit" be with you now and forever."

I've found several ritual dimensions helpful in connection with blessing. First, touch is the tactile expression of what God is doing by his word and presence. The gesture of the laying on of hands is a scriptural sign of God's enacted blessing (Acts 8:17; 19:6; 1 Tim 4:14; 2 Tim 1:6–7). I usually place both my hands on the head or shoulders of a person to be blessed. Then at the name of God the Son I trace a cross on their forehead with my thumb as a physical reminder of his gracious saving work at the cross, bestowed in Baptism.

Since humans are physical creatures, these tactile dimensions are helpful to impress upon a person the intangible blessings being received. But however helpful they are, ceremonies are not essential. For blessings are not magic. There's no power in the ceremony or ritual, but in the word that's enacted by means of the blessing.

L et's call him George. He's greatly distressed over his teenage children who have made poor choices and gotten involved in risky behavior. He's worried about their faith, and he is wondering how best to fulfill his fatherly vocation. Truth be told, he's afraid he's failed them. After exploring the nature of his fears and the specifics of this situation in conversation, you can proceed to give him encouragement and counsel on the basis of God's word. If he suffers remorse over particular failures, harsh words spoken or vindictive actions toward his children, you can absolve his sins using the authority Christ has given you. At the close of your visit you can bring before the throne of the heavenly Father all the anguish and distress of this earthly father, asking his divine intervention and consolation. Then you could conclude your visit by standing and, placing your hands on his shoulders, speak a blessing rooted in God's word; something like this:

> "Every good gift and every perfect gift is from above, coming down from the Father of lights, with whom there is no variation or shadow due to change."
>
> George, God the Father in heaven who has created you, who by blood of his Son has ransomed you from sin and death and adopted you into his family, who by baptism has sanctified your body as the temple of his Spirit, give you confident peace in mind and heart, body and soul, equipping you with everything good that you may do his will as husband to your wife and father to the children he has given you, working in you that which is well pleasing in his sight. And the blessing of God Almighty: the Father, the Son and the Holy Spirit be with you now and forever. Amen.

THE CARE OF SUFFERING SOULS

There's nothing more challenging than pastoral care for people who suffer from intractable bodily pain. Over the years I've witnessed a lot of hurt and tragedy. But the cases that impact me most are those I've seen up close and personal. I'll be candid; the most wrenching is the chronic, unrelenting physical pain my beloved bride has endured ever since she injured her back years ago plus all the complications since. She continues to be an example to me of patient, prayerful endurance despite real suffering every day for more than twenty years. Then there was a lengthy episode of acute, but enduring misery my closest friend went through, the ugly aftermath of a complex combination of injury and disease. Being one flesh with my wife, my vocation is primarily husband, since we have been blessed with competent and sensitive spiritual care from our pastors over the years. During my friend's intense pain, however, I served also as his pastor.

It's hard to watch people you love hurting so badly, wishing with all your heart that by some miracle you could borrow their pain and give them even a brief respite from their agony. I couldn't do that for either one of them, but I did what I could, and it was appreciated. There's some relief, I suppose, when someone who loves you cares about your pain and stands by you when you're hurting. Loneliness exacerbates pain, after all. Let's face it, though: Human empathy can only go so far.

But there is one who has actually entered into human suffering. By his agony on the cross Christ Jesus, who is not just our Savior but our brother in this human flesh of ours, freely embraced the bodily and mental sufferings of all his saints. Though now risen in exalted glory, he has already experienced their anguish and has sanctified their personal agony with the touch of his most sacred body. In their suffering, people come as close as is possible this side of heaven to their Lord who by his presence consoles and comforts them in their misery. This gives meaning to human suffering; I've seen its impact. Martin Luther put this consolation quite vividly in a pastoral letter he wrote his prince, Frederick the Wise, who was gravely ill. Frederick had acquired one of the largest collections of relics of the saints in all of Germany, and Luther deftly uses his prince's affinity for these allegedly sacred objects to point him to his suffering as a holy thing—a reminder and sign of the presence of Christ:

"If you kiss, caress, and embrace as sweetest relics the robe of Christ, the vessels, the water jugs, and anything Christ touched or used or hallowed by his touch, why will you not much more rather love, embrace, and kiss the pain and evils of this world, the disgrace and shame which he not only hallowed by his touch but sprinkled and blessed with his most holy blood, yes, even embraced with a willing heart and with supreme, constraining love?"[4]

THE PASTORAL LETTER

Throughout my friend's periodic bouts with intense pain, I certainly extended ongoing brotherly affection and support. But in his case this was supplemented at times with distinctly deliberate pastoral care. One of the most useful ways I found to distinguish my personal support as his friend from the care I gave as his pastor was to follow up on the pastoral care sessions with a pastoral letter.

We're all familiar with the pastoral letters of Peter and Paul in the New Testament, but not many of us think of written communication as a way to provide cure for souls. Over the years I've found it helpful to follow up pastoral visits with an emailed pastoral letter to reinforce the thrust of my prescribed cure (treatment). I've found this helps the suffering person to repeatedly revisit my care to remember and reclaim the power and thrust of the word of God in the midst of their distress. So I did the same for this dear friend in some of the darkest days of his suffering.

Here's an excerpt from a letter I wrote my agonized friend after a face to face meeting that concluded with prayer and blessing. I outlined a way he could pray when his conscious mind was preoccupied and overwhelmed with pain. Bodily suffering is not only physically tormenting; it can strangle the soul.

Thank God your devotional life is still in place, though no doubt harder and harder and less and less gratifying. Be realistic, my brother. If you're having pain flare ups you won't be

4. Martin Luther, *Fourteen Consolations* (1520), LW 42:143. LW stands for *Luther's Works*. 82 vols. projected. St. Louis: Concordia; Philadelphia: Fortress, 1955–1986, 2009–.

able to sustain long intervals of uninterrupted contemplation. Settle for snatches. Don't rely merely on your intellect and mind, use your imagination to picture Jesus in his suffering not just for the world but especially for you. (The visual/tactile tool of the crucifix may help focus your attention/imagination on this.) Call to him out loud; cry if you will. As you've learned to focus on how he bears the sins inflicted on you and puts them in remission, add in the misery you feel in your body. In proximity to his suffering, yours is sanctified. "Learn of me," he invites. "My yoke is easy and my burden is light." i.e., cast your burdens on him and yours, though no less painful, will be more bearable, for since he bore them ahead of you he will bear them with you now.

Even though in the midst of severe pain the mind cannot pray, the heart cries out and the body itself does the praying, while the Spirit himself intercedes with prayers that cannot be uttered. (Rom 8:26) Thus the paradox; that pain becomes a mark of ownership and an assurance that you belong to Christ. The feel of the crucifix in your hand is the (more tangible than cognitive) reminder that he is with you in your suffering because to know Christ is to know the fellowship of his suffering (Phil 3:10). Even though fear and panic may threaten to overwhelm you, that suffering will not separate you from Christ, exactly the opposite, in fact; it is a sign that you belong to him and you are safely enfolded in his loving arms. While experientially it may be sheer terror, in reality it is holy ground, marked by closest proximity to the Holy One.[5]

This is only one example of the use of prayer in pastoral care. And admittedly it's a special circumstance. But my point is this: When you provide our Savior's cure for souls, don't just personally intercede for them; teach them to pray as well. Our Lord is the real source of all comfort and care. And he has a standing invitation for all his beloved: "Come to me, all who labor and are heavy laden, and I will give you rest. ... You will find rest for your souls" (Matt 11:28–29).

---

5. Personal email correspondence.

Prayer and blessing go together. Rooted and grounded in the word of God, they are important ingredients in the care and cure of souls. Use them well and intentionally and both you and those you serve in Jesus' name will be blessed.

A NEW BEGINNING

So with these ten theses you're off and running regarding the nuts and bolts of the care of souls in its classic form. With these in mind you're well on your way toward developing a pastoral *habitus*—a disposition of mind and heart as a physician of souls, applying God's own healing to souls tormented by the ravages of sin, both their own and others' sins. I hope you're beginning to develop a taste for this— an infatuation, if you will—eager to see God at work through your ministry providing hope and healing to broken and wounded souls.

But just as medical doctors practice medicine as an art throughout their medical careers, so spiritual physicians practice the art of the cure of souls for as many years as God gives them in ministry. We're always a work in progress, you and I. With each encounter with a troubled soul we learn incrementally more of our ancient craft. Actually it's nothing less than learning to "comprehend with all the saints what is the breadth and length and height and depth, and to know the love of Christ that surpasses knowledge" (Eph 3:18–19).

And so our work is never done. That, too, is part of the *habitus* of a pastor. He keeps on keeping on, knowing that in the Lord his labor is never in vain. Through the ministry he performs in Jesus' name and stead, Christ Jesus himself is at work, together with his Spirit, calling, gathering, enlightening, and sanctifying for himself a holy people.

So perseverance is central to our craft. A faithful pastor keeps on keeping on just like a faithful farmer keeps on working daily in his field, looking for the harvest. Thank God, that harvest is sure to come. One day soon the Lord will gather in all his own and we will hear his welcome voice: "Well done, good and faithful servant. You have been faithful over a little; I will set you over much. Enter into the joy of your master" (Matt 25:23).

But not yet. In the meantime there's work to be done, souls to be won and tended in Jesus' name.

CHAPTER FIVE

Sheep-Dogging and Shepherding

The Noble Task

You and I easily pick up the delusions of our age that cloud our vision when it comes to pastoral work. Since the operation of God's Spirit through preaching and sacramental ministration is hidden to the eye, it's easy to set them aside in favor of approaches to pastoral work that promise more immediate and visible results. We're always working in the dark, so to speak. We ourselves cannot detect the operation of the Holy Spirit by the means of the word we speak and the sacraments we administer. We can't apply a spiritual stethoscope or blood pressure monitor to the soul; only God himself sees into the human heart. So spiritual ministry by definition can't be measured. On the other hand, managerial and psychological approaches to working with people are much more easily quantifiable and thus are more satisfying. Especially in a time of declining church membership and attendance, when churches find themselves struggling financially, we pastors are easily persuaded to focus on these helpful and beneficial modes of ministry to the exclusion of the essential.

ESSE VS. BENE ESSE

There's a classic distinction that can serve us well in sorting out how to go about our work. In the church's parlance over the centuries we have spoken of those things that are *bene esse* (beneficial) and those things that are *esse* (essential). Most people have an innate grasp of this concept, but too often it's set aside in practice. For example, most members of a church board understand that Christians worshiping in a comfortable, well-appointed sanctuary in America have no advantage over Christians worshiping under an open air awning in equatorial Africa; the same word and sacrament that enlivens and sustains faith in one setting enlivens and sustains faith in the other. These sacred means are essential; the surroundings—though they can be helpful—are expendable. Yet the average church board in the west spends nine-tenths of its time and energy (financial resources, too) focused on these helpful but non-essential things.

The real rub is when you and I as pastors begin to adopt the same approach. We set aside the essential for the non-essential. We expend nine-tenths of our time and energy on secondary matters and ignore the primary. We focus on approaches to ministry that are at best helpful but unnecessary. But in the process what too often goes begging is the careful application of the word of God and faithful administration of his sacraments.

In part, this is because we've been hoodwinked into believing that the word and sacraments are passé. Most of our formation and training revolves around these sacred means, yet once we're in active practice as ministers, we're handed other job descriptions. Leadership and management principles drawn from the business world lie at the center of most of these alternate approaches, while others revolve around relational skills. Running a church becomes the focus rather than shepherding souls.

PRIMARY AND SECONDARY

I discovered over the years that I needed to pay pretty close attention to matters managerial and psychological. If you want to truly shepherd souls, you also need to know how to run a church. The managerial and psychological dimensions of ministry are important and beneficial. They are truly an important component in the general well-being of any congregation. Balanced budgets, attention to the property and grounds, strategic plans and accurate record keeping are conducive to excellence in ministry. Likewise, the psychological or relational modes of ministry enhance your ability to connect with people and help them develop meaningful connections with the rest of the body of Christ. So the managerial and the psychological modes of ministry are beneficial to the life of the church and dare never be neglected.

Yet as important as they are, these remain secondary to the only truly essential mode of ministry, namely the spiritual. Until Jesus comes again in glory, his gospel must be proclaimed to the ends of the earth. Through the gospel—not through managerial activities or relational skills—the Holy Spirit continues to call, gather, and enlighten souls captive in the bondage of decay and bring them out into the glorious liberty of the sons of God (Rom 8:21). So it's essential that we hang onto our pastoral identity if we are to be faithful and effective in our work. Remember, I contend that being comes before doing in pastoral work. First you need to know who you are; then you will be more confident and satisfied in what you are doing. Shepherding souls is a *habitus* before it is a vocation. Properly understood, it is not a matter of ambition or personal achievement, but rather giftedness.

THE GIFTEDNESS OF MINISTRY

I'm not suggesting that you exalt yourself somehow as God's gift to your people. Perish the thought that any pastor would seek to promote his own reputation by gathering admirers for himself. This work of pastoring is not about you, remember? It's all about Jesus and his gifts. You only work for him. That's where the giftedness comes in. You are not the groom, but the best man, Gregory reminded pastors very long ago. "That man is an enemy to his Redeemer who on the strength of the good works he performs, desires to be loved by the Church, rather than by Him. Indeed, a servant is guilty of adulterous thought, if he craves to please the eyes of the bride when the bridegroom sends gifts to her by him."[1] You are not to court the bride of Christ. That would be adulterous; she already has a husband. You are, however, the friend of the Bridegroom, and as his best man Jesus has commissioned you as his servant to serve his bride in his name and stead. He has certain gifts he wants to give her, and he has entrusted them to you to deliver. Until he returns to claim his bride he yearns

---

1. Gregory the Great, *Pastoral Care*, trans. Henry David, Ancient Christian Writers 11 (New York: Newman Press, 1950), 75.

to lavish his love on her, continually cleansing her in the washing of water with the word, forgiving her all her sins in the proclamation of his gospel and feeding her with the flesh and blood he gave and shed once upon the cross, but is the continual sign and emblem of his forgiveness, life, and salvation.

What a privilege it is to be Jesus' best man! What a joy it is to see him and his bride together, to observe firsthand what happens when she basks in his love and life as they are freely dispensed in the word he has given us to preach and the sacraments he bids us bestow on her. What a privilege it is to see his forgiveness, life, and salvation at work by his Spirit in the hearts and lives of his beloved. No wonder, then, that Paul reveled at the very prospect. He writes young pastor Timothy: "The saying is trustworthy: If anyone aspires to the office of overseer, he desires a noble task" (1 Tim 3:1). Noble indeed! What could be more noble than to be an emissary of the Lord of life to sow life and hope in the midst of death and despair? But the Lord is the noble one, not us. Our nobility comes from the fact that we serve a noble Lord. Despite all the arduous work involved in shepherding souls in these difficult days, we need to keep focused on the nobility of the office we bear and the privilege that is ours in serving the lambs and sheep of Christ. In so doing, we are actually serving Jesus himself. It's simultaneously a humbling prospect and a wondrous honor.

FAILURE AND RESTORATION

And yet it's not that we deserve that honor. Like Peter, we are all miserable failures—poor, miserable sinners, to be exact—unworthy in ourselves to serve in the office we hold when it comes to our own track record. Maybe we haven't blatantly denied Jesus as Peter did in the courtyard of the high priest the night of his betrayal, but by our sins of omission and commission as pastors we, too, have turned our backs on the Savior we serve.

You know that story: how not once but three times Peter reneged on the allegiance he had solemnly pledged to Jesus (Matt 26:35). Under pressure to confess Jesus, instead Peter denied him, even invoking God's sacred name as his witness (Matt 26:69–74). But this Bible narrative unfolds itself routinely in your own life and mine. Time and again by our words and actions—or lack of them—we turn our back, too, on the Lord who bought us with his blood and summoned us to follow and serve him. Worried about our reputation or livelihood, all too easily we sacrifice our integrity as ministers of the gospel on the altar of popular approval. We shrink from teaching the whole counsel of God because it might not be well accepted, and we're constantly tempted to adjust our words and actions to the trends of the day and the whims of people we serve. Rather than giving them what they need, we settle for giving them what they want. But all too often what they want is God's approval apart from repentance and faith; and so feeling good takes precedent over being good.

Add to this the rapidly disintegrating social structure and you have a recipe for faithlessness. Biblical truth and the created order are viewed as confining and negative, and those who stand for that truth and order are viewed as bigoted and repressive. Sadly, pastors often cave under these pressures. We are less than faithful to the Savior to whom we have pledged our faithfulness.

But even though we're often faithless, Christ Jesus remains faithful, because he cannot deny himself (2 Tim 2:13). Love is inscribed on his very nature as the eternal Son of God; wherever and whenever there is a soul that confesses its sin, he is duty bound to forgive, to cleanse, and to restore every broken and contrite heart. "If we say we have no sin, we deceive ourselves, and the truth is not in us. If we confess our sins, he is faithful and just to forgive us our sins and to cleanse us from all unrighteousness" (1 John 1:8–9).

Peter's heart was broken when he realized what he had done. As the Lord Jesus turned and looked at him after his cowardly denial around the campfire that night there in the high priest's courtyard, he went out and wept bitter tears of repentance (Luke 22:61–62). But here's the point: Though Peter had reneged on Jesus, Jesus never reneged on Peter—His love remains forever constant. As Peter not once but three times denied Jesus, so Jesus not once but three times affirmed his continual love for his fallen servant.

After it was all over—the stripping, the flogging, and the shaming, the horrible mockery and agony, the despicable painful death of the cross, and then the glorious rising to life three days later—after all of that, Jesus, by the shores of the Sea of Galilee, deliberately enlisted

Peter for ministry. And that ministry was a ministry of love, let there be no mistake about that.

We're given to eavesdrop on that seashore conversation in John 21. Right after the miraculous catch of fish and the disciples' ensuing shore breakfast, Jesus asks Peter, "Do you love me?" using the word for God's unmerited love. Peter replies in the affirmative not once but twice, and both times Jesus responds, "Feed my lambs; tend my sheep." And then he asks one more question: "Do you love me?" this time using the word for the intimate bond between friends. The way Jesus worded that question cuts Peter to the heart. No doubt the memory of his spectacular fail in the courtyard was indelibly etched in his mind—along with his broken and contrite heart—the bitter residue of his denial. And now his Lord was questioning Peter's love at every level, both human and divine. Peter was grieved, John records (John 21:17).

I dare say we can understand Peter's grief. For we've been there too. At times our love for Christ seems tenuous at best, hanging by a thread. At times our work feels like drudgery and our heart just isn't in it. We go through the motions, but find little if any satisfaction in pastoring the people entrusted to our care.

A MINISTRY OF LOVE

But remember, whenever we are faithless, Jesus Christ remains faithful. He cannot deny himself. He whose very name is love forgives, restores, and renews us by his love just as he did Peter, his fallen disciple. "Lord, you know all things, you know that I love you also as a friend and brother," said a crestfallen Peter. Christ's response was at once terse and comforting: "Feed my sheep" (John 21:17).

With these words, Jesus did two things. First, not once but three times he pronounced a cleansing absolution, obliterating Peter's threefold denial. It was an absolution of love both divine and personal. Second, not once but three times Jesus vividly tied Peter's ministry to his sheep and lambs with his own ministry to them. It was to be a ministry not of obligation but privilege. It was above all a ministry of love. In effect, Jesus was saying "Love me; love my sheep." In feeding and tending the sheep for whom the Great Shepherd laid down his life, Peter was demonstrating his love for the Shepherd himself.

YOUR MINISTRY OF LOVE

What was true for Peter is also true for all of us pastors. Whatever we do for the least of the brothers and sisters of Jesus, we do for him (Matt 25:40). Thus the impelling and compelling power and force for ministry originates not in us but in him. Our own heart will let us down every time. Our own compassion is limited and our commitment nebulous at best. We just don't have it in us to carry on consistent, intelligent, faithful ministry. But what's humanly impossible is accomplished not by human ingenuity or will power, but by Christ Jesus himself as you and I do his bidding in the power and presence of the Holy Spirit, by means of the gospel and sacraments entrusted to us.

What's true in the ministry of Christ's called and ordained servants is also true in the life of discipleship of every baptized Christian. We love because he first loved us (1 John 4:19). And that love can keep us going through the thick and thin of ministry, in times of joy and sadness, in times of fulfillment and emptiness. Christ's love surrounds us and his hand leads us to ventures of which we cannot see the ending, through perils yet unknown. "In the world you will have tribulation. But take heart; I have overcome the world" (John 16:33). Thus Christ Jesus quiets anxious hearts and stills anguished souls. In the cacophony of the conflicting and conflicted messages all around, his calm voice bestows a peace the world can never understand.

This, I'm convinced, is the sole power for consistent ministry as pastors. We love because we have first been loved—then we in turn love others as we ourselves have been loved. We are, in a very real sense, only channels or conduits for the love of Christ that enfolds us, impels us and compels us for faithful work in service of the Great Shepherd who has laid down his life for us all. That love of his knows no bounds, and I have found personally that his love alone keeps me going in ministry when I've got nothing left in myself to bring. Many is the time, in fact, that my call and ordination kept me sane and on target through some very dark and difficult days in ministry. And just as many times keeping a clear eye focused on him was all that kept me going; if Jesus loves these unlovable people so much that he gave his all and shed his life's blood for them, then I can love them too—certainly not because they are loveable in themselves (exactly the opposite in fact), but because he loves them so and has gifts to bring them through me.

A SHEPHERD AND HIS DOG

In the old days when I was young, dairy herds were comparatively small. On diversified farms like ours, cows would be let out to graze in pasture between milkings. A disciplined dog was a great asset in rounding them up and bringing them in. I say disciplined because it was essential for good milk production that the cows not be harried or hurried, but merely guided twice a day along the path toward the barn, where they would be secured in their stalls for the milking routine. The natural instinct of the dog to snap and attack had to be captive to the will of the dairyman. This took some training, but with practice it could be done. When that happened, the partnership between man and beast was beautiful to behold. They worked in tandem as one unit. This partnership, it seems to me, illustrates the desired relationship between pastors and the Lord they serve.

In more recent years I've come across an even better illustration; it comes not from the dairy industry, but sheep farming. Some years ago while traveling in Great Britain I watched a televised sheepdog competition, a contest testing the ability of shepherds and their dogs to guide a small flock of sheep through a maze. It astonished me to see how closely the dogs worked in synch with their shepherd/masters, deftly guiding those unruly sheep toward the intended goal no matter how intent they were to run off in all directions at once.

With that scene in mind, consider this picture of the relationship between a sheepdog and shepherd as a vivid illustration of the bond between a pastor and the Good Shepherd who has enlisted him in service to his sheep. The sheepdog is iconic of a faithful pastor's work: one ear tuned to the voice of the Great Shepherd, the other tuned attentively to the sheep. Picture in your mind's eye the sheepdog contest I mentioned above, then consider this:

> That dog was the docile and faithful agent of another mind. He used his whole intelligence and initiative, but always in obedience to his master's directive will; and was ever prompt at self-effacement. The little mountain sheep he had to deal with

were exceedingly tiresome, expert in doubling and twisting and going the wrong way as any naughty little boy. Even so, the dog went steadily on with it; his tail never ceased to wag.

The dog's relation to the shepherd was the center of his life; and because of that, he enjoyed doing his job with the sheep, he did not bother about the trouble, nor get discouraged with the apparent results. The dog had transcended mere dogginess. His actions were dictated by something right beyond himself. He was the agent of the shepherd, working for a scheme which was not his own and the whole of which he could not grasp, and it was just that which was the source of the delightedness, the eagerness and also the discipline with which he worked. But he would not have kept that peculiar and intimate relation unless he had sat down and looked at the shepherd a good deal. [2]

What enthralls me about this picture of a dog in the service of his master are three things: First, the dog can't possibly know or even begin to grasp the whole of the shepherd's intent. Second, he's not self-assertive, but only and entirely serves as an extension of the shepherd's heart and directive will. He is an agent of another mind, at the willing and eager disposal of the shepherd, doing his bidding and finding great delight in the process. He can afford to take his time, confident and assertive but never aggressive. Finally, despite the frustration caused by the sheep, the dog's tail is always wagging, because he is completely captivated by his love for the shepherd.

VITALITY IN MINISTRY

Do you see it? Can you grasp what a wonder it is that the same Lord who poured out his life's blood as a ransom for souls would entrust them into your care? Can you comprehend what a miracle it is that he should put his words in your mouth to warn and rebuke, to be sure, but even more to comfort, console, forgive, and restore hearts and lives that are broken and bruised under the effects of sin? What

---

2. Evelyn Underhill, "The Teacher's Vocation," *The Mount of Purification* (New York: Longmans, Green and Col, 1946), 182–83.

a privilege it is to be engaged in such precious, healing work in Jesus' name and stead! Indeed, like Paul before us, such a miracle of love in action should give us pause: "To me, though I am the very least of all the saints, this grace was given, to preach ... the unsearchable riches of Christ" (Eph 3:8).

This amazing, ceaseless, reckless love of the Great Shepherd is the secret to vitality in ministry. The work we do in his service to his people is a ministry of love—both his love for us and our love for him. This love of Christ and for Christ impels us day after day, taking up our tasks one after another, in full knowledge that our work no matter how tiring and repetitive is really his own. We have nothing to give to others that we ourselves have not first received. His gifts of forgiveness, life, and salvation are inexhaustible.

But, like the sheepdog, we cannot possibly carry on steadily in such exhausting and depleting work without spending a great deal of time sitting perfectly still, looking at the Shepherd. This is how we find rest for our own souls. I'll have a great deal more to say about a pastor's devotional life in chapter eleven, but for now let me just say you'll never develop a pastoral *habitus* just by practice. This genuinely pastoral character and grace is something you grow into not merely by long habituation, but through your own connection with the Lord Jesus by his word through meditation and prayer. Your time sitting perfectly still, looking at the Shepherd is not time wasted but time well invested—not just for your own sake, but for the sake of his sheep and lambs. By word and by prayer, God habituates and forms you into a true servant of Christ and steward of God's mysteries to bring his gifts to humanity.

TO KNOW CHRIST

With this vivid picture in your mind, it's easier to grasp the essence of pastoral work. For us, it's never just a job—though most of us earn our livelihood and feed our families by the remuneration we receive from our work as pastors. This work is rather a true calling; we are daily engaged in doing what Christ has commissioned us to do.

Make no mistake about it; this work has eternal significance. Baptizing people into Christ, feeding them with his living word and life-giving flesh and blood erases sin, heals broken hearts, cleanses wounded souls, and gives eternal salvation to all who believe. There's nothing more important than to know Christ—that is, to believe in him and so receive life eternal in the life still to come as well as life in all its fullness already now. Everything else in all the world is peripheral to that; this alone is central.

"Indeed, I count everything as loss because of the surpassing worth of knowing Christ Jesus my Lord. For his sake I have suffered the loss of all things and count them as rubbish, in order that I may gain Christ and be found in him, not having a righteousness of my own that comes from the law, but that which comes through faith in Christ, the righteousness from God that depends on faith—that I may know him and the power of his resurrection, and may share his sufferings, becoming like him in his death, that by any means possible I may attain the resurrection from the dead" (Phil 3:8–11).

JUSTIFICATION: THE
CENTRAL ARTICLE

Theologians of the Lutheran confession—others too—call justification the "central article" of the faith. That is, all other teachings of the Bible revolve around this one pivotal truth, that "in Christ God was reconciling the world to himself, not counting their trespasses against them" (2 Cor 5:19). There are many doctrines, or teachings, in the Bible, but this doctrine called justification remains central to all the others. "Justification" via its Latin cognates has overtones of a judicial decree. It means to be declared righteous by God himself for Christ's sake, through faith. That's really the heart of the matter: that Christ Jesus has taken all our sins upon himself and into himself and by his sacrificial death on the cross removed forever the penalty of those sins. Though he had no sin of his own, he borrowed ours, and our sins killed him. It's as simple and profound as that. Trusting in him and that death of his not only are we forgiven, but God also credits Christ's own righteousness to us.

A little digression here may help you get this fixed in your mind more vividly. It's yet another vignette from my childhood, but if you're a germophobe, you might want to skip this.

When I was a kid, we didn't have a bathroom. Yep, that's right; we had electricity and running water, but no indoor toilet. We took care of those necessary bodily functions in an old fashioned outhouse located behind the garage, out of sight and smell. (Do you suppose that's why they called it the outhouse?) On bitter winter nights we had a convenient utensil set up in the pantry that had to be emptied every morning. Maybe that's too much information for you.

But here's my illustration, and it's not really about toilets and pots. It's about baths. You see, since we didn't have a bathroom, baths happened in our kitchen in a big round washtub in front of the woodstove. Every Saturday night, whether I needed it or not I took my bath there in that washtub. As the only kid I was first. When I was done, my mom was next. Last of all, it was dad's turn. All three of us were ready for church the next morning, having bathed in the same water. By the time my sisters were born my parents added a bathroom and laundry onto the old farmhouse built by my grandfather in 1906. But up until then, the last person to take a bath accumulated whatever those who bathed first had left in the water. My dad didn't mind, apparently.

Sorry to offend your hygiene sensibilities, but I think this serves as a fair illustration of what Jesus did for us, taking on our sin even though he had none of his own. The illustration fails on the most essential level though. The whole point of justification is that not only does Jesus take our sin onto himself, but in the process he also gives us his own righteous perfection instead. This magnificent exchange makes us acceptable to God through faith in Christ Jesus; we are justified. Justification is central; in fact, the great reformers contended it's the doctrine upon which the church stands or falls.

TRUTH VS. FICTION

Now when you start talking about doctrine it sounds like just empty talk. But Christian doctrine is never a matter of abstracts or ideas, but realities. Justification is but one example. It's not a concept, but a reality. We ought not regard it merely cognitively, but experientially. There's nothing abstract about justification; by it Jesus takes our sin just as surely as my dad took on my bodily dirt. God the Father really has heaped all our sin on the sinless shoulders of his beloved Son and put him to death as the innocent victim of our sin as the ultimate sacrifice. By that sacrifice he has bridged the gap between God and humans, putting our sin to death with him on his cross and bestowing on us Christ's very own righteousness and innocence. This is not legal fiction or God playing pretend with us. It's not as if we were righteous. In Jesus God deals justly with our sin. The penalty for sin is death, and at the cross that penalty was paid in full. Jesus carried all our sin in his own body on the tree of the cross and suffered the death penalty in our place. He exchanged his innocence for our sin. But the exchange goes in both directions. Not only was he made to be sin for us there on the cross, but we were made to be the righteousness of God in Him; Christ's own righteousness was credited to our account, and so the divine scales of justice are in perfect balance. God looks at believers in Christ Jesus and no longer sees their sin, but only the perfect record of his own Son—He calls rebels and sinners his own beloved children. And so they are (1 John 1:3). No word games here; justification brings life and peace with God for all believers in Christ Jesus. No wonder it's the central article of the faith once delivered to the saints.

But justification is not just central in preaching and teaching; it's also central for the care of souls. We have something to bring to broken hearts and troubled souls. It's much more than just a feeling or an idea. We bring the reality of sins forgiven and broken hearts mended in Christ Jesus. We bring a clean heart and a right spirit for Jesus' sake. We deliver a clear and good conscience before God. We do not preach ourselves, but Jesus Christ crucified and risen, who brings life to the dying, hope to the disheartened, and light into this present darkness by his Spirit.

THE TARGET: CONSCIENCE

The simple fact is that all pastoral work, be it for those outside or inside the community of faith, has to do with the conscience. Everything we do, whether it's evangelizing a soul lost and without hope or comforting a soul torn and distressed by the effects of sin, is geared toward delivering a good conscience before God. You'll recall that's the location and reference point we're interested in as pastors: *coram Deo,* "before God." This pastoral work of ours is always relational; we're interested in relationships of all sorts. A person's relationships with her family, her peers or coworkers and friends are all pertinent and legitimate relationships to take into consideration, but chiefly our ultimate focus is on the soul's relationship with God. And the conscience is the crux of the matter.

Conscience is more than you think it is. In popular usage the conscience is a lawmaker—a person's moral compass, his personal standard of right and wrong. These days the moral compass has lost its magnetic true north; there's no reference point for moral truth and so people live their lives according to their unbridled inner compulsions. That's why teaching God's law as the revelation of his good and gracious will is especially important for pastoral work today, but that's not what I mean when I speak of conscience.

The New Testament word for conscience is *syneidēsē*. From its cognates this word means "to know together with," referring to a soul's perception of its standing before God. Conscience is not so much a moral compass as it is an umpire, or the capacity to see oneself as God sees you. It's conscious sensitivity toward God's judgment and grace. Pastoral work is chiefly concerned that every person has a good and clean conscience so that it functions well, doing its proper work: detecting both sin and righteousness.

Sadly, this is not always the case. Much of life in this fallen world leads to a dysfunctional conscience. Habitual indulgence of sin as well as damaging injury from the sins of other people scars the conscience so that a person cannot rightly see himself as God sees him. When the conscience is under attack the devil drives a person toward despair, pounding home the conviction that he is unlovable and that God could not possibly love him. Tragically this condition is epidemic. To one degree or another, every child of God wrestles with a scarred conscience every day of his life.

This means you and I have a clear focus for our pastoral work. Everything we do, from teaching a Bible class to visiting the sick and dying to counseling the discouraged to confronting the erring—and of course preaching, baptizing, and distributing the sacrament—every pastoral act zeroes in on this one vitally essential task: delivering a good conscience to people who are constantly under spiritual bombardment from every side, being driven to a bad conscience by the devil, the sinful world around them, and the lusts of their own sinful heart.

No wonder, then, that when Paul instructs young pastor Timothy in the art of the cure of souls he targets the conscience as the center of attention for pastors: "The aim of our charge is love that issues from a pure heart and a good conscience and a sincere faith" (1 Tim 1:5). Faith clings to Christ. When you have Christ Jesus by faith you have all his gifts: forgiveness, life, and salvation. In Christ you are therefore justified; all your sins are heaped on him and in exchange you are given his righteousness so that God the Father regards you innocent before him. But by faith in Jesus you are also sanctified; the defilement and impurity of your sin is washed away and you are wrapped in Christ's own holiness, healing all your hurt and bestowing purity and innocence before God your Father in heaven. There you have it: A pure heart and a good conscience go together, all yours by virtue of your faith in Christ Jesus.

Now pastoral work begins to come into sharper focus. While pastors clearly have instructional work to do, helping people to grow in knowledge and understanding of the word of God, you and I are not trainers in a spiritual health center or life coaches of some sort. Our goal is not to build people up to utilize their own inner resources or become better spiritual athletes. The cure of souls is instead geared to address spiritual dysfunction and disease, restoring health and life to souls burdened by guilt and torn by shame. Our task as spiritual physicians is to treat bad consciences, continually delivering the healing balm of the living word of God and his life-giving sacraments.

WATCH YOURSELF

That means we will need to tend our own souls when it comes to conscience too. For if we ourselves have a bad conscience while we strive to deliver a good conscience to others, there will be an inner disconnect. Even as we speak God's efficacious and powerful word, in the innermost recesses of our mind the devil will call that word into question. Our hearts will condemn us, and rightly so. "If we say we have no sin, we deceive ourselves, and the truth is not in us" (1 John 1:8). What's good for others is good for us too. We need to unburden our hearts and minds; we need to confess our sins and receive absolution. Plainly, we need pastoral care just as much as anyone else. Who among us pastors can say we're without sin, or that we've never been wounded by others' sins? Who of us can say we don't have a bad conscience? What we have been given to give to others we need to receive ourselves; the alternative isn't pretty. It feeds robotic, per-functory ministry and leads to spiritual shipwreck for ourselves and those we serve. On the other hand, when we tend our own souls by prayer and meditation and receive pastoral care from another servant of the word, the results are stunningly effective and utterly freeing. "If we confess our sins, he is faithful and just to forgive us our sins and to cleanse us from all unrighteousness" (1 John 1:8–9).

HOLY SPIRIT, HOLY PEOPLE, HOLY CHURCH

Sadly, many pastors don't get this straight for themselves, so it's hard for the people they serve to find much help. They don't get much consolation from abstract information. There's very little comfort in an idea/concept or a theological category. But there's immense comfort in the Holy Spirit. In fact, Jesus called him "another com-forter:" His stand-in sent by himself and the Father to continue his own consoling work.

God doesn't just give us ideas; he gives us himself. God the Father sends his Son, and the Holy Spirit proceeds from the Father and the Son to continue forgiving sins, lifting hearts, and healing souls among us today just as Jesus did when he visibly walked on planet earth so long ago. By his word, God the Holy Spirit continues to call, gather, and enlighten sinners still today as he did back then, bringing them out of the darkness of sin into everlasting light. And day by day even now he continues to sanctify sinners one by one, bringing them into the fellowship of the saints in light as a company of forgiven sinners, newly created in Christ Jesus to be a royal priesthood, a holy people, one church united in Christ Jesus in this world and the next.

So justification remains the heart of the care of souls, just as it is in evangelization, preaching, and catechesis. You and I have our hearts and minds rooted and grounded in one central reality: the justification of sinners for Jesus' sake by grace through faith. In every instance of pastoral care the recurring central theme is one and the same: "I was determined to know nothing among you except Jesus Christ and him crucified" (1 Cor 2:2). As physicians of souls we are always works in process, continually growing in both knowledge and skills, becoming as erudite and adept as we can at both. Yet the simple message of the cross undergirds everything we do in all these areas: "For our sake (God) made him to be sin who knew no sin, so that in him we might become the righteousness of God" (2 Cor 5:21).

CHRIST OUR SANCTIFICATION

Just as surely as justification remains the center of everything we do, it is not all we do. As sheepdogs for the Lord Jesus we are always working simultaneously in the realm of sanctification. The person and work of the Holy Spirit by means of the word is always in the picture whenever we deal with sinners. And that's always the case, you know. There's no doubt: When you deal with a human being, you're always dealing with a sinner. They may be an ignorant or intentional sinner, and that will need to be taken into consideration. Yet the bottom line is that sin always has to be dealt with. A sinner may be penitent, very aware of the impact of sin on their broken heart. Or they could be impenitent, with a heart hardened and calloused, arrogantly intent on continuing in sin. A person could be on the receiving end of sin instead of the instigator. That is, they could be the innocent victim of someone else's sin, crushed and wounded by hateful speech or hurtful actions. A sinner often mislabels shame as guilt. That is, they may believe they have done something wrong when in reality they have been wronged. (I'll have more to say about that in the next chapter.) For now, just remember that the impact of sin may have multiple different manifestations or implications. And it's up to you and me to work through the symptoms as good spiritual physicians, sorting out how best to deliver a good conscience before God.

My point is that although justification always remains the heart of the matter, when we care for souls you and I are always working in the area of sanctification. This side of heaven, sinners have need of the sanctifying work of God's Spirit as he first calls them by the gospel, enlightens them with his gifts, and then sanctifies them by means of the holy things of God: his word and sacraments. Through these sacred means we are given to share in God's own holiness as he daily and richly forgives our sins for Jesus' sake, then cleanses, renews, and purifies us by his Spirit so we may be holy as he himself is holy. As in justification we are given an alien righteousness by God's grace, so in sanctification we live in a holiness borrowed from Jesus. He is not just our righteousness, mind you, but also our holiness, according to Paul, because he is our redemption.

"God chose what is low and despised in the world, even things that are not, to bring to nothing things that are, so that no human being might boast in the presence of God. And because of him you are in Christ Jesus, who became to us wisdom from God, righteousness and sanctification and redemption, so that, as it is written, 'Let the one who boasts, boast in the Lord.' " (1 Cor 1:28–30).

The perfect payment Jesus made at the cross (redemption) applies to us in both directions. Christ's righteousness is bestowed on us through faith (justification) as is his holiness (sanctification). For believers, then, it's not either/or; it's both/and. It's not as though you can be justified but not sanctified. You cannot borrow Christ's righteousness by faith without borrowing his holiness as well. Justification comes first; sanctification follows. It's a package deal in Christ. The difference is that righteousness is a done deal, perfect and complete, while holiness is always continually in process. We are dying to live each day. The old Adam in us is drowned and dies by contrition and repentance and the new man emerges and arises to live in righteousness and true holiness. Christ's righteousness covers us by faith, but his holiness is obscured and defiled each day by our own sin and the sins of others. Thus the process of daily sanctification goes on day by day, the dying and rising again—until the day we die physically, to be raised in glory.

So the struggle ensues: Every baptized believer lives each day on a battlefield in this fallen world, contending not just against the devil but also wrestling with the compulsions and obsessions of his own sinful flesh. These forces conspire to defile and desecrate the holiness that belongs to every baptized believer. That means that the Christian life in this world calls for constant vigilance; the Christian is always under siege and at war with the devil, this sinful world, and his own sinful flesh.

Sanctification is not a do-it-yourself project. Rather, sanctification is the life baptized believers (justified sinners) live in Christ before God. By baptism into Christ, we put on Christ. We are buried with him by baptism into death and raised with him in newness of life (Rom 6:1–4). Joined with him by faith, we sinners receive both his righteousness and his holiness as a gift. Jesus lives in us as we live in him. In fact, Jesus lives out his life through us as we live each day no longer for ourselves, but for him who for our sakes died and was raised (Gal 2:20). In a very real sense, we are both dead and alive spiritually speaking: dead to sin but alive to God through faith in Jesus. Yet in that we are sinners, our life is continually full of ups and downs, twists and turns. "I know that nothing good dwells in me, that is, in my flesh," Paul writes. "For I have the desire to do what is right, but not the ability to carry it out. For I do not do the good I want, but the evil I do not want is what I keep on doing" (Rom 7:18–19). There's only one solution to this dilemma: "Wretched man that I am! Who will deliver me from this body of death? Thanks be to God through Jesus Christ our Lord!" (Rom 7:24–25). Christ Jesus remains himself not just our righteousness, but our holiness before God as well (1 Cor 1:30).

MINISTRY TO RECOVERING SINNERS

Sin is a given. Until the day we die, Christians are always dealing with the impact of sin in one way or another. Remember, it's not only our own sins that are the problem; it's also the sins of others. Christians are not only sinners, but also sinned against. That's the reality you're dealing with in your daily work as physicians of souls for whom Jesus gave his life. You're called to stand in the breach, to venture out in Christ's name and stead to do his work among his beloved, to extend not merely his forgiveness, but also his healing, cleansing touch by means of the word you speak and the sacraments you administer. You are sheepdogs for Jesus, doing his bidding. Like a tenderhearted shepherd, he yearns for every one of his sheep, be they hungry and thirsty or wayward and lost. Every moment of every single day he longs to tend those already in his flock and to gather his other sheep he has yet to bring into his fold.

That's where you come in. Mission and ministry go together. Gathering and tending, evangelization and pastoring are the package work to which you are called. Equipped with his life-giving word and healing sacraments, Jesus sends you out empowered by his Spirit both to gather in those sheep that have wandered far from home and to tend those already gathered. When you deal with people by his divine command, Christ deals with them personally. It's as if Christ were dealing with them himself. When you forgive, Christ forgives. When you console, Christ consoles. You do nothing at your own volition, but you serve the Lord who sends you. You are merely his sheepdog, serving his directive will and extending his work among his beloved sheep and lambs: comforting broken hearts, lifting the unbearable load of their own sins and soothing their wounds from sins committed against them.

At bottom, sin of every sort is fundamentally idolatry. Sin will not let God be God, but insists on elevating the self to sit on God's throne. It says, "My will be done; my kingdom come." Sin turns to the mirror in every time of need and looks to its own reflection for all good; it will not worship or obey the Creator because it prefers to worship created things instead.

So you have your work cut out for you, assisting souls to find their way through this world of sin while contending with the effects of their own sin and the sins of others. It's a tall order and—to be honest—an impossible task. Who of us is capable of these things? There's not a man among us who is up for this job, left to our own devices. Humanly speaking we just don't have it in us to be able ministers of the New Testament and discerning physicians of the soul. But of course that's what I've been telling you all along: Try and do this relying on your own devices and you'll crash and burn, spiraling into depletion and failure. But while you cannot do this work by your own reason or strength, God the Holy Spirit will equip you with every good gift, working in you what is well pleasing in his sight as you serve in Christ's name and stead.

JESUS THE PACK LAMB

Jesus arrived at the Jordan where John was baptizing, preaching a message of repentance for the forgiveness of sins (Mark 1:4). When John saw him, he introduced him to the faithful as a sin offering: "Behold the Lamb of God, who takes away the sin of the world" (John 1:29). In Old Testament terms, Jesus remits sins in two ways: He is both the sacrificial lamb and the scapegoat (Lev 16: 7–10). There were two goats presented before the Lord in Israel's rituals. The first was slaughtered and offered to God as a sacrifice, the second was sent out of the camp, bearing all the sins of Israel away into the wilderness. The sins were first imposed upon the goat ritually, and then the goat was sent out, taking all their sins away with him into the wilderness.

The people at the Jordan understood John to mean that Jesus was forgiving and remitting sins in both dimensions. In that he was the final sacrifice for sin, those sins were to be erased and forgiven. In that all sin was heaped upon him, that sin would be removed as far as the east is from the west. The church's song has wonderfully captured this in the historic liturgy, singing John's proclamation at the Jordan before the faithful receive the redeeming flesh and blood of Jesus in communion as a pledge and guarantee that all guilt has been paid in full. "Lamb of God, Who takes away the sin of the world, have mercy upon us." *Agnus Dei qui tollis peccata mundi, miserere nobis.* That word *tollis* ("bear, carry") implies that sins have been imposed on Jesus so that he might take them all away with him into his death.

THE REMEDY

But this is not just a liturgical trivia game; it's highly significant for your pastoral toolkit. If Jesus has borne away all sin as well as paid for it by his death, that means that sins are not merely forgiven, but remitted. That is, he puts sins into remission in a two-fold way. On the one hand he pays the full price of sin, enduring the wrath of God the Father in our place. But just as significantly, he carries sin away from us, together with all the consequences of sin. We believe not merely in the forgiveness of sins, but the remission of sins as well.

This means that when people have sinned, there is forgiveness for them in Jesus. But when they have been sinned against, there is also balm and consolation in Jesus as he takes on their hurt and injury and bears it all away from them. He puts all sins into remission—both the sins we have committed and the sins that have been committed against us. This remission is increasingly important to bestow in Jesus' name, especially in our dysfunctional and abusive era. Wounds of body, mind, and conscience abound. But they find their solace and healing in Jesus, who is not merely sacrifice but scapegoat. Taking all guilt and shame upon himself and into his own body, he carries it all away. In a very real way Jesus is our pack lamb, taking that whole mess away.

The very same gospel that forgives guilt also cleanses from shame. Jesus Christ frees and liberates us from sin's bondage—in the case of guilt, by erasing our guilt and bestowing his own righteousness instead. In the case of shame, Christ Jesus heals our wounds by his redeeming love, cleanses us from the defilement of sins committed against us, and sanctifies us with his own holiness, thus claiming us as his very own and restoring us to full status as beloved children of our loving Father in heaven.

So you could put it this way: In Jesus Christ and his saving work, God puts all the effects of sin in full remission. The deadly disease of sin is conclusively set aside by Christ. All the sins we've committed against him he removes from us as far as the east is from the west, and all the sins committed against us and the hurt they've caused he sets aside as well, healing our wounds and bestowing on us his loving favor instead. Guilt and shame find their common remedy in the gospel of Christ our Lord.

But remission of sins is not just for a few, you know; it's for you too! So before, during, and after you take up the noble task of being a sheepdog, you'll need to spend a considerable amount of time sitting perfectly still, looking at the Shepherd.

CHAPTER SIX

Guilt and Shame

If you've talked with suffering souls for any length of time as I have, you've discovered that most people have a hard time distinguishing guilt from shame. And that stands to reason, for subjectively they're hard to tell apart; internally they feel very much the same. Many people who have been shamed feel inordinately guilty and are convinced deep in their soul that God is angry at them. Though they may not use the label "shame" to describe what they are experiencing, that's what it amounts to—they've clearly been dishonored or violated by the actions of others. Conversely some who are in fact guilty have convinced themselves that they're perfectly innocent and others are to blame instead. Paradoxically, they think they've been victimized and that others are perpetrators, when in fact it is their own sin that lies at the root of their discomfort. Guilt is sin committed; shame is sin suffered.

There's certainly a fair amount of overlap between guilt and shame. You can see this clearly in the case of our first parents. When first Eve and then Adam caved to the temptations of Satan in serpentine disguise, they experienced both. When they elected themselves God and violated his command not to eat from the forbidden fruit, immediately they came under God's judgment. "In the day that you eat of it, you shall surely die," he had warned (Gen 2:17). Although their physical death was a long way off, that day they disobeyed their Creator something inside them died. Their eyes were opened and for the first time their unclothed bodies felt intensely shameful

137

to them. That evening when God came seeking their companionship in the cool of the day, they were nowhere to be found. And so their Creator graciously went seeking after them: "Adam, where are you?" He kept calling out. That's our God for you; he has never stopped seeking after the lost ever since. "I was afraid, for I was naked," Adam replied, "and so I hid myself."

There you have it. That's shame for you; it runs away and hides. It seeks shelter away from God, rather than in God. Instead of delighting in God's company as they usually did, Adam and Eve hid when he approached them. That's the way shame works. It cripples and shrivels the soul, burdening the heart with an intense and overpowering sense of disgrace and dishonor. Shame strips body and soul of all their glory, leaving people naked and afraid before God.

Note that the root of their problem was sin. It was not sin in the abstract, but actual and specific sin. Eve took the fruit and ate it, and then she gave some to her husband and he ate. They had violated God's will; they did wrong and stood guilty and condemned before him. That's the root of our problem too. We all, like our first parents, have sinned and fallen short of the glory of God (Rom 3:23). All we like sheep have gone astray, we have wandered, every one of us, to his own way (Isa 53:6). Because we prefer our way to God's way, we keep on doing our own will rather than God's will. We sin, and in sinning we violate God's commands and come under his righteous judgment. We're guilty before him, and so there's a price to be paid. The wages of sin is death—both physical and spiritual. Sin always exacts a price, and that price is death.

But the same sin that violated the will of God and placed Adam and his wife under his judgment also shamed them—they were also victims of sin. That is, they had a keen sense of deep and unrelenting disgrace. That's why they took cover; they needed to hide their shame.

Guilt has to do with behavior, while shame is a matter of identity. Guilt is tied to the sinful things I've done; shame is the continuous experience of utter remorse over who I am. A person who experiences shame has an abiding sense of failure and self-disgust. We can see how this works in our children. When you correct your child, he is crestfallen because he knows he's done wrong. But he also knows he's disappointed you and therefore has an intense sense of unworthiness.

He's ashamed. For his guilt your child needs forgiveness because he knows he has wronged you. For his shame he needs cleansing from his deep sense of defilement and degradation. Maybe he wouldn't be able to put it into words, but inwardly he feels dirty and contaminated in your eyes, and just as he would need a good bath if he fell in a mud puddle, he craves restoration in your sight. So besides forgiving him, when you wrap him up in your arms you reaffirm and embrace him as your beloved son.

This is exactly how Jesus pictures God's cleansing mercy in his gripping story about a wayward son and his loving father.

THE WASTEFUL SON

Jesus vividly explores both the distinction and overlap of guilt and shame in his famous parable of the return of the prodigal. "The Prodigal Son" it's usually called, but I like the late Helmut Thielecke's title "The Waiting Father" better. The father figure in the parable is the real hero of the story. Jesus pictures him as the one constant in the two different scenes of the narrative. He is a man with two sons. The eldest stays home to work the family farm; the youngest sets out to seek his fortune. There's just one hitch: He impudently demands his share of the inheritance and then proceeds to waste all the assets his father gave him in reckless living.

The boy soon finds himself in desperate straits. He is hired on with a hog farmer tending pigs. You can't get much more desperate if you're a Jewish boy with no option other than to work among unclean animals. The last straw came when he found himself looking enviously at the hog trough. When pig slop began to look good to him he knew he had reached rock bottom. That's when he decided to go back to his father's house. He knew he had done wrong; he had sinned against both God and his father. But his sin not only resulted in guilt, it also brought a heavy dose of shame. This man had a keen sense of unworthiness; he felt deep in his bones that his brash rebellion had disqualified him from sonship. He even rehearsed a little speech: "Father, I have sinned against heaven and before you. I am no longer worthy to be called your son. Treat me as one of your hired servants" (Luke 18:18–19). That's what shame feels like: It strikes the very core of your being and radically alters your sense of identity.

And so that dejected boy began the long trek home, silently practicing his remorseful speech over and over. He knew he had not only wronged his father; he had failed him as a son. Although he hoped to get back under his father's roof, he couldn't begin to hope that he could ever be a son again. But maybe he could hire on as one of his father's servants.

THE WAITING FATHER

I love the way Jesus tells this story. As the boy trudges on doggedly toward home, we learn that his father has been waiting all along, anxiously scanning the horizon for his beloved son. "But while he was still a long way off, his father saw him and felt compassion, and ran and embraced him and kissed him" (Luke 15:20). Woodenly the dejected boy began the sad little speech: "Father, I have sinned against heaven and before you." That was the voice of guilt talking; it confesses wrongs committed. But then he went on: "I am no longer worthy to be called your son." That was the voice of shame speaking; it speaks of wounds suffered. Remember, guilt has to do with behavior, shame has to do with being and identity. Believing himself to be disqualified as a son, he hoped to be hired as a servant instead.

But his father would have none of it. Interrupting his son mid-sentence, he turned to a servant and gave orders to quickly bring a cloak, a ring, and shoes—all emblems of sonship. Not only were his son's wrongs forgiven, but his shame was lifted and his honor restored. "Bring quickly the best robe, and put it on him, and put a ring on his hand, and shoes on his feet" (Luke 15:22). Although the son had wandered far away from his father's house and squandered every vestige of his inheritance, his father's embrace told him all was forgiven. Dressed and adorned as a son he knew he had come home again.

WELCOMING SINNERS

That's what's so utterly thrilling about the care and cure of souls. Pastors are servants in the Father's house, bringing the signs and seals of sonship to remorseful, broken children of God. Over and over again you and I have the remarkable privilege of welcoming souls back home where they belong. God's fatherly heart yearns to wrap all his erring sons and daughters in his embrace and call them his very own, to restore them to their rightful place within his household. And that's exactly where we pastors come in. Calling wandering souls to repentance by repeated earnest entreaty, we invite them to find themselves and come on home where they belong. And when by God's grace they turn from their sin and shame, we come alongside to accompany them on the way. We teach the habits of heaven to those whose lives have been scarred and broken by habitual sin.

The first step in the journey home is of course simply confessing before God who they are: "I, a poor miserable sinner." Whenever a person admits their sin before God and us, then you and I are under orders. We are duty bound to forgive penitent hearts and cleanse them with the absolving word entrusted to us as emissaries of the living Christ: "All your sin—including that one—has been placed on Jesus' back and he has taken it all away with him in his death. In his name and stead I forgive you all your sin."

Whether by using a formal rite for individual confession and absolution or the simple declaration of forgiveness and cleansing in the name of Christ as I've outlined above, you in that instance have one of the most amazing privileges ever granted to mortal man: to be the mouth of Christ absolving sin and erasing guilt. It's often the very first step leading to lasting renewal and hope for sorrowing hearts that had given up on the thought that God could ever love them again.

That's the first and essential step, but the way home to the Father's house is a lifelong journey, filled with all sorts of twists and turns and ups and downs. Certainly that's what David's life was like. As a recovering addict, he knew the importance of daily repentance; in many ways his life depended on it. The habits of sin are deeply engrained in a wounded sinner's heart, mind, and body. And they die slowly—and often painfully, due to the inevitable objections of the old Adam who always protests that he's too young to die, but keeps on promising he'll reform and mend his ways. But the sinful nature cannot be taught new tricks. Daily sin must be done to death by contrition and repentance. The old Adam simply cannot be reformed; daily he must be drowned and die so that the new man in Christ may emerge and arise, created anew in true innocence and blessedness.

So we physicians of souls are patient with our patients. That is, we go steadily on with it, like the sheepdog in the illustration. Remember, that dog didn't become discouraged when the sheep returned to their old habits; he stuck with doing the shepherd's will. His tail never ceased to wag because he knew the shepherd had things under control. So doggedly he just kept on keeping on doing what he'd been given to do.

That's really the secret to joy in ministry. Like that proverbial sheepdog, you and I can't possibly grasp the whole of our Savior's plan. Yet joyfully we take on what he's given us to do, eager to do his bidding. And that's just it, don't you see? Ours is not just a job; it is a holy calling. Jesus has personally commissioned us to feed his sheep and tend his lambs. He bought those sheep with his own blood, and he's given his flock to us to tend and nourish in his name and stead. What a humbling honor; what a noble task this our ministry is!

More than an occupation, then, being a pastor is a divinely given charisma, in which you and I are continually being shaped and formed into faithful servants of Christ and stewards of God's mysteries. We are called to steadily hold forth the word of life to souls sinking in a quagmire of sin and shame, repeatedly ushering people into the presence of the living God where day after day they receive life in the midst of the death that threatens to engulf them.

LESS THAN THE LEAST

This might be a good spot for me to let you in on a little secret: I've been insecure and unsure of myself most of my life. If you would have asked me when I was a kid growing up on the farm what I wanted to do with my life, likely I would have described things I was familiar with: tilling the soil, tending the crops, milking cows, slopping hogs, gathering eggs. That was an idyllic, comfortable life—and it was all I knew. It turns out that God had other things in mind. As a child, I never would have anticipated becoming a pastor.

There might have been a few early indicators though. Like most kids, I enjoyed playing make believe. Having no television, no siblings until I was ten years old, and few if any playmates, I enjoyed playing cops and robbers as well as cowboys and Indians (we weren't socially aware back then) all by myself. I wiled away many an enjoyable afternoon under the bright western Minnesota skies playing the roles of both protagonist and antagonist, hero and villain.

But I also liked to play "pastor." Week by week on Sundays I was fascinated to see my pastor disappear during the sermon hymn, exit the chancel, and reappear in the pulpit to preach God's word to an attentive congregation. So like all kids I imitated what I saw.

In our barn we had a haymow up above where the seasonal supply of alfalfa and brome grass was stored; every afternoon my dad would toss huge forkfuls of hay down through the haymow door into a racked enclosure below. Then he fed the hay to the cows in their stalls arranged in two rows on either side of the central aisle running the full length of the barn. With their heads secured in stanchions, the cows stood facing the central aisle from opposing sides.

In my childhood imagination, those cows facing each other on either side of the aisle looked kind of like a Sunday congregation lined up neatly in pews—and the empty haymow rack at one end became my pretend pulpit. I can't remember what texts I chose nor the content of those "sermons," but I do recall that those cows gave me their rapt attention.

As an adolescent, people kept telling me I should consider a career in pastoral ministry. Though the idea was appealing to me, I couldn't shake an inherent insecurity; how could I ever get up and preach a sermon in front of *people*? Cows are inquisitive by nature, but humans are a bit more discerning—and a whole lot more critical.

I won't bore you with the details of how I finally bit the bullet and enrolled in prep school and then seminary. But my point is this: When I reluctantly agreed to offer myself as a candidate for pastoral ministry, I could never envision serving in a congregation different from the church I grew up in—that was all I'd ever known. I knew men and women of the soil like my mom and dad, simple people who eked out a living by working with their backs and their hands, living close to the land. I thought that maybe by God's grace he would equip me to serve in a rural church, but any other setting seemed totally foreign and off-putting.

You can imagine how intimidating it was for me, then, when I was assigned to serve my intern year in a congregation in a university town. Key lay leaders were full professors on the faculty; men and women with PhDs. To say I felt out of my element is an understatement. A farmer boy among the intellectuals—imagine that!

One day when I confided my insecurities, an academic set me straight. I think he was a professor of mathematics. "Don't worry," he said, "when I come to church I don't come for intellectual stimulation; I come as a sinner to hear the word of God." A wise man, that guy! He knew how to encourage a simple Minnesota farm lad to continue preparation for his God-given vocation.

And the rest is history. Since then I've been blessed to serve farm people like those I knew as a child, small town businessmen and women, mission converts, university students and professors, suburbanites, ethnic minorities and city folk. I've taught in a seminary classroom, written several books of popular theology and devotion, and now I'm serving as an executive for a para-church organization doing continuing education for clergy and laity around the world.

It has all been purely by the grace of God, without any merit or worthiness in me. To be sure, there is nothing in me really that qualifies me for the pastorate. It's just that God through his church has brought me to this time and place and equipped me for this task, using the faithful people of God around me to enrich me and support me. Like Paul, I can honestly say: "To me, though I am the very least of all the saints, this grace was given, to preach to the Gentiles the unsearchable riches of Christ" (Eph 3:8).

So if you're a man contemplating becoming a pastor, or if you're already serving in that role, but you are wondering whether you actually have what it takes to keep on going, here's some advice from someone who's been there, done that. There's really nothing in you that prepares you for the noble task of serving as a sheepdog for the Great Shepherd. But when he calls you to serve him, surprising things can happen. A pastoral *habitus* isn't acquired overnight. "Be patient, and he who first began a good work in you will bring it to completion in his good time, working in you what is well pleasing in his sight" (Phil 1:6). I know it's trite to say, but in this case it's true:

Today is the first day of the rest of your life. If you've dropped the ball, confess your sins and begin again by the grace of God in Christ Jesus our Lord. He can and will accomplish astonishing things through you if you give him half a chance. The real resources for ministry aren't in you, after all, but in the tools he places into your hands and mouth.

THE MEDICINE OF HEAVEN

The sole instruments of healing we have at our disposal to bring healing to souls given into our care are the word and sacraments. But these are not empty human rituals or hollow gestures. By these sacred means God the Holy Spirit continues his perpetual work of calling, gathering, enlightening and sanctifying for himself one church on earth. The wonder is that he would use such flawed servants as us for such a noble task.

Yet such is the lavishness of his grace that he uses the likes of us to do his heavenly work on earth. He places his powerful word in our feeble mouths to call sinners to repentance, to heal broken and wounded sinners with forgiveness for their sin and covering for their shame. Using our weak and unworthy hands he plunges sinners young and old down into the bath of regeneration where they die with Jesus and then are raised up with him to live his risen life in true righteousness and innocence. Into these frail hands of ours he places the living bread come down from heaven to bring life to the world. Every Lord's Day we are privileged to bring hope to sorrowing souls and courage to trembling hearts as they receive the flesh of Jesus to eat and his blood to drink under earthly bread and wine as a sign and seal of his love and grace.

NOT SLAVES BUT SONS

Broken hearts and wounded souls usually are so battered that they lose perspective on their Father in heaven. Steeped in dysfunction, they're frequently plagued with misbelief, despair, or other great shame and vice. They have blindly embraced the devil's lie that they're alienated from the Father's house, no longer worthy of his love. The best they can hope for is to hire on with him as a servant, hoping to earn for themselves some sort of place within his household. But like the father in Jesus' parable, our God in heaven will have none of that. He embraces every fallen sinner who returns to him and calls them his precious son or daughter. Calling his servant, he bids him come and wraps these children of his in the signs and seals of his love: The robe, the ring, the shoes that indicate he is theirs and they are his. He prepares a feast for them and bids them take an honored seat at the table.

You and I are that servant. The loving Father commands us to preach glad tidings to the sorrowing, hope to the despairing, healing for the brokenhearted, restoration to the fallen. Wrapping broken sinners in their baptismal identity, we bring them wholeness once again as by contrition and repentance their old Adam is drowned and dies and a new man emerges to live by faith in the Son of God who loved them and gave his life for them. Remember David? Deeply wounded by an abusive father, he kept trying to earn his way back into the good graces of his Father in heaven by signing on as a servant. The forgiveness, life, and salvation I repeatedly lavished on him in Jesus' name were indispensable signs that he belonged in the Father's house not as slave, but as beloved son.

Watch yourself, though. You'll be tempted to think that once you've led a baptized soul to contrition and repentance, you're done. Sometimes after initial success we're too quick to pull the plug on one particular soul and move on to another. But of course it's not that easy; you know from your own experience as a Christian that the old Adam is a good swimmer. Drown him by contrition and repentance one day and the next day he's back at it again, alive and kicking and up to his old familiar mischief.

GARDENING AND REPENTANCE

I'm reminded of the necessity of ongoing repentance every gardening season. I've rented a community garden plot now for nearly fifteen years; it's good medicine for my farmer soul to regularly get my hands into dirt. One bad thing about my garden plot, though: It's got a nasty infestation of quack grass. This noxious weed reproduces not just by producing seeds, but via an elaborate underground network of rhizomes that, left unchecked, soon turns a nice productive garden into a solid weed patch. So every season I set out to do battle, laboriously spading up every square foot of my raised beds and then painstakingly sorting through every cubic foot of soil to remove every last root fragment I can find. This spring I think I eradicated ten large five gallon buckets full of quack roots by hand.

Patience and persistence are two cardinal virtues in farming, and that's true in pastoring as well. You can't take any short cuts with sin-damaged souls. When you barge in with the equivalent of a roto-tiller to address the symptoms, temptations only multiply; guilt and shame reproduce. Rather, you need to patiently persist in listening and diagnosing the cause of the injury. When the soul is led to contrition and repentance then the healing power of God's word can go to work, rooting out sin and bestowing life and peace in Christ. So, no short cuts. Above all else we physicians of souls need the patience to hang in there and stay with it, even when it's tough going. We press on, simply doing what we've been given to do again and again.

But what amazing things we've been given to do! We forgive penitent hearts, we comfort anxious hearts, we console weary hearts, we soothe wounded hearts—not out of our own compassion, remember, but from the bottomless well of the Savior's love and in the promise of his continuing presence by means of his word preached and sacraments administered.

TREATING SIN ADDICTS

We are all addicts. Ever since the cataclysmic rebellion of our first parents in the garden every last one of us is prone to sin. Sin is what sinners do. And, says Jesus, "Whoever commits sin is a slave to sin" (John 8:34). Sin is addictive. Even though on one level we know that sin will kill us, we've come to believe that we need to sin in order to go on living. That's the bad news. But the good news is surpassingly good. "If the Son sets you free, you will be free indeed" (8:36). The ongoing story of the Christian life is the unfolding saga of sin addicts continually being set free to live as sons, not slaves.

Addicts never go into recovery without therapy. And thank God, he has provided treatment for sin addiction. In all addictions the human will is powerless to effect change, and that's the way it is with sin addiction too. Try as we might, our own willpower can't quell the compelling urge to indulge the cravings of our sinful heart and flesh. The quandary is exactly as Paul put it: "For I know that nothing good dwells in me, that is, in my flesh. For I have the desire to do what is right, but not the ability to carry it out. For I do not do the good I want, but the evil I do not want is what I keep on doing. Now if I do what I do not want, it is no longer I who do it, but sin that dwells within me" (Rom 7:18–20).

There's only one way out of this dilemma, of course. If we're going to escape the prison cell of our own sinful lusts and desires, God himself will have to break us out. And of course that's exactly what he has done. Taking on our human flesh and bones, the eternal Son of God became one of us, subject to every temptation known to humanity. Actively he obeyed the whole will and law of God as a stand-in for us all. Passively he took upon himself and into his sinless flesh the sin and iniquity of every human being. He dealt conclusively and definitively with our guilt and shame by his sacrificial death at Calvary, being first put to death for our offenses and then raised again for our justification (Rom 4:25). This is what many Christian teachers have labelled the "great exchange" by which Jesus takes on our sin and gives us his very own righteousness and holiness. But all this took place very long ago and very far away. How does this exchange become ours?

BAPTISMAL THERAPY

Baptism is the enactment of Jesus' death and resurrection for every Christian. The limits of time and geography are erased and each of the baptized by this sacrament is linked to Good Friday and Easter. By this sacred washing of water and the word every child of God is taken with Jesus down into his grave to die his death and then raised up with Jesus to live his own risen life from then on.

"Do you not know that all of us who have been baptized into Christ Jesus were baptized into his death? We were buried therefore with him by baptism into death, in order that, just as Christ was raised from the dead by the glory of the Father, we too might walk in newness of life" (Rom 6:3–4).

Baptism happens only once. But its significance goes on and on. For the rest of their life, every baptized child of God goes on dying and rising every day. Dying to sin but rising to righteousness, the sin addict dies and is raised again and again to live no longer as a slave but as a son within the Father's house.

This I've come to call baptismal therapy: the ongoing application of the power of baptism by which the sinner is given a new life to live—no longer fueled by his own measly and inept will power, but by the crucified and risen Savior who lives within him by faith. And it cuts both ways, this therapy. It addresses both guilt and shame. For sorrowing hearts experiencing the crushing weight of their guilt, baptismal therapy brings relief and release in the entire forgiveness of all their sins. For cringing, cowering hearts bearing wounds of shame deeply engraved in their souls by the sins of other people, baptismal therapy brings cleansing and renewal as they are enwrapped over and over in the royal robes of Christ's own holiness.

CURATIVE SKILLS FOR PASTORS

Therapeutic skill is an aptitude essential for medical doctors. So also for physicians of souls. As I explained above, to be good doctors of souls you and I need to develop our skills in both diagnosis and cure. And baptismal therapy is one of the chief curative skills you and I need to acquire. It's essential when treating both guilt and shame. Most often there will be comorbidity. That is, people who have been shamed by others usually retaliate by sinning against those who have wounded them.

That's why pastors need above all to be good listeners. We tend to jump in too quickly with what we regard as a solution. But people aren't mathematical problems to be solved. They are souls for whom Christ died. So what should we remember for quality soul care?

We need to be all ears so that we can bring them what he intends to give them. In chapter four I described the four guideposts for that conversation in which the pastor approaches the soul before him, listening for the telltale signs of spiritual distress—be it guilt or shame. Paying attention in Jesus' name is the first and crucial component in the cure of souls.

Then we need to act intentionally in Jesus' name. Like any good sheepdog, I merely serve the shepherd and do his bidding. I can't cure the soul by my own ingenuity or any human means. My sole responsibility in every instance is to be a servant of Christ and steward of God's mysteries by which he does the healing. My concern is to facilitate a meeting between the soul before me and Christ Jesus the Lord of life. My single burning desire is to apply his healing and help.

Remember the story about that wayward son and his loving father that Jesus told? Once the boy found his way home again he proposed he hire on as staff. His father would have none of it. He ordered his servant to quickly bring a robe, a ring, sandals—all signs and emblems of sonship. You and I as pastors do the same in our ministry. That person sitting across from you in your study or lying in a hospital bed is just another wayward child of God the Father, each in their own way yearning to return to the Father's house. Baptismal therapy is nothing more and nothing less than a return to baptism and the ongoing application of the gifts bestowed once in that sacred bath by which sins are forgiven and life restored. By contrition and repentance prodigal sons and daughters keep on returning to the Father's house and his loving embrace. And within the fellowship of Christ's church they receive all the benefits of the household of faith. No longer slaves to their obsessive sinful lusts and passions, they are set free to live each day as sons within the Father's house. So we pastors stand ready with all the Father's bounty to distribute all his gifts to his hurting sons and daughters.

Daily and richly the Holy Spirit forgives all sins to penitent believers. You and I bestow that forgiveness by means of Christ's absolving word. Whomever the Spirit calls, he sanctifies; he makes holy those who are defiled by their own and other's sins. You and I bestow that holiness by means of the cleansing blood of Jesus and his purifying word. We give sorrowing hearts hope again. We bring life where death looms large; we bestow hope where despair formerly reigned supreme. We use our ears to hear human hurt and pain; we use our mouths to speak God's word; we use our hands to apply his balm by means of water, bread, and wine. We pray for every aching heart and wounded soul, giving voice to the laments and griefs we've heard, helping each soul to draw near to the Father in heaven with full assurance that they will be heard as a beloved child because they approach him through Jesus Christ his beloved Son. Finally, we bestow blessing on each hurting soul, applied in the powerful name of the Holy Trinity: the love of God the Father, the grace of our Lord Jesus Christ, and the abiding fellowship of the Holy Spirit.

A CAUTIONARY WORD

Shame and guilt are far more than just negative emotions. As pastors we must be deeply and attentively conscious of the emotions of God's people; that's indispensable when it comes to accurate spiritual diagnosis. It's crucial as well to be aware of our own internal emotions that could influence the way we respond to people. But we're not merely treating emotions; we are treating people. If you read your Bible you understand that guilt and shame are not only subjective human feelings; they're objective realities. I feel guilty because I *am* guilty. I've done wrong. At the same time, because I have been defiled or had shameful things done to me I'm also ashamed. I feel polluted and contaminated, and profoundly unworthy.

One vivid example of this is in the experience of King David, the "man after God's own heart" (Acts 13:22). In the bitter episode found in 2 Samuel 11 and 12 of his seduction of Bathsheba and murder of her husband, we can see clearly how concrete and real sin and shame are, what impact both have, and how both are addressed by Nathan, whom God sent first to confront and then to heal David from his sin and shame.

King David violated God's holy command in taking Uriah's wife to bed and then attempting to cover up his sin by arranging Uriah's death on the front lines of battle. But by those sins he had also desecrated God's holiness and defiled not only Bathsheba, but his own body. Confronted with his sin by Nathan, the Lord's prophet, he was a broken man. Opening his heart to God, he confessed both his guilt and his shame.

> Have mercy on me, O God,
>   according to your steadfast love;
> according to your abundant mercy
>   blot out my transgressions.
> Wash me thoroughly from my iniquity,
>   and cleanse me from my sin! (Ps 51:1–2)

Notice how David's sin needed intentional cure in two overlapping, but distinct ways. For his guilt he needed forgiveness, or release from the penalty he deserved ("blot out my transgressions"). For his shame he needed cleansing ("wash me thoroughly"). That's exactly what he received by the mouth of the Lord's spokesman. "David said to Nathan, 'I have sinned against the Lord.' And Nathan said to David, 'The Lord also has put away your sin; you shall not die' " (2 Sam 12:13). Note that Nathan's goal was not to make David feel better, but to forgive him and cleanse him from the defilement of his sin. Did he feel better afterward? Undoubtedly. But the feelings flowed from the realities he received: forgiveness for his sin and cleansing for his shame.

HEALED HEALERS

There you have it. Guilt and shame are the twin results of sin. The better you are at distinguishing these two realities that are so often intertwined, the better you'll be able to bring help and healing in Jesus' name. Like all aspects of pastoral work, the ability to make this distinction is the result of long practice as a physician of souls; it is an acquired skill. It belongs to the *habitus* of the pastoral office. You grow into it as you tend your own soul attentively and intentionally and as you are cared for by another pastor. Then, by God's grace, what you yourself have received you give to others. I know I'm beginning to sound like a broken record. But it's true; you have nothing to give that you have not yourself first received. Thankfully the bounty of our gracious God knows no limits. As John put it long ago: "And the Word became flesh and dwelt among us, and we have seen his glory, glory as of the only Son from the Father, full of grace and truth. ... For from his fullness we have all received, grace upon grace" (John 1:14, 16).

Receiving forgiveness for its guilt and cleansing for its shame, the soul is revived, renewed—in fact, re-created in the image and likeness of its Creator. Once hiding in shame and broken by guilt, the soul emerges to live and love in wholeness and purity, made right again and purified by the shed blood of Jesus, the holy, sinless Lamb of God who was made to be sin for us that in him we might be made the righteousness of God. Like David of old, once forgiven and cleansed, the ransomed, renewed soul exults in the God who saves and restores:

The Care of Souls

Purge me with hyssop, and I shall be clean;
    wash me, and I shall be whiter than snow.
Let me hear joy and gladness;
    let the bones that you have broken rejoice.
Hide your face from my sins,
    and blot out all my iniquities.
Create in me a clean heart, O God,
    and renew a right spirit within me.
Cast me not away from your presence,
    and take not your Holy Spirit from me.
Restore to me the joy of your salvation,
    and uphold me with a willing spirit.
Then I will teach transgressors your ways,
    and sinners will return to you.
Deliver me from bloodguiltiness, O God,
    O God of my salvation,
and my tongue will sing aloud of your righteousness.

(Ps 51:7–14)

Notice how the presence of the Holy Spirit was pivotal for King David's restoration. This is the heart of the cure of souls: In proximity to the sanctifying Spirit every soul finds its renewal and cleansing.

CHAPTER SEVEN

Holiness and the Cure of Souls

While justification remains at the heart of the Christian gospel, pastoral work is carried out routinely in the realm of sanctification. The preaching of the cross remains always at the center. This—and this alone—constitutes the gospel: the gracious pronouncement that God was in Christ reconciling the world unto himself, not counting their sins against them. Indeed, Christ Jesus is the redeeming sacrifice for us all. By his death on the cross he accomplishes a glad exchange. Absorbing into himself all our iniquity he bestows his own perfect righteousness to all who trust in him. Now when God looks at the believing Christian he no longer sees a sinner, but his own beloved Son in whom he is well pleased.

Yet for as long as believers remain in this world, sin continues to unleash its devastation. We daily sin much and indeed deserve nothing but God's wrath and punishment; we remain guilty as charged before the unbending standard of his holy law. But there is another equally devastating dimension of sin besides guilt, and that's shame. Besides sinning against other people, at the same time we are regularly sinned against by others. Thus we also routinely struggle with shame and a deep sense of defilement and unworthiness before a holy God.

Remember the case of David, the recovering alcoholic who was reeling from wounds inflicted by an abusive father? Do you recall how he remarked one day: "Sanctification is such good news"? At the time I equated sanctification and good works, so I puzzled over his comment. I wondered how doing good works could possibly erase the lingering effects of his abuse and compulsive behavior. But I've come to discover that David was right. He grasped instinctively the proper biblical teaching that sanctification is God's work, not man's work. David relished forgiveness for his sins, most certainly. But in the holiness God shared with him, he found relief from the disorders, injuries, and remorse that had been a hellish vicious cycle of life for him for decades. Now through the work of the Holy Spirit in his heart and soul he found newness of life and the desire and ability to learn healthy newly ordered patterns of thinking and living. He'd been given a new mind that enabled him to live no longer out of the hurt and shame he'd suffered in the past, but out of Christ's love and grace. In Christ Jesus he was a free man for a change. For decades he had lived with a pile of guilt, that's for sure. But also he had been staggering under a crushing burden of shame. In sanctification he found relief and release from the prison of his former way of life. Guilt was his central issue, but for him shame was the real crippler.

Whether it be by guilt or shame, people are daily polluted and defiled before God. They need spiritual cleansing. And that's where you come in. In your preaching, most surely, but also in all other pastoral acts you're continually cleansing people from their own sin and the defilement of sins others have committed against them. You are delivering to them a good conscience before God as you usher them into God's presence through the means of the Holy Spirit—his gospel and sacraments. They are being sanctified by God the Holy Spirit through his means. The very same power is at work on the Lord's Day in your preaching, baptizing, communing as in all the teaching, consoling, absolving, praying, and blessing you do the rest of the week. It's not your charm or the influence of your dynamic personality that releases from sin's guilt and cleanses from sin's shame; it's nothing less than the presence and power of the Holy Spirit working through his inspired word. As I keep repeating, you are a man on a mission. You're under orders as Christ's servant to speak his word tailored for each circumstance. And that word of Christ is potent, for his words are spirit and life.

In all your work, then, be conscious that you are nothing more—and nothing less—than an emissary of Jesus Christ. You are his sheepdog, remember? You've been sent to do his bidding and to speak the word he gave you to speak. And you can be sure that as you faithfully speak his Spirit-filled word, the Holy Spirit himself will be at work calling, gathering, and sanctifying for himself a holy people called out of darkness to live as lights in this dark and dying world.

WHAT DOES "HOLY" MEAN?

So holiness is the realm in which we work as physicians of souls. But what do we mean by "holy"? Here's a word found all over Scripture and a word repeatedly used in the historic liturgy and Christian hymnody, and yet its meaning remains elusive. I think that's because we keep thinking of it in descriptive terms, when it is actually more definitive than descriptive. True, it's used in the Bible as an adjective, as in "holy people" or "holy things." But before it functions descriptively, it works definitively. For example, in Leviticus 19:2, the Lord God instructs Moses that the foundation of all of Israel's worship and life is fundamentally rooted in the Person of God himself: "Speak to all the congregation of the people of Israel and say to them, You shall be holy, for I the Lord your God am holy." This is both a command and a promise. What God requires, he also gives. Holiness is not only demanded, but provided. Only God is intrinsically holy in himself. Yet in his gracious condescension he shares his holiness with his people.

You can't really define holiness. That's because holiness belongs to the very essence of God. So holiness does not merely describe him, but defines him. Before "holy" is an adjective, it is a noun. This may be a new way of thinking for some of you; I know it was for me. But this is the way the Scriptures speak. The Lord God is the Holy One of Israel. "The Lord our God is holy" (Ps 99:9). The unclean demon cringed in fear of the Lord Jesus: "I know who you are: the Holy One of God" (Luke 4:34). Scripture portrays God as utter holiness in his very being. Wherever God is, there holiness is located. You will search in vain in the Bible for a definition of God's holiness, and this is by design. The holiness of God is not just another one of his attributes, such as "all-powerful" or "all-knowing" or "present everywhere." Nor can God's holiness be understood by way of analogy in comparison to human attributes, such as "without sin" or "transcendently pure." No, the holiness of God involves his very being as God. Holiness is not descriptive of his essence, it is his essence. Holiness is what sets God apart from of his creation, including humans. You might say that God's holiness is his "godness," his divinity.

SET APART

In his famous "Gettysburg Address," President Abraham Lincoln reminded a sorrowing nation that "we cannot dedicate, we cannot consecrate, we cannot hallow this ground. The brave men, living and dead who struggled here have consecrated it far above our poor power to add or detract." The familiar cadence of these solemn words continues to resonate in contemporary ears, yet the language of holiness in which they are couched is a foreign tongue for most of us today. Sadly, even Christians have lost touch with the language of holiness (e.g. its verbal form "hallow") and the idea of the holy or the concept of consecration (making sacred). Yet here in this thoroughly secular setting not all that long ago historically speaking, a beloved American president reminded those gathered for the dedication of a military cemetery that the ground on which they were assembled had already been hallowed. It was consecrated by the blood of the men of the Blue and Grey who gave their lives in the horrific carnage of that historic battle.

Lincoln's eloquent words are rooted in the language of Scripture. What was spoken there at Gettysburg on that hallowed battlefield lends vivid credence to our own experience of sanctification. We cannot dedicate (set apart) or consecrate (make sacred) or hallow (sanctify) ourselves or anything else. We can only acknowledge or maintain the holiness already present. The blood of Jesus Christ, God's Son, not only cleanses us from sin, but consecrates us to live under him in his kingdom to be sanctified by his Holy (sanctifying) Spirit as we draw holiness from him in public worship and by personal meditation on the word and prayer.

We are set apart by God and not by our own will power. Sanctification is not a project, but a gift. As we cannot by our own reason or strength believe in Jesus Christ our Lord, or even come to him, so also we can never sanctify ourselves by improving ourselves morally. Sanctification is not our personal self-improvement project. True, our human will plays a part. We cooperate with God's will.

Yet that will of ours is not of our own making. First, last, and always God himself is at work in us equipping us with everything good that we may do his will, working in us what is well pleasing to him (see Heb 13:21).

POWER AND PRESENCE

If we read the Scriptures carefully we see that the holiness of God is never defined abstractly or by way of metaphor or analogy. Rather God's holiness, wherever it shows up in the Bible, is experienced as the power and presence of God himself. Thus the holiness of God is somewhat like light or fire, which simultaneously both attract and repel. They're dangerous in one way, but life-giving and enriching in another. The sun gives life and light to all creation, for example, but it blinds anyone looking directly into its searing beams and scorches and annihilates anything that approaches it. So too fire gives off heat to warm and enliven, but it also consumes anything combustible.

The Lord's holiness provided life and vitality to Israel, but also destroyed anyone who desecrated it. The sad story of Aaron's sons Nadab and Abihu is recorded in Leviticus 10:3; they offered unauthorized sacrificial fire before the Lord's presence within the holy tabernacle, and Lord's fire came out from his presence and consumed them. Yet at the same time the Lord sanctifies his people by means of his holy name. By that sacred name they are sanctified and God shares his holiness with them. "I am the Lord who sanctifies you, who brought you out of the land of Egypt to be your God: I am the Lord" (Lev 22:32b–33).

GOD IS OUR SANCTIFICATION

Let's see how this transformational understanding of sanctification works in the care of souls. Let's pick just one commandment as an example. How about the sixth? "You shall not commit adultery." Not that sexual sin is the most grievous, but if we are to believe Scripture, it's the most defiling spiritually and degrading subjectively speaking. All other sins are committed outside the body by word or thought or deed, but this sin involves the body most intimately and personally. It's no surprise, then, that sexual sin leaves a lot of damage in its wake. Not only psychologically and emotionally, but spiritually as well.

When a Christian indulges in sexual sin he defiles and desecrates his body, which is God's holy temple.

"Flee from sexual immorality. Every other sin a person commits is outside the body, but the sexually immoral person sins against his own body. Or do you not know that your body is a temple of the Holy Spirit within you, whom you have from God?" (1 Cor 6:18–19).

This is no small matter. As I write this book, the Western world is sinking into a sexual quagmire that rivals the pervasive sexual decadence of the ancient pagan world. The sexual revolution of the 1960s has toppled the sexual standards of previous generations and has become the new norm in contemporary culture. Sex is now nearly completely severed from procreation and has become entertainment—a recreational sport, both participatory and spectator. Marriage is despised and redefined. In an age of gender fluidity, sexual identity is divorced from human anatomy; wide spectrums of self-constructed genders replace the biological binary sexes. Homoerotic liaisons are legitimatized and even prized. Virginity is despised and chastity is ridiculed. Sexual promiscuity of every sort is expected and admired. Thanks to the Internet, pornography addiction has become pandemic, to the extent that many otherwise healthy young men find themselves incapable of normal sexual function.

THE PASTORAL CHALLENGE

In such a sexual cesspool, spiritual physicians have their work cut out for them. How are we to navigate this rising tide of decadence? How are we to provide care and cure for souls wounded and broken by sexual sin—both the sins they commit and the sins committed against them? How are we to minister to the women and men who've been victimized, shamed, and defiled by sexual assault and abuse? How are we to bring healing to the broken souls who have indulged in illicit sex and now stagger under a seemingly insurmountable mountain of guilt, hurt, remorse, revulsion and shame regarding their own bodies?

A vibrant proclamation of rich forgiveness and grace in Jesus Christ is clearly essential. Such broken and contrite hearts crave the forgiveness that Jesus freely gives through his called servants. But to recover from the collateral damage of sexual sin, these souls also need sanctification. Yet always remember this: Sanctification does not come by means of the law. True, the commands of God are not burdensome to forgiven sinners renewed in Christ Jesus (1 John 5:3). And most certainly the moral standards of God's law need to be taught and preached vigorously and without apology—especially in our immoral and promiscuous times. This is no time to let up on God's law, for these are lawless times. Yet the law of God, though it can and does teach us the way of holiness, can never bring us holiness. The Lord God alone remains our sanctification.

DÉJÀ VU ALL OVER AGAIN: A PAGAN RESURGENCE

Sexual sin is nothing new. The first Christians lived in a culture drenched in sexual decadence. That stands to reason, for paganism by definition inevitably entails a life of unrestrained hedonism. The relentless pursuit of pleasures of every sort means that sexual indulgence inescapably becomes a way of life. The Western world, for long centuries shaped and influenced by Christian teaching, is reverting to its pagan roots. We see the results around us everywhere in rapidly unraveling moral standards and a pervasive tsunami of sexual decadence and debauchery.

As physicians of the soul, you and I need to remember that this sexual disaster is not the core problem. It's only a symptom; the real quandary we're in is not primarily moral, but spiritual. You can't straighten out this mess just by launching a moral improvement campaign. Nor can you heal broken and wounded souls who suffer the consequences of bodies defiled with sexual sin by means of the law—as if these poor sinners could by their own reason and strength make themselves more holy. No, God alone is holy and he himself is our sanctification.

A SEXUAL CASE STUDY

There are many parallels between the world of ancient antiquity and our own world of late modernity; both are environments mostly devoid of Christian morality. It's highly instructive for us as contemporary physicians of the soul, then, to see how Paul taught first century Christian men to maintain their holiness amid the defilement of a sexual cesspool of perversions and decadence very much like our own.

"Finally, then, brothers, we ask and urge you in the Lord Jesus, that as you received from us how you ought to walk and to please God, just as you are doing, that you do so more and more. For you know what instructions we gave you through the Lord Jesus. For this is the will of God, your *sanctification*: that you abstain from sexual immorality; that each one of you know how to control his own body in *holiness* and honor, not in the passion of lust like the Gentiles who do not know God; that no one transgress and wrong his brother in this matter, because the Lord is an avenger in all these things, as we told you beforehand and solemnly warned you. For God has not called us for impurity, but in *holiness*. Therefore whoever disregards this, disregards not man but God, who gives his *Holy* Spirit to you" (1 Thess 4:1–8).

You will notice that I've taken the liberty of emphasizing four words in this passage. This is simply to call your attention to the obvious: In the original text all four words are cognates of *hagiasmos* (holiness). Our English words "sanctification" and "holiness" are exactly the same word in New Testament Greek. The implications are striking for any Christian man struggling to maintain sexual purity in a depraved world. And they are absolutely transformational for any pastor who seeks to provide faithful soul care in our sexually indulgent climate.

As we look at this case study from the pen of the apostle written to real flesh and blood people, we note six things:

1. *We need to work at improvement in Christian living.* "*As you received from us how you ought to walk and to please God, just as you are doing, that you do so more and more.*" (v. 1)

Where there's faith, there is love. And that love is always expanding. This is common in any genuinely loving relationship. Love is never static. For example, I might say to my wife: "I love you more than yesterday but less than tomorrow." Friendships likewise deepen and expand over time through mutual joys and tribulations shared.

In the same way the Christian continually grows outside of himself to live increasingly by faith in God and by love in his neighbor. Faith lives by love. So wherever faith increases, love grows too.

Thus pastors will urge their men to please God more and more in their behavior, being careful to ground that growth in Christ, not in the unaided human will. For the sinful mind is always at war with God (Rom 8:7). Paul the pastor stresses that his exhorting and urging toward sexual chastity is "in the Lord Jesus." The Christian life always remains rooted in baptism, as noted above. Christian virtue flows from baptism into Christ. As we live in him, so he lives in us. Manly sexual virtue is accomplished not just by imitation of Christ, but by baptism into him. Thus Christ with all his virtues takes shape in bodily life by the daily cycle of death and resurrection. Each day the lusts and desires of the sinful flesh are drowned and die by contrition and repentance and a new man continually emerges to live before God in righteousness and true holiness. And that emerging new man looks very much like Jesus.

No wonder, then, that there's an implied progress in moral living in a Christian's life.

2. *Yet sanctification is never equated with moral improvement. God alone always remains our sanctification. "For this is the will of God, (who is) your sanctification" (v. 3).*

We are called to be holy, yet we can only become holy and maintain our holiness as we share in God's holiness by participation in his divine life. He doesn't expect us, nor are we able, to come up with our own sanctification by working harder at it. We cannot by our own reason or strength believe, nor can we sanctify ourselves by human reason or strength.

Sanctification is not a personal project, but a gift of the Holy Spirit. And it's an ongoing gift. Our moral track record goes up and down. Good works present a checkered pattern in a Christian's life, always mingled with sin. Because of the sinful nature within us the good we want to do we don't do, and the evil we don't want to do we do instead (Rom 7:19). Good works are the result, not the cause of sanctification. Our works of love and faith flow from sanctification, but sanctity is

God's gift. The life we live in these bodies of ours we live by faith in Christ, daily drawing on his transforming power. He, the Holy One, remains the inexhaustible source of true holiness.

3. *Chastity is therefore an acquired virtue.*

Men can never gain control over their sexual appetite or maintain sexual purity by their own willpower. Neither can women, for that matter. But Paul was clearly referring explicitly to males in this instance: "that each one of you know how to control his own body in holiness and honor" (v. 4). The original word for "body" in this verse is more accurately translated as "vessel." While scholars debate its precise meaning here, that specific word was used widely in the ancient Greek-speaking world for the penis.

So here we have Paul, the physician of the soul, speaking bluntly and quite frankly to Christian men about how they use their sexual organs. The habits and sexual mores of their pagan brothers should not determine how they live sexually, he instructs them.

In his wisdom God created men and women with strong sexual desire; it was his way of ensuring bodily union within marriage and the resulting procreation and ongoing nurture of children. The male sex drive is an especially potent force. Paradoxically, its immense power can be used constructively or destructively. Like the irresistible current of a vast river, it can be channeled for great good or, spilling over its banks, it can decimate everything in its path. This was the widespread condition among pagan men in the sexual degeneracy of ancient Thessalonica. "Gentiles who do not know God" give free rein to their libido, Paul writes.

Of course. How could it be otherwise? Post Eden, the great positive potency of the male sex drive wreaks great havoc wherever it flows unchecked out of its naturally created marital boundaries. Like a great river in flood stage, it then engulfs and consumes everything in its path. Sex gone wild decimates and destroys. Decadence had been unleashed among many men in Thessalonica. Raw animal appetite drove these pagans to indulge their sex drives freely. Sexually, they were incontinent; their urges went unbridled. They ravenously used their organs in "the passion of lust." They did whatever felt good.

But there's a dramatic difference between Christians and pagans, the apostle reminded them, especially in their sexuality; Christian men are certainly no less manly than unbelieving men. They are no less potent; their libidos are just as forceful. The distinction is that they know the Lord Jesus. In a very real sense their bodies are not their own. Their bodies, including their genitalia, were first purchased and cleansed by the blood of Christ. Then in baptism their bodies are sanctified as temples by the indwelling of the Holy Spirit. This means all their bodily parts are members of Christ, managed under his control and direction. Sanctified and guided by Christ, the male libido is thus harnessed and redirected for the glory of God and the good of others—in conjugal relations with one's wife and, contained and redirected, empowering chaste and fraternal relationships with one's brothers and sisters in Christ's church toward the welfare of the neighbor.

It's common to think of Jesus as a sexless human. Yet he is a man's Man in every way. Incarnate in male flesh, Scripture teaches that he was tempted in every way just as we are, yet without sin (Heb 4:15). That means that though he remained sexually abstinent, he knows the tug of every man's sexual temptation. We do not have a high priest who is unable to sympathize with us in our weakness. This explodes the myth that chastity is not only improbable, but also impossible for virile men.

Virtue and virility have the same Latin root: *vir* means man. To be genuinely manly and virile involves more than musculature, hormones and sexual prowess; it means to be virtuous by baptism into Christ, exhibiting Christ-like baptismal virtue. The truly masculine traits of courage, honor, and strength are used for others rather than selfish pursuits. Likewise the manly virtue of sexual chastity: It empowers both abstinence apart from marriage and faithfulness within it.

By baptismal union with Christ Jesus men increasingly learn how to direct their sexuality and control their genitals "in holiness and honor." However, that holiness is not dredged up from within. Such holiness is always "in the Lord Jesus." Sexual sanctity is derived by continual connection to God, who is holiness himself. That changes things. By the holiness God provides, a man is no longer enslaved to his lustful passions. Now he's a free man, set at liberty to serve God and his neighbor in every way, including his sexuality—in abstinence if single and in faithfulness to his bride if married. Thus the noble power and energy of his virility becomes a potent force for good. Like a great dynamo generating electricity to power thousands of households, the Christian's sanctified sexual energy directs his whole life to the glory of God and the common good of humanity rather than self-indulgent erotic gratification.

4. *Sex is a public issue. "That no one transgress and wrong his brother in this matter" (v. 6).*

In our sexually decadent society, this sounds like heresy. In our world, every individual is a free agent when it comes to sex. Whatever sexual indulgence he or she engages in is perfectly fine, so long as it's mutually agreeable in the case of two (or more) individuals. Strangely, though sexual acts of all sorts are brazenly and openly displayed in media and public entertainment, there's a puritanical obsession with privacy when it comes to sexual experiences. Most men think their sexual obsessions and proclivities are a matter of both individual choice and personal privacy. They assume, "Since it's my body I can do whatever I want with it and moral limits don't apply; I should be permitted to do anything I feel like doing sexually."

Paul, in contrast, sets private sexual acts within the public life of the church and the fraternal bond of brothers in Christ. "No one (should) transgress and wrong his brother in this matter," he writes. Within the Christian church what men do with their bodies sexually reflects on the whole church, which collectively is the body of Christ in this world. A Christian's sexual sin defiles his brother's honor as well as his own. Fornication is not merely a sin against God and his sexual partner, but against the brother with whom he is united in holiness.

Conversely, each man's chastity builds up his brother's. By living a sexually pure and decent life, he encourages his brother in sexual fidelity as a husband if married or in sexual abstinence if he is single. Holiness is catching, it seems. Borrowing his holiness from God, who is our sanctification, each man's holiness encourages and edifies his brother toward greater sexual faithfulness and purity.

5. Holiness (sanctification) is a gift of the Holy (sanctifying)
   Spirit. "God has not called us for impurity, but in holiness.
   Therefore whoever disregards this, disregards not man but
   God, who gives his Holy Spirit to you" (v. 7–8).

Far from a mere moral infraction, sexual sin defiles and pollutes
a person spiritually. Paul urges these men "in the Lord Jesus" to
offer their bodies to God for his service. In a decadent, debauched
world of promiscuous sexual license Christian men are called to
sexual purity—which includes abstinence apart from marriage and
faithfulness within it. However, if a Christian man mimics his pagan
neighbors by indulging his passions and living a promiscuous life
like they do, not only does he sin against God, but he also defiles
and desecrates the entire body of Christ, especially the Christian
brotherhood.

Thank God there is forgiveness for penitent sinners. Turning in
contrition and repentance to Christ, there is forgiveness and restoration in his shed blood also for sexual sin. In your ministry as a
spiritual physician, remember to bring broken and contrite hearts
absolution and cleansing by the blood of Jesus. But having desecrated
the honor of his Christian brothers by sexual sin, a penitent who sins
sexually needs more than simply forgiveness and cleansing through
the righteousness of Jesus. He also needs covering for his shame and
the restoration of his honor through the holiness of Jesus as well.
Sexual sanctification is always a work in process; it is an ongoing gift
of the Holy Spirit in Christ Jesus. And what the Holy Spirit does for
one recovering sinner in his church, he does for all. Sanctity is the
common possession of the saints of God collectively: The church is
a communion of saints. We're all in this together.

6. Thus there's more at stake in sexual issues than "values" or
   mere morality. "For God has not called us for impurity, but
   in holiness" (v. 7).

Baptismal virtue is at the heart of the matter. It's a matter of defile-
ment/desecration and holiness. It's a question of sanctification. As
physicians of the soul we are not moral policemen or sexual traffic

cops. Rather we are genuine physicians for souls—embodied souls, to be sure, but souls nonetheless. When caring for souls in sexual matters we need to take into consideration not merely guilt, but the whole spectrum of spiritual defilement, purification, and sanctification.

CLEAN AND HOLY

This case study in sexual soul care from ancient Thessalonica translates well into our own hyper sexualized world. Sexual promiscuity always contaminates and defiles a person before God. Christian men (and women) have not been called to impurity, but to holiness, Paul reminds them.

The question is, where does that holiness come from? This passage clearly teaches that holiness is always a gift of God, not a work of man. Clearly in this lawless world of ours, rapidly sinking ever deeper into flagrant crass paganism, you and I as pastors need to teach explicitly and directly what it means to live according to God's will and commandments. Yet such knowledge of God's law alone does not have the power to change human hearts. Only God himself can do that by his Spirit.

Once more, for good measure: Sanctification is not a project, let alone a do-it-yourself project. Sanctification is rather the gift given by God's Holy Spirit through his divinely appointed means: the word of God preached and his sacraments administered. These are the sacred channels of the Holy Spirit's cleansing and sanctifying power. By these sacred means people are not only forgiven of all their sins, but they participate and share in the very holiness of God, "who gives his Holy Spirit to you" (v. 8).

PHYSICIANS OF SEXUAL SOULS

I hope you're beginning to grasp a clearer picture, dear brother, of the high privilege you've been given as a servant of Christ and steward of God's mysteries. He sends you out every day on his vital mission: to bring the Holy Spirit with all his gifts to suffering and wounded souls by the very word you preach and the sacraments you administer. Remember, all sins are not created equal. Amid the wreckage left in the wake of the sexual revolution, pastors need to be keenly aware that sins of the body defile and contaminate the body, which is the temple of the Holy Spirit. They profane the holiness of God, placing the Christian in grave spiritual jeopardy.

"Flee from sexual immorality. Every other sin a person commits is outside the body, but the sexually immoral person sins against his own body. Or do you not know that your body is a temple of the Holy Spirit within you, whom you have from God? You are not your own, for you were bought with a price. So glorify God in your body" (1 Cor 6:18–20).

Yet even the toxic mental havoc and spiritual contamination of sexual sin can be erased—not just eradicated in the forgiveness of sins and the righteousness of Christ, but also healed and made whole by his holiness as well. Thus the discerning physician of souls intentionally applies both: the righteousness of Christ to convey forgiveness and cleansing to broken and contrite souls, and his own holiness as well to bring sanctification and wholeness to desecrated and wounded souls.

DYING TO LIVE

By baptismal therapy, you are given both to kill and to make alive pastorally as you lead suffering souls to repentance. Repentance comprises a genuine turning and renewal in mind and heart, which leads to a new life in Christ. By contrition and repentance the old Adam in these souls is put to death and they are raised up each day renewed in the spirit of their minds to put on the new man created after the image of God not only in righteousness, but true holiness as well (Eph 4:23–24). Obviously, then both law and gospel are at the heart of baptismal therapy.

God's law serves three essential functions: It prescribes, it proscribes, and it describes. We need the instruction/prescription of the law to know what pleases God. Especially as human culture grows ever more pagan, the clear and consistent teaching of the law of God is more important than ever; it prescribes what is God-pleasing. People need direction; they need to know how to live lives that are pleasing to God instead of simply conforming to the increasingly decadent world around them. "The law is holy, and the commandment is holy and righteous and good" (Rom 7:12).

Likewise God's law proscribes. Without the commandments of God, there would be no barriers to the sinful inclinations and obsessions of the fallen human heart. And that would be a pretty scary situation, for Jesus warned that out of the heart comes all kinds of mischief and mayhem: not just adultery and all kinds of perverse sexual sin, but also lies, slander, theft, and murder—all originating in evil thoughts that flow unchecked from the human heart ever since Eden (Matt 15:19). So when the law proscribes it also serves society as a protecting wall against public mayhem.

Finally, the law of God also describes what the new life in Christ looks like: "Love is patient and kind; love does not envy or boast; it is not arrogant or rude. It does not insist on its own way; it is not irritable or resentful; it does not rejoice at wrongdoing, but rejoices with the truth. Love bears all things, believes all things, hopes all things, endures all things" (1 Cor 13:4–7).

Thus for the Christian, the commandments of God are not burdensome (1 John 5:3). God's law indeed describes the new life in Christ. The mind set on the fallen flesh is in rebellion against God. "It does not submit to God's law; indeed, it cannot" (Rom 8:7). But the mind made new in Christ delights in the law of God and always strives to please him. "If the Spirit of him who raised Jesus from the dead dwells in you, he who raised Christ Jesus from the dead will also give life to your mortal bodies through his Spirit who dwells in you" (Rom 8:11). And so we see how baptism is pivotal, the hinge on which the Christian life depends, the door to ongoing renewal and repentance all life long. Martin Luther eloquently summarizes the ongoing impact of baptism into Christ: "In baptism, therefore, every Christian has enough to study and to practice all his life. He always has enough to do to believe firmly what baptism promises and brings— victory over death and the devil, forgiveness of sin, God's grace, the entire Christ, and the Holy Spirit with his gifts."[1]

Sinners who have been plunged into Christ's saving death and resurrection by baptism into him are freed from bondage to sin to live in freedom as the sons and daughters of God. They no longer

---

1. Martin Luther, *The Large Catechism*, in *The Book of Concord: The Confessions of the Evangelical Lutheran Church*, ed. Theodore G. Tappert (Philadelphia: Fortress, 1959), 442.

live for themselves but for the Lord who bought them with his blood and set them free to live before God in righteousness, innocence, and blessedness. Indeed, for them the old way of life is gone and the new has come. It's just as the apostle wrote: "I have been crucified with Christ. It is no longer I who live, but Christ who lives in me. And the life I now live in the flesh I live by faith in the Son of God, who loved me and gave himself for me" (Gal 2:20).

With the above three functions of God's law in view, we can see how God the Holy Spirit therefore uses his law—not just to curb the destructive impact of sin in the world, but also as a mirror to show us our sin, and then finally as a guide to show us how to live. Certainly the law of God is good and wise and true; "the law is spiritual," writes Paul. But I'm not. "I am of the flesh," he continues (Rom 7:14). And that's the problem. As long as we are in this world, people are plagued with the ceaseless compulsions of their sinful minds; though we set out to do the right thing and please God, we end up falling right back into sin again.

Have some compassion on the sinners you work with, then, in Jesus' name. You should be able to empathize with them, after all. For just like you, they're continually hounded by the urges of a sin-obsessed mind. When they set out to do the right thing, they end up doing the wrong thing. The good things they want to do, they don't do; instead they end up doing the evil things they wanted to avoid (Rom 7:19). So don't try reforming them. You can never tame the sinful nature. Sin cannot be reformed; it has to be killed. Daily, sin must die so that the new man can arise and live again. And that, my friend, in a nutshell is what baptismal therapy is all about: applying law and gospel to lead sinners into ongoing repentance—genuine change and renewal in Christ Jesus.

THE RIGHT PRESCRIPTION

One caveat: For all its benefits and blessings, the law of God should never be used to motivate or empower the Christian life. David, my recovering alcoholic friend, knew all too well what God demanded of him. Yet he could not bring himself to do it. His only hope was to live one day at a time, putting sin to death by contrition and repentance, so that the new man he was in Christ might daily emerge and arise to live in righteousness and purity. That's baptismal therapy at work. And that's the treatment you need to prescribe as a doctor of souls— especially in these lawless days.

It's pastoral malpractice to prescribe the law to penitent sinners as the source of a God-pleasing life. The law can direct and guide, but it cannot motivate or empower. The only legitimate motivation for the life of faith is not the law, but the gospel—the good news that God was in Christ reconciling the whole world unto himself, not charging their sins against them, but against his own sinless Son. Putting sin to death by his sacrificial suffering, death, and resurrection, Jesus has opened the kingdom of heaven to all who trust in him. By baptism he has joined himself to them and them to him; he lives in them as they live in him. The life they live in the flesh they live by faith in the Son of God who loved them and gave himself for them. (Gal 2:20)

Sinners need to go on dying and rising in Christ every day of their lives. Repentance is the key, and it's worked by God himself by means of both his law and gospel, properly distinguished and applied. And that's where you come in; this, too, is part and parcel of the pastoral *habitus*. The art of the right distinction and application of law and gospel is a skill you never master, but continually acquire in the school of experience as you minister to both proud/arrogant sinners and broken/contrite sinners with the goal that they might serve God with a clean and free conscience in Christ Jesus.

CARING FOR SEXUAL SOULS

It's utterly crucial that when dealing with sexual sin you keep this baptismal therapy uppermost in mind and heart. For daily dying and rising is the ongoing hinge to the new life in Christ, also in this most intimate dimension of human experience. The sexual drive is a force to be reckoned with. As I noted above, God himself designed sex to be a powerful force for good. Yet like the proverbial Humpty Dumpty, sex has experienced a great fall. Humanly speaking, it cannot be restored to its good and holy purpose in God's pristine creation. Sadly, contaminated by sin it has become a destructive compulsion polluting the soul and potentially harming other people. Yet what is impossible with man is possible with God. What the human will cannot control, God can re-create and restore. In his letter to the Galatian Christians Paul unpacks how daily sanctification by the Spirit contains and re-directs destructive sexual impulses for good.

"Now the works of the flesh are evident: sexual immorality, impurity, sensuality, idolatry, sorcery, enmity, strife, jealousy, fits of anger, rivalries, dissensions, divisions, envy, drunkenness, orgies, and things like these. I warn you, as I warned you before, that those who do such things will not inherit the kingdom of God. But the fruit of the Spirit is love, joy, peace, patience, kindness, goodness, faithfulness, gentleness, self-control; against such things there is no law. And those who belong to Christ Jesus have crucified the flesh with its passions and desires" (Gal 5:19–24).

VICE AND VIRTUE IN THE
CARE OF SOULS

Physicians of souls should take note of the proper use of vice and virtue. In this text the apostle does not prescribe godly virtues as the antidote for sexual vice as though somehow each sexual sin can be negated and countered with a corresponding sexual virtue. Rather, vices and virtues collectively become tools for valid diagnosis of the spiritual dimension of sexual sin as well as proper treatment of the underlying spiritual ailment. Note the vices listed in verses nineteen to twenty-one; all are listed as "works of the flesh." They are products of the sinful nature. Giving free rein to the sinful nature leads to indulgences forbidden by God and destructive to others.

On the other hand, the virtues listed in verses twenty-two and twenty-three are not called "good works" or "works of the renewed will," but rather "fruits of the Spirit." Genuine virtue is produced by the Holy Spirit, not dredged up from within. Virtues are the result, not the cause, of sanctification. Sanctification always remains the holiness bestowed by the Holy Spirit through faith. Good works and Christian virtue flow out of sanctification; they are not sanctification itself.

So also, Christian virtue is not a human achievement. Each virtue most properly belongs to Jesus Christ. Yet having been baptized into Christ, his virtues are bestowed on every believing Christian. The life baptized believers live in the flesh they live by faith in him. In a very real sense Christ Jesus lives out his life through every member of his body, the church. As Paul would put it: "I live; yet not I, but Christ lives in me" (Gal 2:20).

SELF-CONTROL

This is the key to sexual chastity. Urges that seem all consuming and overwhelming can be tamed and redirected by God's Spirit. The sexual tsunami of self-indulgence and its attendant tide of moral pollution can be averted. Instead of caving in to lustful passion, men whose bodies are temples of the Holy Spirit can exercise sexual restraint, combining moral strength with gentleness and self-control.

One caution, however: In this translation the English word "self-control" is misleading. The sanctification of sex doesn't magically make men masters of their own bodies. Sexual continence is always a gift of God. The virtue of self-control—this fruit of God's Spirit—is better translated as "holding in" or "containing." Not suppression, mind you, for no man can suppress his potent sexual drive just by his own personal willpower. Rather sexual chastity is the gift of God's Spirit by which the powerful force of sex is first contained and then redirected, harnessed, you might say, for godly purposes. So abstinence apart from marriage and faithfulness within it is not the impossible dream, but a blessed reality for the man who in co-operation with the Holy Spirit uses his masculinity in service of God and his neighbor.

As someone has noted, one is a whole number. Singleness should never be despised in the church. Some people are single by choice, some by circumstance. Some pastors are single as well; maybe you are among them. Remember, singleness too is a holy calling within the family of Christ's church. Unmarried men and women may be alone, but God forbid they should be lonely in the church; they have brothers and sisters in Christ and share each other's burdens and joys. They are truly members one of another as the apostle writes so viscerally and compellingly about the organic and intimate unity within the body of Christ (1 Cor 12:12–31). For all the legitimate and necessary teaching on marriage in our time, we need to uphold the integrity and worth of every member of Christ's body. Singles are not second-class citizens in the kingdom of God.

Yet marriage also is a holy calling. In fact, in 1 Corinthians 7 the apostle writes quite candidly that marriage is in fact God's remedy for sexual immorality. "It is better to marry than to burn with passion," he writes (v. 9). Lifelong celibacy is a rare gift. Both men and women were created with a natural instinct for sexual union within marriage that cannot be ignored. In a day and age in which marriage is commonly delayed well past puberty, Paul's practical pastoral directive needs to be taken seriously. Sexual urges may be contained and redirected, but they cannot be disregarded or denied.

Marriage is the holy estate designed by God in which man and woman are joined as one in body, mind, and spirit. In the union of husband and wife their sexual drives are consecrated and directed to the spouse for mutual benefit instead of selfish gratification. The procreation and nurture of children is God's intent through the lifelong comprehensive union of husband and wife. In fact, holy matrimony is iconic of the marriage of Christ, the heavenly Bridegroom and his earthly bride, the church (Eph 5:32). In their mutual giving and receiving—especially in the marriage bed—husband and wife mirror the union of Jesus and his bride. This is, as the apostle writes, "a great mystery" transcending mere romantic bond or orgasmic release.

MARRIAGE BEDS UNDEFILED

A word to the wise: If you're married, my brother, don't neglect your wife. You once pledged your lifelong devotion to her and that includes not just your mind and emotions, but your body too. God has given her to you, most certainly. But remember he has also given you to her. Tragically when you and I neglect our wives, they may begin to see the congregation we serve as "the other woman"—a sad condition that breeds wounded marriages and dysfunctional congregations. So you and I need to tenderly woo our brides all life long. That starts with setting aside calendared time for domestic chores, quiet talks just between the two of you, and family time around the table. But it also includes your bedroom; your calling as her husband there is just as holy as your calling as a pastor. The marriage bed is a holy place in God's design, and the sexual union of the two of you is an important part of keeping holy what God has made holy. (Heb 13:4) In giving yourself to her completely there you serve the Lord who has joined the two of you as one flesh. In a time of sexual decadence much like our own, Paul reminded husbands and wives that their mutual nuptial joy was an important guard against temptation to the prevailing immorality. "Do not deprive one another, except perhaps by agreement for a limited time, that you may devote yourselves to prayer; but then come together again, so that Satan may not tempt you because of your lack of self-control" (1 Cor 7:5)."

Remember, chastity is our mutual calling in Christ's church, no matter if we're married or single. Whether sexually active (as in marriage) or abstinent (as in singleness) a man's body is not his own; he has been bought with the price of the blood of God's own Son. By the power of the Holy Spirit he learns how to control his sex organs "in holiness and honor, not in the passion of lust like the Gentiles who do not know God" (1 Thess 1:4–5). This is the life of holiness, genuine sanctification. It's not a project, but a gift. And it is most certainly not a do-it-yourself project.

Since God himself is our sanctification, it's clear that we will need to be in proximity to him to be sanctified. So let's explore what this means for the care of souls—and how this is done.

CHAPTER EIGHT

Drawing Near to God

Proximity and Holiness

When we're dealing with spiritual care we're not merely operating in the realm of ideals or concepts. Too often righteousness, holiness, peace, and joy, on the one hand as well as guilt, shame, sorrow, anxiety, or fear, on the other are regarded as mere categories or notions. Nothing could be farther from the truth, however. These are not just conceptual ideas. All of these biblical words describe realities experienced by human beings in relationship with God and others. They most definitely are not simply dogmatic categories. And they aren't just feelings either.

Our goal as pastors is not to help people feel better. Now don't get me wrong; mental pain is as real and debilitating as physical pain. Suffering of all sorts certainly calls for compassion. So emotions are clearly on the radar screen for every conscientious physician of the soul. In fact they are crucial in the diagnostic phase of spiritual care. Like bodily temperature, respiration, pulse and blood pressure are signs of physical health or sickness, emotions are indispensable to me as a physician of souls. I can't accurately discern what's going on spiritually with anyone unless I'm aware of their emotional state. Likewise, I'd better get a good grip on what's going on inside me emotionally as I listen and care for a person or else I'm likely to misdiagnose or mistreat that soul. Nevertheless, as a spiritual physician I'm treating the whole person, not just their emotions. When the soul is at rest in God, emotions will stabilize.

CURING VS. FIXING

Of course my first instinct as a pastor is to alleviate any pain I run across. And quite frankly, as men you and I are inveterate "fixers." We move quickly toward strategizing a fix for every problem we run across. That's a common male characteristic, and it's a good one. It equips us well as protectors and providers for our households. It's the same in the household of God; qualities of good leadership are highly desirable in pastors. We need to be men of action, first analyzing and then addressing various circumstances.

Yet in caring for souls, especially in the initial stages of dealing with acute spiritual need, we need to restrain this natural instinct of ours and devote a whole lot of time and energy to listening more intently before moving to action. As I said, our ultimate goal is not to help people feel better. We have a much more important goal: to help them be better. We want to bring every man or woman into the fullness of their stature in Christ. We want to give them a good conscience by the gospel. We want to bring them healing and wholeness in the One who gave himself for them that they might live no longer for themselves, but for him and others for Jesus' sake. When they find their life and peace in him, their souls will be at rest and their emotions will follow.

But you never "fix" souls; you care for them. Like any good medical doctor, you provide precisely what is needed in each circumstance so that health can be achieved and maintained. The cure you provide is of divine origin: God's efficacious word and the sacraments. These are the sacred means of the Holy Spirit who creates and sustains faith. And spiritual care operates the same as medical care. There's a curative treatment for every ailment, and yet that cure is never complete. All life long health is interrupted by illness. So the cure of souls, like medical cure, is ongoing. Spiritual health, like physical health, is a lifelong process.

The truth is that sin has so radically ruined God's perfect ordered creation that even in its beauty it is profoundly disordered. I used to think that my job as a pastor was to bring suffering people to perfect health spiritually speaking. I've gained some wisdom through the years; with disorder comes dysfunction. Every one of us in this fallen world has a fallen nature, and that means that all of us—pastors included—are dysfunctional in one way or another. And dysfunction is a chronic condition this side of heaven. Therefore spiritual cure is always needed.

Our job is not to usher in perfection, but to bring people to Jesus and him to them. He provides the healing with his righteousness and holiness. Already now God beholds them perfect and whole in Christ Jesus, which is the basis of a good and clean conscience before our Father in heaven. But in the meantime you and I see through a glass darkly. We are incomplete in body and soul; perfection awaits us in all its fullness in heaven. So as physicians of the soul we keep treating suffering sinners in Jesus' name and stead with the medicine of heaven: his life-giving and life-restoring gospel and sacraments. Through these God gives the Holy Spirit who works faith when and where it pleases him in those who hear the gospel.

So ultimately the Spirit of God is the real curate, then. He sanctifies by his healing proximity. But that too continues all life long.

A NEW MIND

Since the cure of souls is an ongoing project, don't be surprised if sorrowing hearts and anxious souls remain unmoved by the word you bring. To be sure, the word of God brings life and light. Yet souls long accustomed to death and darkness find it hard to embrace the promises of God. As Scripture says, the thoughts of a person's heart determine his condition (Prov 23:7). Recent studies in brain science and neuroplasticity have shown how physical and emotional trauma can impede and impact mental, emotional, and physical functions. It shouldn't surprise us, then, if such traumas also impact spiritual care. If the pathways of the mind are strewn with the wreckage of life, God's promises may sound like a foreign language, and such a person likely needs more comprehensive treatment than you can provide. You are neither trained nor licensed as a therapist. That's why as a pastor you will do well to find a competent psychologist who is skilled in the relationships between cognition and behavior. A skilled therapist like that will be of great assistance in helping an emotionally scarred individual to hear and appropriate the transformative spiritual treatment you've been called and authorized to deliver in Jesus' name.

Yet remember that learning new habits of thinking and acting is not easily done. It's always a work in process. That shouldn't surprise you. After all, that's the very definition of repentance: a new mind. Every child of God needs spiritual renewal every day. Such daily repentance brings life and hope to souls dwelling in darkness and the shadow of death. So feelings are definitely in the picture for soul care, yet they are not the whole picture. Our focus as physicians of the soul is on the soul, not merely feelings. When the person is sanctified, his emotions will be sanctified as well.

SANCTIFICATION AND PROXIMITY

To understand how sanctification works in the cure of souls we need to get a firmer grip on how sanctification was first delivered to Israel in the Old Testament and then fulfilled in the person and work of Christ Jesus in the New Testament. Since Jesus is not merely the payment for our sins (our redemption) but also our righteousness (justification) and holiness (sanctification), all of pastoral care involves bringing people to Christ and Christ to people.

It's a question of proximity, you could say. Picture sitting around a campfire. The closer you are to the fire, the better you can see and the warmer you are. It's no different when it comes to sanctification; proximity to the source of sanctification is essential. Since Jesus is our holiness, whenever he draws near to people and they to him, they are sanctified for service to God and others. The further away they are from him, the more their hearts and lives will be defiled and their bodies contaminated by the influence of the ungodly world, their own sinful nature, and of course the power and influence of the Evil One.

HOLY GOD, HOLY PEOPLE

The worship life of Israel in their desert wanderings is where this first comes into focus. The Lord appeared to his people initially at Mt. Sinai. They were strictly warned not to touch the mountain, for it was holy with God's presence (Exod 19:11–25). Yet Moses and the seventy elders of Israel were invited to the top of the mountain where God dwelt invisibly within the glory cloud (Exod 24:9–18). Though the entire mountain was holy, the top of the mountain was most holy because it was God's dwelling place. God's presence is holiness.

There at Sinai God gave Moses instructions on the construction of the tabernacle, which served Israel all during their desert journey as a portable sanctuary (Exod 25). It was a mobile Mt. Sinai, in effect. It consisted of an outer courtyard cordoned off by curtains and an inner courtyard in which there were two tent enclosures: a holy place where the priests were to perform the daily rituals and a most holy place between the wings of the cherubim which flanked the lid of the ark of the covenant, the mercy seat where God himself sat invisibly enthroned to meet with his people and to sanctify them by his presence. This innermost sanctuary was out of bounds to everyone except the high priest, who entered the most holy place only once a year, on the Day of Atonement, when he performed the rituals to cleanse the tabernacle and its furnishings of defilement. The people of Israel did not enter the holy place, but gathered in the outer courtyard where the Lord came to meet them at the altar during the presentation of the morning and evening sacrificial offerings (Exod 29:38–42).

If anyone claims God is indifferent to questions of worship, he's never read Exodus or Leviticus. In these books of Moses the Lord prescribes in minute detail the furnishings, the sacred vessels, the priestly vestments, indeed the very rituals that were to be used to enact his presence among his people Israel. And that's the whole point, of course. These rituals were prescribed to impress upon Israel that all holiness proceeds from the presence of God. The tabernacle of Israel, their portable sanctuary, was literally heaven on earth for them. By means of the sacrificial system that he prescribed, God intended to sanctify his people for their daily journey. By these sacred means, he came to them personally to bless them with his presence and—consequently—to bestow his holiness. Through their participation in this divinely prescribed worship, the Israelites participated in the divine life of the Lord their God; they were sanctified by his presence with them on earth.

Perhaps nowhere is the sanctifying influence of God's liturgical presence more vivid than in his directions regarding the sacrificial offerings on the Day of Atonement (Lev 16). This constitutes the Lord's instructions on how his people, his priests, and indeed his sanctuary itself might be cleansed of sin's defilement and sanctified for his service. Detailed directions are provided for the preparation of the animal sacrifices, their ritual slaughter, and the appropriate application of their blood for cleansing. It all sounds quite foreign and distasteful to our contemporary ears until you realize that blood is a sacred fluid for Israel: "For the life of the flesh is in the blood, and I have given it for you on the altar to make atonement for your souls, for it is the blood that makes atonement by the life" (Lev 17:11).

BLOOD FOR CLEANSING

After appropriate personal preparations and careful attention to liturgical directions to avoid desecration, the high priest was instructed to take the blood of the sacrificed bull with him into the innermost sanctuary, the most holy place where God dwelt, and sprinkle it there on the very throne of God. That sacrificial blood, having been consecrated as most holy, was then brought out into the sacred courtyard where it was used to sanctify the altar of burnt offering, the place where Israel's daily sacrifices were offered to God and the altar from which they themselves ate in order to participate in God's holiness. This was proximity to the presence of the Lord God. Holiness proceeded outward from the most holy place where God dwelt. The blood brought out of that most holy place sanctified the rest of the sanctuary and—by proximity—all those who participated in the services of the sanctuary. This sacrificial blood was the means of sanctification for the people of God.

Of course, these prescribed Old Testament offerings were only preparatory. Jesus is the true Lamb of God who takes away the sin of the world. By the atoning sacrifice he offered at Calvary he has surpassed and supplanted all the sacrifices the Lord gave to ancient Israel. "But when Christ appeared as a high priest of the good things that have come, then through the greater and more perfect tent (not made with hands, that is, not of this creation) he entered once for all into the holy places, not by means of the blood of goats and calves but by means of his own blood, thus securing an eternal redemption" (Heb 9:11–12).

So the blood of Jesus is the sacrifice to end all sacrifices, offered once and for all. Yet what was true at Sinai and in the desert wanderings of Israel still pertains. Holiness is participating in the presence of God yet today. Jesus took his own blood not into any earthy sanctuary, but into heaven itself, where he presented it to the Father as the final offering for sin. And now, as our great high priest, he regularly comes among us by his word and sacramental meal to sanctify us by his most holy blood—the means of our sanctification.

You see, sanctification always revolves around proximity. Wherever Jesus is, there is actual righteousness and true holiness. By faith in him we are given to participate here on earth in his divine righteousness and holiness. His blood speaks a better word than the blood of Abel; it cleanses not merely bodies, but hearts and souls, giving them a good and clean conscience before God himself.

"For if the blood of goats and bulls, and the sprinkling of defiled persons with the ashes of a heifer, sanctify for the purification of the flesh, how much more will the blood of Christ, who through the eternal Spirit offered himself without blemish to God, purify our conscience from dead works to serve the living God" (Heb 9:13–14).

PROXIMITY AND SOUL CARE

But what practical use is all of this talk about holiness and proximity? How can you and I as physicians of souls use this to call struggling and strangling sinners to a life of repentance? How does this insight inform our baptismal therapy, helping people turn from sin and find their life in proximity to Christ Jesus, who is their righteousness, their holiness and redemption (1 Cor 1:30)? When I met "Ned," he was an insecure young man in his late twenties trying to find his way into his chosen profession. He was likeable enough, but beneath his friendly exterior, I soon discovered, were some deep emotional and spiritual scars—the residue of childhood wounds inflicted by an abusive, alcoholic father who was apparently not only incapable of loving his children, but blamed their mother for all his own misery. By the time I met him, Ned had been in and out of alcoholism treatments several times himself and was deeply enmeshed in habitual masturbation that he couldn't conquer, despite heroic efforts and episodic periods of sobriety.

Ned was a mess spiritually speaking. He was convinced deep down that he was unworthy of God's love and would never amount to much as a Christian. Basically he had the sense that something within him was irretrievably broken and that it was up to him to somehow fix it. He lived in morbid fear that he would be found out and that his sexual compulsions would further isolate him from the connections with fellow Christians he so desperately craved.

Porn is a solitary sport. It cuts a man off from God and isolates him from community, driving him deeper and deeper into himself. It's a vicious cycle; the lonelier Ned felt, the more he indulged his obsessions. He didn't use alcohol or porn in order to feel good; he indulged his addictions so he could feel nothing. He sought blissful escape from the deep inner pain that stalked him day by day. But alcohol and orgasm, besides offering only a brief and fleeting respite, left behind lingering regret, remorse, and profound inner revulsion.

Ned made good use of professional therapists. Besides alcoholism treatment, he sought the help of a competent sex addiction therapist. Cognitive behavioral therapy has a proven track record in addressing the destructive patterns of thought that feed destructive lifestyles. However, addiction therapists recognize there's a crucial spiritual component to recovery. So Ned came to me for what I was qualified and authorized to provide: care and cure for his soul.

It took a long series of patient, attentive listening sessions to uncover the depth of Ned's dysfunction, the extent of his emotional and spiritual scars and the ensuing callouses on his soul that enabled him to function with some semblance of normalcy but hid the fact that inside Ned was still a scared, lonely, hurting little boy.

Ned's father had died by the time I met Ned. In his last illness he made an effort to reconcile with his son, but he was never able to fully recognize—much less confess—the damage he had inflicted on Ned during his fragile childhood years. There was no going back, of course. No amount of insight and compassion on my part was ever going to undo Ned's injuries or his lingering wounds. The core of the treatment I provided for his wounded soul was not my personal empathy or compassion, but the holiness of Jesus.

Certainly Ned had sinned much in thought, word, and deed as a result of his addiction to both alcohol and sexual arousal. He was more than willing—eager, even—to confess those sins. But they had become a vicious cycle; the more remorseful he was over his sin, the more he loathed himself and his own body. And the more repulsed and disgusted he was with himself, the more he was irresistibly drawn to indulge his addictions. He seemed to punish his sin with more sin.

Whenever Ned confessed his sin, his contrition was raw and visceral and genuine. Of course I forgave him every time; I'm under orders to forgive every penitent sinner all his sins in Jesus' name. The blood of Jesus Christ, God's Son, cleanses from all sin. But it also sanctifies. And for ongoing recovery, that's what Ned needed: the holiness of Jesus. He certainly had none of his own.

So whenever we met, as we did quite often, I gave Ned my undivided attention and compassion. But there's no lasting healing in that. He needed intentional treatment with the means that God supplies. For his guilt I applied Christ's righteousness by the absolution I was commissioned to speak in Jesus' name and stead. But for his lingering wounds and shame only Christ's holiness would do.

It all revolved around proximity to God. The more Ned's sins isolated him from God, the more he needed to be called back into the community of faith and communion with God. Baptismal therapy for Ned involved a repeated cycle of death and rebirth, restoring him the innocence and purity he had long ago been given by baptism into Christ, the Holy One. Ned's willpower was helpless to overcome his compulsion, but in Christ he was given a new mind and a new will day by day.

There's a common practical motto among addicts: "one day at a time." And it's true: Recovery is best tackled not all at once, but piece by piece and day by day. The same is true in spiritual recovery. Ned's baptismal therapy included daily contrition and repentance by which his old Adamic nature could be daily drowned and die. As the new man Ned was in Christ emerged each day, he was freed from compulsion to live a life of righteousness, innocence, and blessedness in proximity to God's Spirit working through his sacred means.

In practical terms, my care of Ned's soul included a whole lot of patient teaching of God's word plus ritual enactment of that word. Not only was Ned enslaved to his compulsions, but like all addicts he was plagued with a ton of misbeliefs and lies he had accepted as true. And so I repeatedly reviewed the nature of sin and grace, law and gospel, contrition and repentance, and the baptismal life in Christ.

But I did more than teach the word. I enacted (implemented and applied) that word by hearing his confession and pronouncing Christ's absolution, by praying with the word and blessing him with the word. I invited him to regular communion at the Lord's Table where he was fed the medicine of immortality to heal his spiritual wounds and salve his inner scars. In the flesh and blood of God incarnate in male flesh Ned was regularly not merely reminded of the Savior's redeeming love, but united with Jesus' sacred body so he could present the parts of his own body no longer as instruments of sin, but as instruments of righteousness (Rom 6:13).

Proximity to Jesus—the Holy One—was the key to Ned's ongoing recovery. Isolated from Jesus, he remained enslaved to his addictions and passions. Connected to Jesus by his sacred word and sacraments, Ned was freed to live each day not as slave but as son within the Father's house, created anew in righteousness and true holiness.

Now don't misunderstand me; baptismal therapy in proximity to Jesus didn't cure Ned of his sexual addiction. Habits die hard; especially bad and destructive habits. Ned was not free of all temptation. But this approach was precisely the cure— the treatment—that Ned needed so his compulsions lost their obsessive power over him. The holiness he found in proximity to Jesus via his word and sacraments broke the vicious cycle of his addiction. Wrapped in Christ's own righteousness and holiness, Ned had a new and right spirit within, so he no longer needed to act out to numb the emotional pain inside.

Now a whole new life was open to Ned in Jesus—a "liturgical life," I've come to call it.

LITURGICAL LIVING

The worshiping assembly God designed for his people Israel in the Sinai wilderness was his way of sharing his holiness— his presence— with his people. Having first cleansed them of their sins by means of the prescribed sacrificial offerings, he then appeared to them in the glory cloud to bless them and give them rest in his divine presence. This is genuine sanctification: to live liturgically.

Let's take a moment to define that term, since it may be foreign to some and off-putting to others. When I speak of liturgical living I mean that everything we have to give as Christians we first receive from God by entering repeatedly into his presence. All of life first flows from God the Father through his Son, Jesus Christ, our Lord in the power of the Holy Spirit. And then everything we do in life is offered in praise to the Father through the Son in the Spirit. "And whatever you do, in word or deed, do everything in the name of the Lord Jesus, giving thanks to God the Father through him" (Col 3:17).

SPIRIT AND TRUTH

In his remarkable conversation with the Samaritan woman at Jacob's well, Jesus underscores this. She wants to debate matters of ritual, whether worship should occur in Jerusalem on Mt. Zion or in Samaria on Mt. Gerizim. Jesus directs her away from questions of locale to the heart of genuine worship: the presence of God. "The hour is coming, and is now here, when the true worshipers will worship the Father in spirit and truth, for the Father is seeking such people to worship him. God is spirit, and those who worship him must worship in spirit and truth" (John 4:23–24).

Since Jesus is himself embodied truth (John 14:6), he teaches here that all authentic worship is directed to the Father via the Son and the Holy Spirit. This is counterintuitive. Most people think still today that worship is "bottom up," so to speak. They assume worship is humanly devised in order to give God praise. In contrast, the Scriptures teach that worship is "top down." God seizes the initiative. Worship begins when God forgives, cleanses, and blesses his people. First God speaks, and then we speak as we are spoken to. God takes the initiative and then we respond. First he gives and then we respond. He first opens up our mouth, and then our praise flows forth.

Worship therefore always has to do with proximity to God's presence. Wherever God's name and word are, there he is. And where God is with all his gifts, there worship takes place—in the presence of God. All that we have we receive from God the Father through his Son in the power of his Spirit. Then and only then do we respond in the Holy Spirit through the Son to the Father. This is what I mean by "liturgical"—the triune shape and direction of God's gifts and our response.

What's true in Christian worship is also true in Christian living. There's a liturgical shape to the Christian life as well as our worship.

Our life of love and good works begins by receiving God's love and the fruits of our salvation in his Son in the power of his Spirit; then these gifts flow from him through us to others. As we have freely received, so we freely give (Matt 10:8).

SANCTIFIED BY GOD'S PRESENCE

Sanctification, once again, is not what we do but what God does to us and through us. You don't become sanctified by doing good works. Rather, you do good works because you are being sanctified by the Holy Spirit. Holy people lead holy lives, but holiness is not self-generated; it is borrowed from God and received in proximity to his presence.

Jesus remains the heart of sanctification just as he is the heart of justification. The forgiveness of sins through Christ our Lord is the center of both. First, we are cleansed from our sins by contrition and repentance and absolved through the blood of Jesus, which cleanses us from all unrighteousness. Being cleansed from the pollution of sin and its devastating effects we may safely enter into the presence of the holy Trinity, there to pray, praise, and adore his holy name. Thus, like Israel before us, we are sanctified, or made holy, by the most holy things: his blessed word and sacraments. Through these God gives the Holy Spirit, who works faith when and where it pleases him, in those who hear the gospel. And such saving faith lives by love; good works flow from sanctification by God's Spirit. See what I mean, then, by "liturgical living"? It all has to do with the presence of God, for all holiness flows from him.

So if you want to be sanctified, you need to enter into God's presence. because he alone is holy and the source and goal of holiness. You can't dredge up holiness from within yourself any more than you can rid yourself of sin. God alone forgives, and God alone sanctifies. You, on the other hand, are called upon to maintain the holiness God has given you—to keep holy what God has made holy. This involves daily contrition and repentance so that your sins may be washed away first of all. But the holy life always revolves around the presence of God. Sanctification is a matter of participating liturgically in the divine life of the holy Trinity; to draw near to him where he draws near to us.

That's why God's word and prayer are pivotal, both personally and corporately as Christians.

The wonderful thing is that although human beings are not holy in themselves, in Christ Jesus you and I share in the very holiness of God (Heb 12:10). That's why I keep stressing that although justification is always the central article of the faith, the majority of our work in the care of souls is carried out in the realm of sanctification. Everything you and I do in pastoring people originates in and leads back to the holiness that God shares with them by giving himself to them. While they cannot make themselves holy, neither can you or I make them holy. On the other hand, God can and does make them holy because he alone is holy and bestows his holiness on them. The responsibility of Christians is to keep holy what God in his mercy has sanctified. For example, by his presence the Lord God sanctified the Sabbath. He does not command Israel to make that sacred day holy, but to avoid the desecration of his holiness: "Remember the Sabbath day, to keep it holy" (Exod 20:8). Christians guard and preserve their God-given holiness by avoiding sinful thoughts, words, and actions that defile God's holiness.

Our goal is to keep holy what God by his word and sacrament has made holy. Our responsibility in the care of souls is to maintain their holiness by bringing Christ to people and people to Christ for their sanctification. He alone is the Holy One, and he alone does the sanctifying. He is, to quote Paul, "wisdom from God; righteousness, sanctification [lit. "holiness"] and redemption" (1 Cor 1:30).

LITURGICAL LIFE IN THE WORLD

Liturgical living is not confined to the sanctuary where God is present with his gifts. The holiness received there is carried out of the sanctuary into daily life. Baptized into Christ, believing Christians have put on Christ (Rom 6:3–4). They live no longer for themselves, but for the One who died for them (Gal 2:20). Virtuous living in a world filled with vice would seem arduous and impossible were it not for one glorious fact: Everyone who has been baptized into Christ has put on Christ (Gal 3:27). The life they live in the flesh they live by faith in the Son of God who loved them and gave himself for them.

By virtue of baptism into him they now live in him and he in them. Jesus now lives his life through them. The key to an increase of love and good works in Christians' lives is baptismal therapy: the death of the old Adam and the resurrection of the new man. Daily their old sinful nature with all its vices is drowned and dies and a new man created in Christ emerges to live a new and virtuous life by faith. And here's the thing: Those virtues displayed in the Christian's life are in reality the virtues of Jesus. Christian virtue does not merely involve the imitation of Christ; in a very real way it is the virtue that Christ himself exhibits among all those who are being sanctified.

BEYOND MORALITY

The perennial error is to equate holiness with morality and good works. Whenever sanctification is equated with good works, spiritual mischief follows. Then people are directed to their own inner disposition and spiritual preparations in order to achieve the level of sanctity that God demands in his law. But God's law is not the motivation for the holy life. It is an essential guide, to be sure, and it is an infallible mirror to show all humanity that they have sinned and fallen short of the glory of God, that they are consequently under his wrathful judgment and in desperate need of the salvation that only he can provide. The law serves humanity also as an effective protective barrier against the mayhem and ruin that would be unleashed if the lawless inclinations of the sinful heart were not constrained by social customs and legislation that reflect to some degree the commands and prohibitions of God's moral law.

Yet, as the old saying goes, you can't legislate morality. We can enact laws that protect the unborn and feeble elderly, that serve to encourage and support God's institution of marriage and the family, etc. Pray God that we will. Yet legislatures can't make people conform to God's will just by legal decree. Nor can pastors make people more sanctified by giving them rules to live by.

True, holy people live holy lives. However, just as you and I cannot by our own reason or strength believe in Jesus Christ our Lord—or even come to him, so we cannot by our own works or effort make ourselves holy. Ours is not an inherent, but derived holiness.

The wonderful thing is that ever since the dawn of creation God has kept on approaching humanity to share his holiness with them by his presence. Since holiness is received through contact with God, we can keep holy what he himself has made holy only by being in proximity to him as he approaches us in his word and sacrament. On the other hand, separation from God and his holiness leads to the inevitable loss of holiness.

WATCH WHAT YOU'RE DOING

One thing about my dad and all the farmers I knew: Their *habitus* was always showing. Farming was so ingrained in them that they acted with deliberate intent informed by habitual instinct. If a cow was off her feed, they soon noticed and worked to find a cure. If the grain was turning ripe, they readied their harvesting equipment. If the clouds threatened a squall, they hurried to get the hay crop in. Their craft informed their work.

In contrast, it seems to me that it's easy for us as pastors to go on autopilot, just going through the motions of ministry, performing the roles we were trained to do without giving much thought to what we're doing. No wonder we become bored and discontent in ministry. No wonder that so many of us burn ourselves out or are such easy prey for temptations of various kinds that ruin us and end our ministries. I therefore plead with you: Watch what you're doing as a pastor. Remember who you are, whose you are, and whom you serve as a servant of Christ and steward of God's mysteries.

Once it dawns on us that we're not just religious activity directors or spiritual life coaches, but genuine emissaries of the living God, then we can't be satisfied with just going through the motions. As agents of the living Lord we find new contentment and fulfillment in our work. We develop a real and genuine *habitus* for the cure of souls. As you and I become more and more aware of what it means to bring genuine life and healing to people who are the lambs and sheep of Jesus, we become all the more attentive and intentional in our work as sheepdogs for the Great Shepherd.

ATTENTION AND INTENTION

A proper biblical understanding of sanctification opens whole new vistas in pastoral work. Once we grasp that holiness is not a human achievement but a divine gift having to do with the presence of God on earth, we're better equipped to bring added hope and consolation to souls alienated from God and isolated in their misery. The whole arena of holiness becomes part and parcel of our pastoral *habitus*. We become more keenly aware of questions of conscience involving both guilt and shame. We develop a kind of sixth sense; we become alert and attentive to those factors that keep people isolated and distant from God. Best of all, we become all the more intentional in our application of Christ's righteousness and holiness in soul care, zealous to bring people closer to him by the means he has provided.

As we grow in our awareness that the word of God is living and active, piercing to the division of soul and spirit, we will increasingly use it to discern the thoughts and intentions of hearts struggling under the burden of guilt and shame (Heb 4:12). As we become more conscious that baptism is not just water, but joined with God's powerful word it is a gracious water of rebirth and renewing in the Holy Spirit (Titus 3:5), we will grow in our ability to apply baptismal therapy, helping hurting souls to daily die to sin and rise to newness of life in Christ. As we come to a fuller understanding that the blood of Jesus Christ, God's Son, cleanses from all sin, our reverence for the sacrament of the altar and our conscious application of the sanctifying power of his flesh and blood will develop in our pastoral practice.

PROXIMITY TO JESUS

Sanctification is God's work, not man's work. The closer people are to Jesus, the greater his sanctifying influence in their lives and the more healing they find in him. They don't get closer to him by their own reason or strength or through spiritual exercises, but by drawing close to him where he makes himself available: in his word and sacraments. And of course that's exactly your calling: to proclaim not yourself, but Jesus Christ as Lord with yourself as his servant (2 Cor 4:5).

True, you serve Christ's suffering people, and such work is not for sissies. Conscientious ministry is often difficult and complicated, especially in these confusing and conflicted times. But you serve for Jesus' sake. That's why there's no need to burn yourself out in ministry. Proximity, remember? Your job is merely to bring people to Jesus and Jesus to people. If you do that, though you may be hard at work, Jesus is working with you and through you all the while.

And he does all the heavy lifting.

CHAPTER NINE

Invisible Powers

Spiritual Warfare

F or all the skirmishes we get involved in as pastors, I've come to believe that we make it harder on ourselves because we're fighting the wrong enemy with the wrong tactics and the wrong weapons. It doesn't help much that while we get a lot of training in leadership strategies and conflict management, we receive precious little instruction in spiritual warfare. I think that's why a lot of pastors are sitting ducks in ministry; they're flying blind and don't grasp what they're really up against. No wonder so many are so highly stressed and so often on the brink of burnout.

You know what it's like when you get a group of pastors together talking shop. If they're honest with one another, they have horror stories to tell. Unrealistic expectations of parishioners are a favorite topic. Then there are those notorious "alligators" that seem ready to snap at every turn. And of course every congregation seems to have its share of cantankerous personalities who find fault with even the most innocuous and well-intended comments or actions of the pastor. On top of that, it's a perpetual hassle to keep people committed and active in the practice of the faith. Not that ministry has ever been easy, but the situation has certainly intensified these days now that the church is statistically on the decline in America. For a multitude of reasons, churches have become battlegrounds and pastors are an endangered species in our time.

BATTLE STATIONS

However, if we take Scripture and the longer experience of the church seriously, there's a whole other dimension to conflict and hardship in ministry. The source of dissension, distress, and difficulty in ministry ultimately is satanic in origin and spiritual in its essence. That means it's delusional to think that real pastoral work can be accomplished in perpetual peace and tranquility. If we're serious about the ministry, we'll need to man up for battle. "Fight the good fight of the faith," Paul counsels young pastor Timothy (1 Tim 6:12). But of course the crucial question is this: Who are we fighting against? I'll give you a hint; it's not the people you serve.

I once had an acquaintance who had invested in several advanced theological degrees and was then in the middle of acquiring a third. He confided to me one day: "I love the ministry but I just can't stand people." I'm sure this man loved theology, but it's clear he didn't love the ministry; not really. If pastoral ministry is anything, it's a ministry of love for people. Jesus taught us well: All ministry flows from his love. If we love him, we are to love the sheep for which he died.

This all makes sense. But it's a whole lot easier said than done. Sometimes the people we serve are quite unlovable. Sometimes seemingly harmless sheep turn into predators. When pastors come under attack, they often fight back. And that's when things can get ugly. Because they're fighting the wrong enemy. You and I assume our problems are of human origin when their real source is actually a lot more sinister.

I didn't make this up; God said so: "Put on the whole armor of God, that you may be able to stand against the schemes of the devil. For we do not wrestle against flesh and blood, but against the rulers, against the authorities, against the cosmic powers over this present darkness, against the spiritual forces of evil in the heavenly places" (Eph 6:11–12).

THINGS INVISIBLE

This changes the conversation on problems in the ministry immensely. Yet most of us still don't get it. We keep focusing on visible things and neglect the spiritual. Ironic, isn't it? You and I both know that most of our work involves things that are invisible, yet very real. No one has ever seen God, after all, and yet you and I daily teach and preach about him to others. We console, comfort, rebuke, and exhort the faithful using the invisible power of the Holy Spirit mediated through the word and sacraments. Forgiveness, peace, holiness, joy, consolation—all these are intangible and beyond the range of the senses, and yet our work revolves almost totally around these invisible things. It's strange, then, that when confronted with roadblocks and obstacles in ministry we address only things we can see, touch, and measure externally.

And so do lay leaders and church councils. Declining membership and depleted budgets create a lot of concern, and rightly so. Yet how are these problems tackled? Usually with approaches borrowed from business and industry: advertising, human relations and financial management tactics. Dissatisfied members are treated much like stockholders in a corporation. Church leaders scramble to figure out a way to keep everybody happy and invested. Now of course good management principles, better communication, and the personal touch are all important in the life of every Christian congregation. Paul exhorted the Corinthians that all things should be done "decently and in order" (1 Cor 14:40). That exhortation certainly applies beyond the narrow confines of the liturgical assembly. Yet at its core the church is not an association like other earthly governments and agencies, but a fellowship of faith and the Holy Spirit in human hearts. Ultimately churches grow and flourish not by sales or business tactics, but by the power of God's Spirit working through his word.

So hear me out on this: You've got to pay closer attention to invisible things. Behind every complication and difficulty encountered by pastors and churches, yes by every Christian, lurk the machinations and intentions of the Evil One. The devil is the sworn enemy of Christ and his church. That goes without saying, really. And yet too often otherwise savvy pastors remain oblivious to the whole dimension of spiritual warfare. Thus by default we relegate the field to fundamentalists and charismatics who see this conflict with Satan in terms of demonology. In that kind of thinking, Christians need to fight the devil out in the world to prevent him from taking over. But Scripture teaches that Satan is the prince of this world; the ungodly world is already in his corner. So he focuses his attacks and assaults on the church instead.

This means that our spiritual battle is a defensive one. You and I as pastors are called to do sentry duty, watching for the enemy's attacks. And believe you me, they're sure to come. In fact, I'd say the more faithful and diligent you are in ministry, the more certain it is that you will come under attack. You can't blame the devil. For if you were the enemy of God and his church, where would you focus your offensive? Would it not be where the word of God and his sacraments are preached and administered, and where that's happening most consistently and faithfully? Through these means, after all, God gives his Spirit and creates and nourishes faith. If you could derail that process, you could undermine God's kingdom. So it only stands to reason that if you are called as Christ's servant and steward of God's mysteries, you're going to be in for trouble spiritually speaking.

TARGETED FOR ATTACK

I've got some bad news and some good news for you. The bad news is that you're on the hot seat. Since you've been called and ordained into the office of the holy ministry, charged with preaching and administering the means by which God the Holy Spirit goes on calling, gathering, enlightening, and sanctifying a holy people, you're targeted. You and your wife and your children are going to come under spiritual assault; there's no way around it. Sadly, Satan doesn't fight fair and square. He doesn't always attack you directly, sometimes he targets those you love instead: your family and your closest friends. But by any means possible, the devil and his minions strive to drive a wedge between you and your Lord. His favorite tactics are misbelief or despair. If he can distract you with chronic worry over your loved ones or bring you to the point of giving up hope, then he's got you where he wants you.

Of course let's not give the devil more than his due. He is, after all, only one measly angel. He's neither omniscient nor omnipresent. Like you and me, he is a created being, albeit incorporeal. Yet he has allies: not only the other fallen angels who make up the demonic horde, not only the tug of the unbelieving world around us, but also your sinful nature and mine. The old Adam in us is a hardened idolater and refuses to let God be God. There's something inside us, then, that's in league with the devil and does not want God's kingdom to come or his will to be done. This complicates things when it comes to the spiritual dimension of our personal and professional life. We need to be constantly on guard not merely against Satan, but our own sinful flesh as well. Sometimes we're our own worst enemy.

CALL IN THE HERO

Yet there is good news too. We're not alone in this battle; we have a hero who fights for us. Like a medieval champion that took on challengers on behalf of his liege lord, Christ Jesus has fought against Satan in our place and won the victory. In his death and resurrection, he routed all the forces of death and hell. And he still fights on our behalf, interceding for us before the throne of his Father on the basis of the atoning sacrifice in his blood. Keep that in mind next time you come under spiritual attack. Never attempt to go it alone and fight these battles by yourself.

Some years ago Jane and I were vacationing in Britain and visited Hadrian's Wall in northern Yorkshire. It's still an impressive sight even in ruin. It must have been quite the feat of military engineering back in the second century when it was constructed to guard the northern frontier of the Roman Empire. At regular intervals along its 73-mile length, fortresses were erected, each containing barracks for a Roman garrison. Soldiers patrolled the full length of the wall, continually watching for invaders. But if an attack came, they were not to venture forth to fight. Rather their job was to blow the whistle, so to speak—to sound the alarm and call in the troops to fight the enemy.

FIGHTING DEFENSE

The striking picture of a Roman soldier dressed for battle in Ephesians chapter six is familiar to us all. What often escapes notice, however, is that his equipment is all defensive, not offensive. This particular gear wasn't furnished to the famous legionnaires who went out to conquer territory for Rome. Rather it was issued to the soldiers garrisoned along the borders of the Empire to fend off attack. Likely the men who lived in the barracks Jane and I visited in Yorkshire were equipped with just such arms. They were fighting a defensive battle, so they needed different equipment than the attack troops.

There's a lesson here for you and me when it comes to our own spiritual battles. Rather than attempting to fight off the assaults of devil, world, and flesh on our own, it's important that instead we don our armor and sound the alarm at first sign of attack. We have One on our side who has already fought that fight and won. The devil is a defeated enemy. Christ Jesus is our champion who even now intercedes for us at the Father's throne. "Christ Jesus is the one who died—more than that, who was raised—who is at the right hand of God, who indeed is interceding for us" (Rom 8:34).

FOREWARNED

Given the fact that Satan and his demonic horde are simultaneously repelled by holiness yet strangely attracted to it, you should be expecting trouble. It's the norm in ministry, not the exception. Remember, you work continually in the realm of sanctification. Holiness attracts satanic attack just like bugs are drawn to light. God the Holy Spirit is calling, gathering, and enlightening a holy people through the sacred means he has appointed. The fact that you've been entrusted with the responsibility of preaching Christ's holy word and administering his sacraments puts you right in the middle of the fray. Because you're constantly dealing with holy things, there's no way you can escape Satan's notice, so you'd better be ready for a rough time. Just don't panic when you come under attack; it's perfectly normal that the kingdom of darkness strikes back when threatened by God's kingdom of light. Like any soldier under battle conditions, every Christian—and especially every pastor—should anticipate incoming attacks and be ready at all times.

Always keep in mind, though, that you're on defense, not offense. You're called to be on guard against enemy attack. But when it comes— as you can be sure it will—call on Christ Jesus to deliver you and your flock. Don't try fighting these onslaughts relying only on your training in psychology, leadership, and people skills. Though dark times in ministry usually have social dimensions that require these approaches, you neglect the spiritual dimension to your peril and the detriment of your congregation. For inevitably these rough patches are spiritual at the core. A competent soldier never ventures out without his equipment because he never knows when the attack will come. Neither should you.

FOREARMED

Your Lord has furnished a full array of defenses for you by his blood and suffering. The apostle details them one by one. The belt of truth, the breastplate of righteousness, and gospel of peace are foundational (Eph 6:14–15).

A soldier's belt bound up his flowing garb so he could move rapidly and unhindered in battle. In an age where there is no absolute truth, but only infinitely varying personal values, the truth of God is essential to keep you at the ready for battle even while everything around you is in flux.

A soldier's breastplate protected his vital organs from deadly wounds. When the righteousness of Christ covers you by faith, you're safe from lethal spiritual injury.

A soldier's footwear equipped him for dexterity on the battlefield. When you're at peace within, you'll not be paralyzed in fear or immobilized in battle. The peace of Christ that surpasses all understanding will guard your heart and mind so you can calmly fight in the hour of attack.

When under attack from invaders, garrisoned troops were issued three indispensable pieces of gear: a shield, a helmet, and a sword (Eph 6:16–17).

A soldier's large wooden, cloth-covered shield was often soaked in water to extinguish any flaming arrows shot by attackers. It's your faith that quenches the fire of spiritual attack. Not, mind you, the faith by which you believe, but the faith that you believe. Christ's saving work douses the destructive flames of the Evil One.

A soldier's helmet protected him from fatal head blows. Just so, your salvation guards you for eternal life. In fact, since Christ has already conquered over sin, death, and hell, you can be sure that you will win in the end. All the sufferings of this present time put together aren't worth comparing to the glories that have yet to be revealed when Christ shall come to claim his own.

The Roman soldiers' famous double-edged sword led them in conquest, but the technical word used here is apparently the shorter dagger-like sword employed to defend the empire against marauding attack. You're well equipped to defend yourself when under spiritual attack. You've been issued the Spirit's sword, the word of God. Note that God's word is best wielded in prayer: "praying at all times in the Spirit" (Eph 6:18). You fight this battle not by preaching the word, but by praying the word. Word and prayer go together for any Christian, but especially for pastors. That's why a rich life of prayer and meditation is essential.

IDENTIFYING THE ENEMY

We shouldn't be looking for the devil under every rock. The demonic realm is just one front in this spiritual battle. The ungodly world and the impulses of our own sinful nature are also in league with the devil. Misbelief, idolatry, and despair constantly stalk everyone, even fervent Christians. The sinful heart stubbornly refuses to let God be God and causes all kinds of havoc in the church. As I've already mentioned, you can always count on sinners to sin. So when they do, don't go at them with both barrels blazing. Remember that the ultimate enemy remains unseen.

If there's to be a fight in your church, make sure it's a good one. Fight the good fight, not the bad fight. A bad fight is with your parishioners or among them. The good fight is against the devil and his minions, not against human flesh and blood. Antagonists and allies in the church alike need pastors. Even so-called alligators in the congregation are not your enemies, though they certainly act like it. They always remain souls for whom Jesus died; never make the mistake of writing them off as adversaries. You're called to serve every sinner in Jesus' name, calling them all to repentance, absolving and sanctifying them by the word you preach and the sacraments you administer.

Serving critics is difficult. Every internal instinct will tell you to avoid detractors and pander to fans—yet there's no surer way to shipwreck your church and ruin yourself for ministry. There's a way through this mess; just don't make the mistake of relying on your own ingenuity or steely resolve to do it. I know a man who nearly destroyed himself emotionally and physically trying to outwit opponents by his own dogged tenacity. His stomach was often in knots and his mind was a muddle, but he slapped on his game face and kept on trying to gut it out as best he could. The turning point for him came when he admitted his deep inner pain to a brother, sought pastoral care for the hurt and misbelief inside, and began to see himself as a servant and sheepdog for Jesus rather than a solo entrepreneur, pulling ministry out of his own rapidly diminishing inner resources.

So what do you do when you're at odds with members of your church? First, remember that you and your flock are enlisted together in the same army. So don't take shots at each other. You fight jointly in the same struggle against the dark forces of evil in the heavenly places. Remind your people you're on their side in this fight. If someone objects to something you've done or taught as a faithful steward of God's mysteries, ask them not to kill the messenger.

Now of course it could be that you're the one that's off base. Maybe you've been abusive toward God's people. Perhaps you've been using power instead of authority, making your ministry all about you. Maybe you've been guilty of manipulating people to conform to your ideas rather than serving them with the gifts of Christ. If so, you need to repent and become a servant, not a tyrant.

But if you've been faithful to the word of God and people still oppose you, then their real quarrel is not with you but with him. In that case, tell them, "We're in this together, you and me. We're allies in the fight against the devil; we can't afford enmity between us." Invite them to join forces with you in the good fight to which you've been jointly called as the company of the baptized.

PRAYER UNDER SIEGE:
THE OUR FATHER

The prayer that Jesus taught his disciples is a prayer for his enlisted soldiers engaged in battle. Here in these seven petitions our Lord gives us not merely a prayer to pray, but a way of prayer. First he invites Christians to pray his very own prayer along with him, joining their prayers to his. "Our Father," he invokes, by these words implying that any Father of his is our Father too. Since we pray in and through Jesus to the almighty Maker of heaven and earth, we have the privilege of approaching him as beloved children. Since Jesus is God's true Son and we are baptized into him, we are God's adopted daughters and sons through faith in Jesus. No holding back, then; boldly and confidently we cast all our cares on him, confident that he cares for us.

Jesus shows us in the Our Father how to pray as he does. He lists all the primary concerns: God's name, his kingdom, his will, our daily bread, and the forgiveness of our sins. Then significantly he concludes with two petitions that focus our attention on the spiritual battle that we're daily engaged in. "Lead us not into temptation but deliver us from evil." Unlike the first five petitions, these last two are connected by the conjunction "but," implying they go together when fighting this battle. Escaping temptation and deliverance from Satan and all his works are two sides of one coin.

Since temptation is the front porch of the devil's strategy to undermine and destroy faith, we need to learn how to handle it strategically.

LEAD US NOT INTO TEMPTATION

From the time of Adam's fall, temptation is the common experience of all humanity. Ever since Eden the lust of the eyes, the lust of the flesh, and the pride of life are forces to contend with (1 John 2:16). The devil isn't called the father of lies for nothing; he continues to twist God's good creation for his own purposes. Things that God declared "very good" at the close of his creation Satan now commandeers to lure God's children away from the salvation he planned for them.

You know how easily your heart can deceive you: how quickly thankfulness changes to greed, appreciation morphs into envy, gifts become idols, hunger escalates to gluttony and healthy sexual desire spirals out of control into ravenous lust. The combined pressures of devil, world, and flesh ensure that constant vigilance is required; we're forever being seduced into misbelief, despair, and other great shame and vice.

That's why Jesus instructs us to pray for protection. His "lead us not into temptation" does not imply that God is the cause of evil or that he brings on all these assaults on our faith and life. God cannot be tempted with evil and he himself tempts no one, James writes (1:13). The real source is much closer to home: "But each person is tempted when he is lured and enticed by his own desire. Then desire when it has conceived gives birth to sin, and sin when it is fully grown brings forth death" (Jas 1:14–15).

So our very first line of defense in spiritual warfare is protection from the enticements and allure of temptation of all sorts. As I've stressed above, you can't keep them from coming your way. They're the common experience of every Christian. You can't avoid temptation when you're in continual proximity to the holiness of God; the demonic forces are strangely attracted to holiness. Yet they are also repelled by holiness, and an important work of God's unseen agents, the holy angels, is to guard and keep the faithful: "For he will command his angels concerning you to guard you in all your ways. On their hands they will bear you up, lest you strike your foot against a stone" (Ps 91:11–12).

THE SIGN OF VICTORY

Remembering you do not fight alone in this struggle is nine-tenths of the battle in spiritual warfare. Christ Jesus is the mighty victor over Satan in his death and resurrection, and he dispatches his angelic hosts to guard all those who bear his name. Troops entering a battlefield need to know who has them covered. Seek cover daily. In his catechism Martin Luther instructs the baptized to begin and end each day with the sign of the cross, the emblem of their baptism into Christ, and by invoking the presence of God the most holy Trinity. Morning and evening catechetical prayers both conclude with the petition: "Let your holy angel be with me, that the wicked foe have no power over me."

Like Jesus in his own private prayers, pray out loud, giving voice to what's on your heart and mind. Invoke God by name, mark yourself with the blessed sign of your redemption by Christ's cross and insignia of your baptism into him. Pour out your heart before your Father in heaven and seek the protection of his holy angel. Even if you haven't been accustomed to praying this way, I commend it to you. I've found it a vivid and practical way to don all the spiritual armaments of Ephesians 6 daily (the shield of faith, the breastplate of righteousness, etc.). Peace of mind and heart can be greatly enhanced despite some chaotic surroundings, I've discovered. Often we have not because we ask not.

WATCH YOUR STEP

Of course in any skirmish it's helpful if the troops are well prepared for what they're about to experience. You'll want to avoid all the land-mines and IEDs you can, so you need to be on high alert. Of course the temptations common to pastors are as many and varied as the number of pastors there are. But allow me to highlight just two. Not because they are any worse than others, mind you, but because in my experience they are so common among us.

The first, as you might guess, has to do with sex. By now you're probably thinking I'm kind of hung up on this topic. But a moment's reflection will remind you why this area demands constant vigilance. I won't retrace the material I shared with you in the pastoral care case study from Thessalonica in chapter seven. But the fact is, you and I are sexual creatures. Every moment of every day even our most platonic activities are carried out in male bodies. We are not pure intellects or disembodied brains. You know as well as I do that erotic thoughts are inescapable and lust creeps into our consciousness unbidden. The question is not whether sexual temptation will occur; the question is how will we respond? The spirit is willing, but the flesh is weak, as every man knows from personal experience. The trick is to avoid situations that you know can easily compromise your defenses. Many a man has shipwrecked his marriage, family, and ministry by adulterous relationships.

By now I hope you've learned strategies to avoid compromising situations. Conducting private pastoral care in settings that maintain privacy, yet avoid secrecy is one thing. Ensure there are glass insets on your study door, for instance, or go for a walk with a troubled person; or sit in public places for private conversations if possible. Probably most important of all is to take care to invest in your relationship with your wife. Quality time isn't enough; set date nights and keep them. Cherish her and nourish your marriage's intimacy—not just physically, but also emotionally.

THE PORN TRAP

But today the most menacing adulterous temptation does not involve flesh and blood sexual partners, but virtual ones. Like it or not, you and I spend large chunks of our time in front of a computer screen. Like all technology, it's neither good nor bad in itself, but depending on its use it can be a tool to edify or destroy.

You're well acquainted with this ominous side of computer technology. It's increasingly a major factor in the broken souls and fractured marriages you minister to. The dark world of Internet pornography promises not merely diversion and titillation, but near instant gratification. Some men are drawn in out of curiosity, thinking that they need to experience it for themselves so they will know better how to help others. Others fall prey to the ingenious marketing devices of the porn industry via click bait accessed on social media. Still others deliberately seek sexual indulgence at first sporadically, then with increasing frequency. Like all addicts, porn users find themselves quickly hooked, moving from so-called soft porn to hard-core pornography, then progressively perverse and vile images to meet what inevitably becomes a bottomless craving to feed an ever-escalating and insatiable sexual appetite.

Pastors are not immune. If you recognize yourself somewhere in this last paragraph, know two things: First, you are not alone. Hundreds of thousands of sincerely dedicated Christian men have been caught in the porn trap just like you. And among them are a goodly number of clergy, more than you'd think. Second, there is hope for you. Jesus is not only your righteousness, but also your holiness. What you cannot do yourself, you can do by faith in him. But you will need help.

RECOVERY

A trusted friend may well be your first contact. This habit, like all sin, grows when kept under wraps. Bring it out into the light; share it with somebody else. Together plan a strategy to tackle this head-on. Firewalls should be installed which prevent your computer from accessing porn—and automatically report any attempts to access it to your friend. Don't kid yourself. Left to itself, the vicious destructive cycle of porn quickly becomes habitual. Every indulgence brings immediate remorse and corresponding self-loathing and revulsion, which then only fuels the obsessive compulsion for more and more indulgence. This tragic pattern must be broken, and the first step is to initiate a fast. A competent therapist can be of immense help; your own will power is powerless to break the toxic cycle of addiction.

But that's only the first stage of recovery. Of course you need to stop your compulsive destructive behavior, but you'll need much more than that. You need to build a healthy life mentally, emotionally, spiritually, and sexually. For that you need forgiveness, cleansing, and healing. That's pastoral care. And that's why you need a pastor. I know this may sound scary to you, but I'm quite serious: You need a pastor, just like every other sinner.

Satan lives up to his name. As our accuser before God, he attacks a pastor in his most vulnerable area: his vocation. He taunts us: "How can you call yourself a Christian, much less a pastor, after what you've been doing? How can you mount the pulpit and preach the holy word of God when you've so severely defiled your own body and desecrated God's holy orders by what you've been doing?"

You know the answer to those questions. The blood of Jesus Christ, God's Son, not only cleanses from all iniquity, but it also brings the sanctifying power of the Holy Spirit to create a clean heart and a new and right spirit. With the two-sided coin of Christ's righteousness and holiness he puts together what seems to have been irretrievably and utterly broken. Our God is surpassingly rich in his grace. He provides consolation and help not merely in abstract ideas and concepts, but through concrete, external means: the sacred meal by which Jesus gives us the very body and blood with which he once paid for all our sins, the washing of water with the word by which we were once buried with Jesus into his death and raised up to live his never-ending life, and the word of the gospel, which is proclaimed to release sinners from their prison cells of guilt.

PASTORAL HELP

But please don't try tackling this compulsive sin all by yourself, self-medicating with the gospel. Help must come from the outside; you'll need to hear that saving gospel from somebody else. Your Lord loves you enough to place his freeing word in the mouth of a brother pastor to address you personally and confidentially in your abject remorse. Habitual porn is the proverbial perfect storm of temptation. A toxic concoction for the old Adam, it whips up together the lust of the eyes and the lust of the flesh, then tops off that delectable delight with a great big dollop of the pride of life. It thrives in secret, fed and nourished on the insatiable, voracious passions of your private imagination. Get rid of them, spit them all out, and bring them out into the light. Find a pastor in whom you can confide. Confess your sins. Pour out your regret, shame, and remorse. That pastor will be your soul's physician to forgive your sins, to heal your wounds, and help you live in freedom again.

You need to find a solid foundation on which to build your recovery, and that foundation is Christ Jesus. But Christ approaches you in the word he places in your brother's mouth. He works from the outside in: Faith comes from hearing, and hearing through the words of Christ spoken to you. In the mutual conversation and consolation of brothers God is surpassingly rich in his grace; he will create in you a clean heart and renew a right spirit in you. He will break the sad nightmare of your bondage and set you free to live again, pure and clean and undefiled. This is baptismal therapy in action—for you.

If you've been dabbling in porn your wife will need help too—both psychological and spiritual. Since you are one flesh with her, sinning against your own body is sinning against her. You can imagine how absolutely devastating it is for a woman to discover that her husband finds gratification in the naked bodies of other women. So if that's what's been going on in your marriage, your wife will likely need concentrated help long after you're well on your way toward recovery. Make sure your wife finds a caring, competent counselor and an attentive, intentional spiritual physician to tend her wounded soul. It's bad enough when pastors are deprived of pastoral care. But the tragedy is exponentially compounded when their wives are spiritually abandoned too, left behind without pastoral care for themselves.

SPIRITUAL BOREDOM

There's one more area of temptation especially common among clergy that I want to bring to your attention. The porn trap is pretty well known; it's common enough that I would suspect you've run into its devastating effects frequently—if not personally, then in your pastoral care of others. But the other prevailing temptation I dare say is nearly unknown, though its sad results litter the wreckage of many a ministry. I'm talking about something the ancients called *acedia*. It's commonly translated sloth, but that's misleading. We're not just talking about habitual laziness or being a slacker at work. Our spiritual ancestors saw beneath superficial sloth and laziness to its underlying spiritual cause: disappointment with and disaffection from God's divinely ordained gifts, be they in the realm of creation or redemption.

Acedia means a lack or absence of care. And that's deadly. Whenever we grow numb to Christ's saving work and the Father's gracious gifts by which he makes us and preserves us, spiritual boredom takes hold, followed by apathy and subsequent despair. Where *acedia* takes root in the soul of a pastor, the flock suffers greatly.

The Care of Souls

The complex demands placed on pastors in our time call for extraordinary management and leadership skills, and many of us have an increasingly difficult time keeping up with the demands. Parishioners and church judicatory leaders are quick to point out a rise in dysfunctional pastors who are simply not at the top of their game. But you and I know that pastors are not trained seals. Ministry involves a lot more than a job description and performance evaluation. Still, I'm sure you'd agree that if we lose our zeal for the gospel and the service of Christ's people, it's a matter of grave concern. Unaddressed, that kind of spiritual apathy can quickly gut our pastoral *habitus* and ruin our ministry.

CLINICAL DYSFUNCTION

Research has shown that increasing numbers of clergy suffer from debilitating emotional dysfunctions. Collectively called "burnout," some of these disabilities stem from something now identified as Compassion Fatigue—the consequence of constant immersion in the emotional rollercoasters of the people to whom they minister. Likewise, research shows that clinical depression among pastors exceeds rates common in the general population. Sadly many pastors don't seek care from licensed clinicians, though emotional dysfunction responds very well to treatment by mental health professionals. Sadder still, far too many church leaders and ecclesiastical supervisors remain uninformed about the extent and impact of these illnesses and available treatment.

But remember: Mental illness and disorders involving the mind and emotions have clear spiritual dimensions as well. If it's tragic that too many pastors remain undiagnosed emotionally speaking, it is doubly tragic when those who preach the gospel to others themselves become spiritual casualties (1 Cor 9:25). How sad it is when pastors who care for others live effectively in a spiritual desert with no pastor to care for them. Likewise self-care is essential. We who take up the Savior's calling to tend the souls of others need to tend our own soul first. Watchfulness and prayerful vigilance are crucial when it comes to *acedia*, which I've come to believe is pandemic in its spiritual impact on clergy today.

Just a head's up: *Acedia* can be chronic or episodic. In my own experience and from what I've observed while caring for other pastors, spiritual boredom comes and goes for most of us throughout our ministry. But then *acedia* can also sink in its talons and take hold for long stretches of time. Whether chronic or acute, *acedia* always calls for watchful vigilance as well as intentional treatment—both your own spiritual self-care and in the care you receive from your soul's physician.

WARNING SIGNALS

How can you tell if you suffer from *acedia*? Here are some of the clear warning signs:

- Ministry begins to lose its luster and you find it harder and harder to rouse yourself to tend to the souls entrusted to you.

- Or conversely, you might throw yourself into frenetic ministry to others just to avoid having to tend your own soul, since you've grown cold and numb to the things of God.

- You lose touch with both the art and craft of ministry; you find yourself acting not out of your pastoral *habitus* but just going through the motions and impersonating a pastor.

- Ultimately the word of God and prayer become more and more an official duty and less and less a personal treasure.

If any of these cluster of symptoms become the norm for you rather than the exception, I think you can be pretty sure you're experiencing *acedia*.

Acedia is certainly not child's play. I've seen it take a good man down to near capitulation and bring him to the brink of despair. Here's how it usually unfolds: It's as if your soul has been injected with spiritual morphine. You become listless and unresponsive to the work of the Holy Spirit through his means. A pervasive numbness prevails; a numbness not just of emotion, but of heart and soul. I'm convinced that's why some pastors turn to porn. It's their way of treating their own unbearable emotional and psychic pain. It jolts them out of their bleak, numb world of *acedia*. What they're seeking is not really pleasure, but the ability to feel something again.

But *acedia* doesn't always present as a porn propensity. It can cast its toxic shadow in any number of ways.

One pastor I eventually treated for *acedia* came to me initially because he wrestled to contain an inexplicable simmering rage while quietly becoming more and more detached from all that he knew to be good and holy and true. Ministry for him became first a chore, then a burden. He no longer had the emotional energy to connect with his wife and children as he wanted to, though he knew he was robbing them of the husband and father they loved. The holy things of God began to lose their luster; he found himself less and less inclined toward prayer and God's word. He grew impatient in his ministry, and it became harder and harder for him to listen to the troubled hearts and souls of his parishioners.

Eventually he and I began to recognize in these symptoms *acedia*'s telltale signs. Besides the medical help he was already receiving for his anxiety, I advised him to change his work habits, take more time out for his family, etc. But here's what I wrote him during some of his darkest days:

> You also need to take on yourself the full armament that Christ supplies (Eph 6): Take up the sword of the Spirit, and pray at all times in the Spirit (which for me simply means to pray to the Father through the Son by the power of the Spirit). *Acedia* regarding holy things: No desire to care/pray, no ability to hear, no sense of peace ... all are symptomatic of demonic attack. There's no reason to fear, however. (This is) the normal result of what happens when a man takes up the mantle of the ministry and begins to do real work in service of Christ and his kingdom. Like moths to a flame, the forces of darkness are drawn to the light; demonic influences can't help but be drawn to such a man doing quality work in the kingdom in order to undermine his work, drive him to desperation, get him to sin in any possible way (pride is of course a favorite) and to break his bonds of love with others closest and dearest.
>
> But he's a defeated enemy. He can harm you none. The One who fights for you is stronger than he. In fact, the devil is God's devil: He inadvertently does God's work; attempting to separate you from Christ, Satan drives you closer to him. Go to Jesus; he has the words of eternal life, as you preached so well last Sunday. Take those words as your own even when you don't feel anything; embrace them and revel in the promises he brings you. What you have taught and embodied so well for others believe for yourself.[1]

I'm happy to report this pastor is well along the road to recovery today. While *acedia* still rears its ugly head occasionally, it's clearly in remission. While his vocations as husband, father, and pastor can at times be overwhelming and exhausting, they are fulfilling for him now, and he delights in them once more. He's infatuated with the care of souls again. Best of all, he knows the telltale signs of *acedia* and

---

1. Personal email correspondence.

knows when and where to seek help and how better to address them himself by prayer and the word of God.

DELIVERANCE FROM EVIL

None of us can be at the top of our game at all times. You know as well as I do that good and effective pastors have their ups and downs emotionally speaking, as well as episodes of greater or less productivity. But when you become chronically disillusioned with holy things and apathy toward God's work becomes unrelenting, it may be that you're not dealing just with an emotional low, but *acedia*. That's a spiritual temptation, part and parcel of the enemy's attack in spiritual warfare. And just as sexual temptation, it needs to be addressed spiritually—both in terms of self-care and most likely also the care of another pastor. Every pastor needs a pastor, and I'll address that in chapter eleven: "The Shepherding of Shepherds." But quality self-care begins, according to our Lord's direction and example, with prayer for protection: "Lead us not into temptation." Then we pray for our Father's intervention: "But deliver us from (the) evil (one)."

Ultimately there's not a man among us who can save himself under the continual onslaughts of the devil, world, and our own sinful flesh. Some things we can handle, but others are above our pay grade. If it were just a matter of working harder or working smarter, we could tackle that. Usually, that is. But you can't outwit Satan. You can't single handedly tackle the sinister influences of this fallen world any more than you can keep a lid on the raging impulses and obsessions of your own sinful nature.

It's true, frustratingly and consistently true. We do not wrestle with flesh and blood in either of these matters: sexual lust, *acedia*—or for that matter a whole raft of other temptations. Ultimately this whole struggle is a spiritual battle, beyond the range of our puny intellect and feeble willpower to curtail. That's why you can't fight this battle, not really. You can only defend yourself and call in the champion to fight for you. Christ Jesus, who by his blood and cross has conquered in the fight already, intercedes for you at the Father's right hand.

And God your Father in heaven for Jesus' sake will take care of you, of that you can be sure. He is the almighty Maker of heaven and earth, and yet at the same time he is your true Father. That means you are his true son, dearly loved. He is guardian and keeper of all his beloved children. He guides you waking and he guards you sleeping. Under his protection you can safely rest even in the most distressing hours of your life.

So call upon him in every trouble, won't you? Pray, praise, and give thanks to him. He is good, and his mercy endures forever. Whenever you are at the end of your rope—mentally, physically and spiritually exhausted—he will then be your strength and stay.

You won't know this, of course, relying on your five senses. Ministry can be not only exhausting, but depleting. And then when you're at your lowest ebb, Satan stirs the pot. He plays his trump card. He calls your attention not merely to your sins, but to the frightening developments around you and the fearsome unknown future ahead of you. All of these are things you can see, and hear, and touch, and feel. Any one of them can be terrifying enough, but collectively they will do you in. For left to your own devices, you will most certainly cave and give up.

PERSISTENT SENTRIES

But you can stand against this attack, provided you are arrayed in the protective armor of Christ Jesus your Lord: his truth, his righteousness, his gospel, his faith, and his salvation. Wield the sword of his Spirit with prayer and supplication, knowing that your Father in heaven delights in hearing your prayer and will most surely deliver you in his own time and way from all that ails you. So don't cash it in. Never ever give up; be just as persistent in meditation and prayer as the devil is in his attacks against you and those you love.

Remember: In this battle you're never a warrior. You're a sentinel. Your primary task is to do sentry duty, guarding against enemy attack. You can never tell where the next attack will come from, or where it will be directed. It could be against you, of course, but frequently the devil is too cagey for that. Coward that he is, sometimes he launches his most vicious assaults on those nearest and dearest to you: your wife and children, your closest friends, your parishioners. In every offensive and by any means possible his sworn, relentless goal is to uproot and utterly destroy God's good and gracious work in Christ.

But he's already judged, and the verdict is in. "It is finished," Jesus cried in his dying breath. All the work of Satan to destroy, all his lies and accusations, all the sin and mayhem he has imposed on God's good creation—all of this has been obliterated and eradicated in the death of our enfleshed God for the sins of the world. Christ's dramatic victory was affirmed and attested by his triumphant resurrection from the dead three days after his stone cold body was laid in its tomb.

So you can be confident, dear brother, that there's nothing in all creation that can ever separate you from the Father's love for you. Stand your ground, then, in the evil day. Some days are sure to be worse than others spiritually speaking. That goes with the territory in ministry. Temptations are sure to come; if not for you, then certainly for those you love. Therefore always remain alert to fend them off. Wield the word, the Spirit's sword. Pray persistently in the power and presence of the Holy Spirit, who sanctifies you already now and then in eternity hereafter forevermore.

And always remember this: The sufferings of this present time can't hold a candle to the joy that still awaits us (Rom 8:18).

CHAPTER TEN

Christ's "Other Sheep"

Mission and the Care of Souls

T he care and cure of souls is not only for those who
already belong to the kingdom of God by faith. Every
single person on earth, whether an elite Wall Street banker or
an impoverished third world islander, is created in the image
and likeness of God. People don't have souls; they are souls.
So soul care isn't an option, it's a given—also in mission. God
would have all people repent and be saved, from the simplest
to the most learned, from the greatest to the least. All must
first be gathered in, then tended in Jesus' name. And that
is soul care to the max. Both the gathering and the tending
comprise the proper care of souls.

We're coming off a solid half-century of concerted evan-
gelistic efforts and concentrated emphasis on the growth of
the church. Billions of dollars and untold lifetimes of energy
have been spent in proclaiming the gospel to win lost souls
for Christ. Yet statistically the number of committed confessing Christians continues to decline precipitously. Part of the
reason for this may be that despite all the effort toward winning souls, little has been invested in keeping them. Winning
souls and keeping souls comprise the two-sided coin of the
church's mission. In this chapter I hope to join back together
what well-intentioned people seem to have put asunder:
evangelization and soul care.

There is no division between the care of souls and mission. God has joined them together in Scripture. Our Lord's
famous mission directive, "Make disciples, baptizing them
in the name of the Father and of the Son and of the Holy

Spirit" includes exhortation to faithful training: "teaching them to observe all things I have commanded you" (Matt 28:19–20). His clear intent was that when souls come to faith by the working of the Holy Spirit through the gospel and then brought into the communion of his church, they should be tended and nurtured with the same Spirit by means of his gospel and sacraments. Mission and ministry, outreach and in-reach, evangelism and care of souls are all linked by God's own design. And what God has joined together, we dare never separate.

Evangelization always leads the way. It's the crucial first step in soul care for an unbeliever. After all, "How then will they call on him in whom they have not believed? And how are they to believe in him of whom they have never heard? And how are they to hear without someone preaching?" (Rom 10:14). A physician of the soul is by definition a missionary. But any real missionary had better be a physician of the soul as well, for souls that are brought to Christ need to be kept in Christ. Infants in the faith need to grow up in every way into him who is the head (Eph 4:15). Mission and ministry belong together.

Yet what God joined together is often divided in contemporary practice. Pastors are increasingly pressured to make a choice. They can either be an evangelist or a shepherd, a missionary or a pastor. Likely you've faced some pressure on this yourself either overtly or subtly, asked to choose between two options that are actually false alternatives. It's usually put this way: Would you rather be a missionary, actively gaining souls for Christ in an increasingly godless world or will you settle for just being a mere chaplain, quietly tending the faithful as a kind of soul custodian? Refuse to play that game. That's an arbitrary distinction detrimental to the church's life. It's time to reject this false dichotomy and set aside the caricatures and exaggerations being lobbed from one camp to the other.

FIELDS WHITE FOR HARVEST

Because organized religion no longer enjoys the prominence and impact it once had on social values and norms in our land, the newest generations are a blank slate spiritually speaking; they've never professed belief in any god other than allegiance to their own expressive self. This presents an obvious challenge to every confessing Christian.

Yet it is also a marvelous moment of opportunity. Today's pastors are surrounded with thousands of suffering, wounded souls, loaded with guilt they don't acknowledge and burdened with shame that escapes their notice. Worst of all, these same souls are in mortal danger, for the soul that sins shall die (Ezek 20:18). Like the convulsive devastation of an earthquake or the utter wreckage a tsunami leaves in its wake, our world is littered with the refuse of spiritual calamity. Souls are broken and wounded; souls are dying. And you are a physician of souls called to the kingdom for just this very time, chaotic though it be. You might only be aware of the challenges of these convoluted times, but I encourage you to see the opportunity before you.

Human history is littered with suffering and mayhem, but in God's estimation it's always harvest time. Jesus taught his disciples to look at the world with a farmer's eyes: "Do you not say, 'There are yet four months, then comes the harvest'? Look, I tell you, lift up your eyes, and see that the fields are white for harvest" (John 4:35).

EYES PEELED FOR THE HARVEST

In my childhood on the farm it seemed like every summer was endless sunshine, punctuated by the regular rhythm of daily chores. The grain grew steadily from seedlings in the spring to tall plants gleaming in the summer sunlight, their seed-laden heads undulating in the wind like waves on a great inland sea. But gradually the color of those heads changed from deep green to lighter shades, and then to golden hues that signaled harvest was approaching.

In late July my dad's typically calm demeanor changed. He'd walk out into the fields each day, breaking off heads of golden wheat or white oats, grinding them between his calloused palms. When the hulls were ready and the kernels were dry, he'd be primed for action. There could not be one day lost; to wait too long to begin the harvest meant that precious grain would fall wasted on the ground as harvesting machinery jostled them off their stalks. Timing was everything. No farmer worth his salt can ignore a field that is ripe for harvest.

So I urge you to look at the world around you like a farmer looking at ripening fields. Better yet, look at people as Jesus does: souls for whom he died. He's given you his harvest tools. In water, word, and meal he's provided you with the implements of his grace. He's sent you to bring hope and life to despairing, dying souls. And best of all, he's promised his presence to his church in every age, including yours: "Behold, I am with you always, to the end of the age" (Matt 28:20).

THE EYES OF JESUS

A pastoral *habitus* is developed over time. You learn by doing. A medical doctor begins by mastering a whole body of physiological science, but that's only the first step. For the rest of his career he practices medicine. The science he has learned informs the way he diagnoses and treats his patients, but the true *habitus* of a physician is an art acquired over time in the pursuit of appropriate care and cure for suffering people. So also you, my friend. You may have mastered theology to some degree, but you are a work in progress when it comes to the care of souls. You remain an apprentice, you might say, every day you work among the lambs and sheep of Christ for whom he died. And like every good and faithful sheepdog, the more time you spend with the Shepherd, the more apt and able you will be for tending his sheep. Your pastoral *habitus* develops in direct proportion to your own meditation and prayer, your personal time with the Great Shepherd.

Spending time in this school of experience, then, you begin to develop the mind of Christ. While conversing with a troubled person, instinctively you seek to discern the root of their distress, then bring healing tailored to that ailment in the gospel and sacrament applied. As I've suggested, pastors do everything by God's word. They listen with ears tuned to the word of God, they speak words taught by the Holy Spirit in his word, they pray by means of the word, and they bless by means of the word. By constant exposure to these words of Christ, you begin to see things from his perspective. You develop the eyes and ears of Jesus. You watch and listen with his outlook. And that includes the lost. When Jesus beheld the milling crowd by the shore of Galilee, "He had compassion for them, because they were harassed and helpless, like sheep without a shepherd" (Matt 9:36). It was a pitiful sight. Sheep without a shepherd are in dire straits. His heart went out to that vulnerable throng.

When you have the eyes and ears of Jesus, you instinctively know his heart. You know that since his heart yearns for all his sheep, he yearns also for the ones who do not yet know him. "And I have other sheep that are not of this fold. I must bring them also, and they will listen to my voice. So there will be one flock, one shepherd" (John 10:16). Jesus' eyes are always scanning the horizon for harassed and helpless sheep. He yearns to give rest to the weary and burdened. He longs that they would listen to his voice to bring them peace. You know of course that his words are Spirit and they are life. And he has given those very words to you to speak, so that all humanity may know him by faith and have life in his name.

A STRANGER'S VOICE

A bunch of sheep without a shepherd is a calamity in the making. Prone to wandering off in strange directions, sheep need to be herded together to protect them from predators and guard them from natural disaster. Then there's the necessity of food. Sheep in an arid land must be led to watering streams and into the nutrient-rich pastures they need to survive. A shepherd's relationship with his sheep is a beautiful thing to behold. They're dependent on him, and they know it. They recognize the sound of his voice and respond to it. For dumb animals, they're pretty bright. They can distinguish their shepherd's voice from the voice of a stranger. They detect differences in vocal timbre and pitch and they react accordingly.

We had no sheep on the farm I grew up on, but something much like this happened in my father's small dairy herd too. When it was time for evening milking, my dad or I would climb up the hilltop behind our barn and call the cows. Every day we used the same long, languid, resonant call: "Come b o s s, Come b o s s, Come b o s s." The second word was accented; I'm not quite sure why. But it worked like a charm. Looking up from where they were grazing—usually in the farthest corner of the pasture—the whole herd would set out for the barn at a slow, deliberate pace.

There was a social order of sorts among them, so the lead cow headed out first. Then the others plodded along behind on the well-worn cow path in stately single file. From long experience they knew what to expect: not just relief for their swollen udders, but also a treat. By long habit each cow entered the very same stall every night, eager for the generous helping of tasty corn silage we'd shovel into the trough in front of her stall, with a delectable ration of milled oats and corn piled on top.

On the rare occasion we hired someone to handle the morning or evening milking chores, he never got the same response we did. He might use the exact same call with a similar vocal inflection, but the cows would simply look up as if to say, "Who are you?" and then go back to munching grass. Then he'd have no choice but to hike out into the pasture, round up the cows, and herd them all the way back to the barn. The cows recognized the voices of those they trusted. They weren't about to respond to the voice of a stranger.

THE SHEPHERD'S VOICE

"My sheep hear my voice," says Jesus, "and I know them, and they follow me. I give them eternal life, and they will never perish, and no one will snatch them out of my hand. My Father, who has given them to me, is greater than all, and no one is able to snatch them out of the Father's hand. I and the Father are one" (John 10:27–30).

In his grace our Lord has provided a way by which contemporary ears in every era can hear his words, though separated by space and time. He puts his mighty word within earshot of people still today through the ministers he has authorized to speak in his name and stead: "The one who hears you hears me, and the one who rejects you rejects me, and the one who rejects me rejects him who sent me" (Luke 10:16). Through the pastoral office the barriers of time and space are transcended and people are given to hear the voice of the Good Shepherd.

HEARING JESUS

Amid the cacophony and frenzy of our harried world, the comforting voice of our gracious Savior still invites: "Come unto me, all you who labor and are heavy laden, and I will give you rest" (Matt 11:28). This is the mission of the church: that souls purchased and won by the saving work of Christ may hear his voice, believe his word and so find life eternal in his name. Notice that it's not hearing about Jesus that saves, but hearing Jesus. There's a big difference between the two.

For example, I could tell you about my wife. She's a wonderful woman, compassionate and caring. Jane is a warm and generous spirit with a ready laugh and great sense of humor. (It's a good thing because she's had to live with me all these years.) And she has a special place in her heart for pastor's wives. Quite a few women have taken courage over the years from her example of living graciously but robustly within the uniquely challenging vocation of clergy wife. I could go on and on telling you about her. But no matter how long I wrote about Jane, that would be nothing compared to actually meeting her and talking with her.

Listening to someone personally beats hearing about that person second hand. Yet strangely when it comes to the mission of the church we settle for the latter. Too much of what passes for gospel mission is second hand information; it may be factual and instructive, but it's not personal. It resembles advertising more than anything else. Testimonials about Jesus and historical biblical travelogues may be interesting and to some degree helpful, but they're no substitute for an audience with Jesus. People need to hear the voice of Jesus today firsthand just as they did two millennia ago.

That's where you come in. The called servants of Christ are not advertising agents or salesmen, but spokesmen for Jesus. When you open your mouth to speak the gospel you've been given to proclaim, people receive the words of Jesus. In a very real way, they hear Jesus himself. One of the greatest compliments I ever received about my sermonizing was from a young man who said: "As I listen to one of your sermons, you seem to fade away and I hear Jesus." No, he was no mystic nor was he describing an ecstatic experience. He simply reported his experience of me delivering the goods Jesus sent me to proclaim: not merely information about Jesus, but Jesus himself, crucified and risen—Christ the power of God and the wisdom of God.

WORDS OF JESUS

The words of Jesus— 'that's what people need to hear. They don't need to hear merely words about Jesus, but the words from Jesus. Because his words are spirit and life, as Peter confessed, they enact reality—they actually do something. By his word, Jesus in fact bestows his Spirit and life. Jesus himself put it this way in the earnest conversation with his Father that dark night of his betrayal in Gethsemane. He prayed not just for his beloved disciples, but also for those who would believe in him because of their words. Just think: He had you in mind!

"I have given them the words that you gave me, and they have received them and have come to know in truth that I came from you; and they have believed that you sent me. … But now I am coming to you … I have given them your word, and the world has hated them because they are not of the world, just as I am not of the world. I do not ask that you take them out of the world, but that you keep them from the Evil One. … Sanctify them in the truth; your word is truth" (John 17:8, 13–17).

Christ's mission and your ministry go together. You're a man on a mission because you are a minister of Christ, chosen and commissioned to do his bidding in this world. You have been given the words of Jesus to proclaim. So just do it. Do what you've been given to do; don't settle for anything short of that.

Too many sermons stop short of preaching Jesus; they are content to preach about Jesus instead. We may hear a lot about his glorious deeds and his astonishing mercy, his compelling and exemplary love, but we don't really hear from Jesus himself. The compassionate words of Jesus are not proclaimed viscerally into the mess and misery of real life where people struggle on day after day under an oppressive pile of guilt and shame. Nor for that matter does his penetrating word ever pierce the calloused hardened hearts of people who live carefree, self-indulgent lives, blissfully ignorant of their impending doom. To heal those hardboiled hearts and comfort those sorrowing, suffering souls, people need to hear the words of Jesus proclaimed into their ears so that faith can take root in their hearts. That faith lives by love all life long, then blossoms into fruition in heaven's glory.

Christ's sheep need you, but only because they need Jesus. In your ministry you bring Jesus to them. Specifically they need to hear his voice—the voice of the Great Shepherd. His voice is the difference between life and death in this world and the next. Jesus said so: "My sheep hear my voice, and I know them, and they follow me. I give them eternal life, and they will never perish, and no one will snatch them out of my hand" (John 10:27–28).

EVERYONE A WITNESS

Now keep in mind that the words of Jesus are not your private possession as a pastor. He has given them to the whole church to speak, not just the called servants of the word. Whenever and wherever the baptized faithful speak the word of the gospel, it remains the power of God for salvation to all who believe (Rom 1:16). In their daily vocations as father, mother, son, or daughter within the family or in society as worker or employer, every Christian is called upon to bear witness to a watching world concerning the hope that is within them. And by the gospel the Holy Spirit continues to call, gather, enlighten and sanctify the whole Christian church on earth.

Mission is not something extra or added onto the life of the church; it belongs to her very essence. As faith lives by love, so the church lives in mission. She cannot help but speak of what she has heard and seen. What she first receives from her glorious Lord she then passes on to those who do not yet confess him. Mission is nothing more than the church in motion to dispense the gifts of life and salvation that are in Christ Jesus. The beating heart of her life together is the person and work of Jesus and his powerful words that are spirit and life. Statistically the church may currently be in decline, but the way by which she grows is no mystery: As long as the earth remains souls are won and nourished by the word of the gospel.

S ome of my most rewarding years in ministry were spent as a missionary and church planter in Madison, Wisconsin. You can well imagine what a country hick like me felt like going to a comparatively large university town—and one not noted as a hotbed of social conservatism, at that.

Jane and I were apprehensive at first about even raising our family of young children in "the big city"—especially one that the head of my denomination's area judicatory called "the New York of the Midwest." He told me it was as close as a pastor can get to foreign missions in the continental U.S. God had something good in store, however. My six years there as missionary and then first pastor of a new and growing congregation were not just golden for me; they are years that our family looks back on gratefully to this day.

Madison was a melting pot of ethnicities, cultures, ideas, and professions. We soon gathered a little flock of mission-minded folk who met in our family room for Bible study and prayer, then began regular door-to-door canvassing and visits. Soon the gospel bore fruit. New converts joined a cadre of members from sister churches in the area, forming a small, but vibrant Christian community.

As the church outgrew its temporary rented space in a local business, we worked together to build the first stage of a large sanctuary that today stands on an imposing hill in West Madison. Most wonderful of all, of course, were the souls who were being built together as living stones to become a spiritual temple for the worship and service of God. When I was called away to serve another congregation, it tore my heart out; we had worked together for so long and so hard that close ties were built among us all.

But here's what I learned as a missionary: In gaining souls for Christ, you need to tend those souls in his name as well. Not only did they need basic instruction in God's word and ground floor training in the historic faith, they also needed individual care and cure for the whole range of spiritual issues you can find in any cross section of humanity. In my relatively brief tenure there I brought the correction, balm, and healing of God's word to bear for people who faced the full gamut of the ravages of sin; not just physical sickness and death, of course, but marital discord and unfaithfulness, bitterness, anger, doubt and uncertainty, same sex attraction, and more.

The wonderful thing about the precious souls who formed the leadership of that mission congregation was this: They believed the word of God to be at the heart of the church's life. They went to extra lengths to ensure that preaching and teaching remained uppermost in the life of our little mission as it began and then as it grew spiritually and numerically. "Pastor," they said, "let us handle all the many details in getting things up and running. We want you to devote yourself to study of God's word and preparing quality sermons for us."

When first things are kept first priority, missional outreach and the care of souls are a seamless whole. Through God's word and sacrament God gives his Holy Spirit, who works faith in those who hear the gospel. That's the secret to vital mission in apostolic times, and it's true still today.

Jesus taught his disciples that his word is like leaven, growing slowly and imperceptibly until it leavens the whole loaf (Matt 13:33). As it was then, so it is now in this our generation. Day by day, year by year, and era by era the Holy Spirit continues to call, gather, and enlighten people by the gospel. That word of the gospel is put into the mouths of the called servants of Christ to proclaim, but it's also placed on the lips of fathers and mothers to teach their children, to tell their friends and neighbors, to share with colleagues and coworkers.

NO SECRET AGENTS

In the increasingly pagan world that Western civilization has become, Christian witness is bound to stand out like a sore thumb. It's only normal that light attracts notice in the dark. "You are the light of the world; a city set on a hill cannot be hidden," said Jesus (Matt 5:14). As public mores deteriorate and the social fabric comes unraveled, those who govern their lives by their baptismal identity in Christ can no longer blend into the wallpaper of society; they will stand out in sharp contrast. But this is as it should be. Christians are not called to be secret agents operating incognito, but witnesses for their Lord and Savior by their words and example. No one lights a lamp and then hides it under a bushel basket, says Jesus, but sets it on a stand so it may shed light in the whole house. Christians are called to let their lights shine (Matt 5:15–16).

Such witness in word and deed is part and parcel of mission—the church in motion. The good news of Jesus is just too good to be kept to ourselves. Yet not everyone will see it as good news. Christians will meet with opposition and sometimes outright persecution because their life and message threatens the comfortable pursuit of self-indulgent pleasure that has become a way of life for many. Paradoxically, some see the message of life and freedom in Christ as a dangerous menace. But then, that's the norm in the life and mission of the church. Early Christians experienced that very thing: "For we are the aroma of Christ to God among those who are being saved and among those who are perishing, to one a fragrance from death to death, to the other a fragrance from life to life" (2 Cor 2:15–16).

Soul care at its most basic level is simply this: bringing suffering souls the good news of the gospel. This is what Christ Jesus sent his church to do. "As the Father sent me, even so I am sending you," (John 20:21) he said to his disciples after breathing out his empowering Spirit upon them. Learners (disciples) no more, they were now apostles ("sent ones") newly commissioned and authorized to proclaim Christ's saving words to the ends of the earth. Just as they were sent, so they went—both they and those they had gathered in by the gospel and sacraments. The called servants of Christ together with his precious lambs and sheep held forth his word of life in a dark and dying world. That's the way the church grows yet today.

MISSION IN MOTION

The formula for the growth of the church now in this confused and confusing world is still the same as it was during the apostolic era: faithful teaching and administration of Christ's saving word and sacraments. Through these, God sends forth his Spirit, who works faith—when and where it pleases him—in those who hear the gospel. Then in turn those who come to faith bear witness to others by what they say and do. This is the church in motion; mission in action. Impelled by God's Spirit, the wheel that moves the church revolves around his word.

You could see this cyclical mission at work in our new church plant in Madison. Its beginnings were notably humble: gifted carpenters constructed a portable altar that doubled as storage for hymnbooks and other materials. They built carpeted modules that we assembled into a portable sanctuary for the altar every week in our rented facility. These furnishings were the center of our fledgling church. I stood behind the altar to preach God's word of life every Lord's Day. A silver bowl borrowed from a parishioner was placed on the altar for baptism, a bath of regeneration and renewing in the Holy Spirit. Our first major purchase was a simple but dignified chalice and paten, and our growing flock regularly gathered around that altar to eat the bread of heaven and drink the cup of salvation for our forgiveness, life, and salvation. The wheel that moves the church kept on moving around these sacred gifts. And at the hub stood none other than Christ Jesus himself.

A diverse group of sinner/saints gathered around that hub. There was Pedro, a Mexican immigrant whose wife managed the low income apartment complex where they lived. Mei Ling brought an Asian flavor to our church—quite literally. Her homemade spring rolls were the hit of our potluck meals. Her young son Billy played a respectable violin; he teamed up with our son Mike on the cello as part of a transcultural children's string ensemble that enriched our church's music regularly. Our church reflected the community in its diversity and a cross section of humanity: college professors, mechanics, real estate agents, corporate executives and common laborers.

What brought these men and women together despite all their differences? Certainly not the charm and abilities of their pastor. Rather, the secret to our vitality was in God himself. By the gospel his Spirit was gathering them as one and making them all one body in Christ. Daily and richly the Holy Spirit was forgiving all their sins and blending them into a cohesive whole, then sending them back into their daily lives to live as his emissaries and ambassadors in their daily vocations.

Vessels for the Lord's Supper: Chalice for the wine, paten for the bread

This is the wheel that moves the church. Not human ingenuity or effort, but God the Holy Spirit working through his means. This was mission for us thirty years ago, and that is mission for you still today. And while the look and feel of mission may vary from age to age, the ingredients in mission today remain the same as what we see among the very first Christians in Jerusalem. They were devoted "to the apostles' teaching" (doctrine) "and the fellowship" (unity in faith and life), "to the breaking of bread" (Communion) "and the prayers" (the sacred liturgy) (Acts 2:42).

True, that first Christian congregation faced some unique circumstances. Due to persecution, they pooled their earthly goods and shared them with each other. But just like Christians still today, they also shared their joys and sorrows with one another. Their love for each other was part and parcel of their public witness, and Luke records that "they enjoyed favor with all the people." God does not imbed Christians in the world to work an undercover operation. Rather, he sends forth his beloved as lights in a dark world to shed the light of his mercy and grace in Christ Jesus in their homes and communities. In their interaction with their neighbors by word and example others are drawn to Christ and his church. That's the way it worked in Jerusalem and that's the way it works today. As a result, "the Lord added to their number day by day those who were being saved" (Acts 2:47). Notice who is driving the verb in that sentence; God is always the actor in mission and people are the recipients of his gifts.

CARE FOR SUFFERING SOULS

At its core the church is a fellowship of faith in human hearts, and that faith cannot be produced by the social sciences or business methods. The church is the body of Christ (1 Cor 12:27), and like the human body it is an organism, not an institution. God himself has provided the blueprint for the growth of Christ's church. It grows one member at a time being grafted into the whole body, drawing nurture and sustenance from the head. When people join a church they don't become affiliates in some sort of service agency; they are linked with each other intricately as members of one body. Membership in a church means a lot more than names on a roster. Like the various limbs of the human body, they are joined into one organism: the living body of

Christ with Jesus Christ himself as head. Within this spiritual union. When one member suffers, all suffer with it and when one member rejoices, all share in that joy. The connections within this one body transcend mere human sociability and affection. We cannot be content to run a church like any other social entity. Even though the church does have social dimensions, at its core it's a union of hearts and lives joined together as one in Christ.

That means that the evangelists of the church need to be good shepherds of souls. The Lord of the church has joined mission and ministry together even though many try to pry them apart. Evangelization is but the first stage in soul care.

DIVERSE SINNER/SAINTS

Take Sonia, for example. She and her husband Rick were the very image of success and respectability. But something was missing in their lives. They found it in our little mission congregation. For the first time since childhood Sonia took delight once more in the promises of Christ Jesus her Savior. Her enthusiasm and zeal for her Lord were infectious. She and her husband were in regular attendance at worship whenever they were not taken out of town by frequent business trips. Their suave sophistication stood out among the more pedestrian tastes of many of our members. It was exciting then to see Sonia's new-found faith take shape in the key roles she assumed among our church's volunteers.

Yet I soon discovered that beneath Sonia's façade of sophistication and sincere faith lay a tortured heart wounded and impacted by cumulative years of sin—sins she had done, to be sure, but also sins she had suffered from the sins of others. I was reminded once again that evangelists are also physicians for souls; new converts need a physician of the soul just as long time members. A lot of listening, consoling, absolving, praying, and blessing was just as important for Sonia, the zealous new convert, as it was for George, the patriarch of a family known as "pillars of the church" for generations.

The very first step in spiritual diagnosis is to rightly discern whether a person is a baptized believer: Do they confess a living faith in the Lord Jesus? The proper cure of souls for an unbeliever is God's law and gospel leading to repentance and faith.

But once a person confesses Christ, the evangelist becomes a physician of the soul. Many who come to faith have lived for a long time in the far country, like the prodigal who wasted his father's inheritance in reckless living. Deep spiritual scars are inflicted by sins of two kinds: whether committed or suffered. As the church goes about the missionary task of welcoming in the walking wounded of this world she needs to exercise responsible soul care as well. Whether these wounded are perpetrators or victims of sin (and usually they are both), careful triage is in order. Accurate spiritual discernment precedes appropriate spiritual care. It won't do to merely bring new believers into the church and neglect their wounds. That's when evangelization turns to care of the soul. Broken and tortured souls brought to faith need deliberate intervention and treatment to bring healing to each complex case.

DIAGNOSIS AND CURE

There are other sheep to gather in; refugees from a lost and dying world need to be brought into the fellowship of the baptized. Our calling is not to build a safe refuge from the storms all around, but to be an oasis of life in a desert of death. We've been given an eternal gospel to proclaim to every nation and tribe and language and people (Rev 14:6). This is the very first stage in the care of dying souls: to bring them the word of life of a gracious God in Jesus Christ and then to wash them in the name of the Father, Son, and Holy Spirit to welcome them into the company of the baptized from every land and nation.

In the post-apostolic era of late antiquity the church tied missionary zeal and spiritual scrutiny together. Extensive catechesis was essential not just to inculcate Christian teaching, but also to provide cleansing and healing for defiled and wounded souls. It's my conviction that necessity will force conscientious missionaries in our time to pay more attention to the cure of souls. We'll be forced to review and recover the church's ancient approach to mission that included both diagnosis and cure for spiritual ailments.

In the turbulent and chaotic world of the twenty-first century, skilled physicians of the soul are essential to mission. As social orders collapse, spiritual wounds are etched all the more deeply on hearts and souls. The church will increasingly become a haven of order in a disordered world. It will be an ark of refuge on an increasingly tempestuous sea. As we welcome refugees from the collapsing world around us into our fellowship, those refugees will need skilled spiritual physicians. "Have mercy on those who doubt; save others by snatching them out of the fire; to others show mercy with fear, hating even the garment stained by the flesh" (Jude 22–23).

You'll need a practiced eye to provide spiritual care for refugees from an increasingly fractured world. You'll be dealing with complex spiritual ailments and co-morbidities that call for careful discernment. New Christians cannot be left to their own devices to contend with the aftermath of a life lived apart from God. They'll be coming under spiritual attack. The demonic realm does not take kindly to someone who renounces Satan and declares allegiance to the Lord who by his cross and resurrection has defeated death and ransacked hell. The missionaries of the future will need to be savvy and competent physicians of souls.

MISSIONARY/SHEPHERD

You've got your work cut out for you. Mission and ministry are a package deal. You wear both hats as a called and ordained servant of Christ: missionary and shepherd. He wants you to do first things first, but not to neglect the second things. Proclamation and nurture, evangelization and soul care go together.

You as pastor play a central role in the Spirit's work, for by your ordination and call you've been set aside and placed into the public preaching office. The Great Shepherd has authorized you to act in his name and stead to forgive sins, to heal sin-sick souls and bring his light and life to souls locked in darkness and death.

PARTNERS IN MISSION

But you do not act alone. The entire company of the baptized have a key role in the life and mission of Christ's church.

Pastors and the people they serve are partners in mission. They each have a distinct role, to be sure, but there's no need to pit laity against clergy. He has joined his church and their called servants together in his mission. Each has a different calling. Not everyone is a minister, but all are priests. All Christians are called to offer up their prayers and praises together with their works of love in thanksgiving to our gracious God for all his mercies in Jesus Christ his Son. Ministers are called to serve to the royal priesthood the gifts of Christ in his name and stead, while the whole company of the baptized are called to meet their neighbor's needs with deeds of love in Jesus' name.

So this is God's mission in sum: Christians are passive in faith, but active in love. First we receive, and then we give to others what we have first received. You as pastor by your call and ordination have been given the solemn duty to publicly preach the gospel and administer the sacraments. By these sacred means God the Father sends forth his Spirit, who works faith according to his will in those who hear the gospel. But where faith is present, it flows forth in works of love. Consequently mission spills over from sanctuary into daily life. The wheel that moves the church spins on week by week. What is received on the Lord's Day from font and pulpit and altar changes hearts and lives all week long. Mobilized into Christ's service, every Christian is enlisted in his mission in daily life. All Christians by their baptism have been called into service of their neighbors day by day, bearing witness by word and deed to him who is their life. As it was in the beginning, so it is now and ever shall be until Jesus comes again: Mission is nothing more than the church in motion. Mission leads to ministry, and ministry to mission.

What God has joined together let no man put asunder.

CHAPTER ELEVEN

The Shepherding of Shepherds

E very baptized believer needs care and cure. Continually the soul needs the direction and admonition of God's law as well as the consolation and comfort of his gospel. But at times acute wounds and ailments of the soul call for specific curative treatment.

So that brings us back to you. Who takes care of your soul? I'm just guessing that if you are like most of us you try and shrug off your own spiritual needs. After all, we're trained theologians, aren't we? We've been to seminary and that means we should have all the answers. We're avid Bible students and we have soaked up the wisdom of the ages when it comes to Christian doctrine. If that's the way you've been handling your personal spiritual needs, I have two words for you: STOP IT! That's right, you need to seek out care for your soul; you need to place yourself under the care of another pastor. This is not a sign of weakness; rather, it shows you respect the office that you yourself hold.

I doubt that you would return to a dentist whose teeth are decayed and falling out or a barber whose hair is a mess. Every profession proves its integrity when its practitioners themselves seek out the services of a colleague. So if you value the art and craft of the cure of souls to which you've been called, why wouldn't you seek someone to pastor you?

FINDING A PASTOR

But where to look? Those who have been given responsibility for your ecclesiastical supervision would likely be the first option. However, most of these men that I know recognize that their dual role as both pastor and supervisor creates a formidable barrier when it comes to quality pastoral care. The threat of disciplinary consequence—whether imagined or real—is going to make a pastor somewhat hesitant to be transparent with his supervisor. That's why men in leadership positions in the church tend to encourage pastors under their supervision to seek out a brother or father confessor for themselves who can provide the care they need on an ongoing basis.

Pastors often ask me how they should go about finding a pastor who can shepherd them. The first thing I tell them is don't gravitate toward friends. Like I already told you, a pastor needs every friend he can cultivate, and having pastors in your circle of friends is a treasured gift. They know firsthand the joys and stresses of pastoral work, and with them you can be completely candid. But pastoral care is a lot more than empathy, camaraderie, and understanding. Here and there I've known pastors who are good at keeping these roles separate and can serve in both vital capacities: friend and pastor. But that's a dual role, and it involves conscious and deliberate vigilance, so normally I advise men to look beyond their circle of friends to identify their personal pastor.

So how to proceed, then, in seeking a pastor for yourself? I advise men to use their eyes and ears. How does the pastor you're considering view the congregation he serves? Is it clear he's able to love his people despite their weaknesses, with all their warts and blemishes? Is he a man of theological integrity and good humor, who takes himself lightly, but his office seriously? Does he demonstrate a healthy reverence for the word and the sacraments as instruments of God's Spirit in creating and sustaining faith? Does he present himself as a servant of Christ and steward of God's mysteries? If so, approach him with the request to meet with you regularly to receive the gifts of God: to listen to you, pray with you, bless you, or hear your confession as needed.

I was blessed during the most taxing years of my service in the parish ministry with such a pastor who served me well and faithfully. He was a real pastor's pastor, a man of utter integrity theologically speaking, but also possessing a gentle and caring spirit. Jane and I had known him ever since we used to take our young children on an annual vacation to a lake near the church he served at the time, and we grew to love the depth of his preaching and the warmth of his personality. It seemed only natural, then, that in those years when I needed a stalwart servant of Christ I turned to him and placed myself under his care. Our visits always began in his study, where we began with pleasantries but moved naturally to the things that had been cluttering my mind and worrying my spirit. Then we moved to the sanctuary where we both knelt before the altar and I was able to unburden my heart, pouring out both my sins and the sorry wounds of my soul to God.

After I had finished my confession he stood and, with the crucifix behind him, my pastor spoke in the place of the Crucified One to forgive me in his name and stead. Usually he prefaced his absolution with a marvelously crafted brief homily of encouragement and hope. Using the text he was preparing to preach that week, he skillfully wove together the hurt and horror of my sin with the healing balm of my Savior's wounds. "Do you believe that my forgiveness is Christ's forgiveness?" he concluded. Upon my assent, he forgave me all my sins in the name of the Father and of the Son and of the Holy Spirit. I made it a regular habit to go to him for pastoral care and cure. I sought a time to meet with him on a rotational basis, monthly or at least seasonally. This was the ongoing care that I needed because of my chronic need for forgiveness and encouragement.

But there were also times of acute need. During a crisis of congregation discontent and disarray I suffered late in my parish ministry, I called on him for help. It was then I discovered that my pastor made "house calls;" he came to visit me in my own study, armed with God's word and the power of his gospel absolution, in which I found help, hope, and renewal. So seeking out this cure in times of acute need was also part of my pastoral *habitus*. I commend it to you as well. I'm convinced there should be a concluding admonition added to the rites of ordination and installation: "Don't try this alone." The work is too difficult and fraught with danger to be tackled relying on one's own resources. Thankfully God, who is surpassingly rich in his grace, provides help in multiple ways—including the exhortation and comfort he provides through the mutual conversation and consolation of brothers.

I'm hoping these couple of pages on why pastors need pastors has convinced you; I'm quite serious about this. And I believe that Jesus is too. You'll notice that when he sent out his disciples (Mark 6) and the Seventy-two (Luke 10) he sent them two by two. Not just because there's strength in numbers, but because in the Lord's kingdom, faith comes by hearing. Therefore the servants of the word themselves deserve—and need—to hear the word that brings them life. I urge you, then, by the mercies of God, that you make the regular reception of the word from the mouth of another pastor part and parcel of your ministry. You'll discover, as I have, that having a pastor for your own soul is an essential part of the pastoral *habitus*.

CARING FOR YOUR OWN SOUL

I've made my case that every pastor needs a pastor of his own. But there's another aspect of the care of your soul that is critical; it belongs to the essence of personal spiritual health. And that's the care that you give your own soul.

Again, if spiritual self-care sounds like foreign language to you that's only one more indication of the spiritual disarray into which we've fallen. By training and inclination our instinct is to prioritize the care of others. Selflessness in ministry is an admirable quality to which we all aspire. And in our " self-help" world it sounds almost narcissistic to pay attention to our own spiritual welfare. Who wants to be a spiritual navel-gazer? Yet when we look to the Scriptures we see that faithful care of others' souls includes care of our own. You can't give away what you don't have, after all. We pass on to others what we ourselves have first received. And the plain fact is that you're in no shape to help others spiritually if you yourself are starving spiritually.

Remember the drill you hear on an airplane just before take-off? The flight attendant launches into a familiar litany that goes something like this: "In the unlikely event of a loss in cabin pressure, oxygen masks will descend from the ceiling. If you're traveling with a child or someone who needs assistance, put your own mask on first before assisting others." It only stands to reason: You can't provide oxygen to anyone else if you yourself are asphyxiated. The same holds true when it comes to the gifts the Holy Spirit gives by his word: You can't give them to others if you're suffering from gift depravation. Paul underscores this in two places. First, in his farewell to the pastors of Ephesus he charges them: "Pay careful attention to yourselves and to all the flock, in which the Holy Spirit has made you overseers, to care for the church of God, which he obtained with his own blood" (Acts 20:28). And then again in his first letter to Timothy he writes: "Take heed to yourself and to your teaching; hold to that, for by so doing you will save both yourself and your hearers" (1 Tim 4:16, RSV). In both instances the verb he uses implies careful tending and nurturing on behalf of the Great Shepherd who laid down his life for the sheep. Notice that the pastor's care for himself comes first, before either care for the people of God or the doctrine to which he is pledged.

There's an important lesson here. You neglect your own personal spiritual care not only to your own peril, but to the detriment of the church of God and your fidelity to the doctrine of his word. Therefore time spent in private prayer and meditation is not time wasted, but time invested in quality ministry.

BY WORD AND BY PRAYER

It's become customary to speak of private meditation and prayer as "devotion" or "quiet time." There's nothing especially wrong with those terms so long as you define them properly. Yet many falsely assume personal meditation is quieting the mind and getting in touch with the self. All meditation and prayer is built on the premise that God draws near to us and speaks to us in his word. Thus healthy devotion and quiet time involves ongoing conversation: God first speaks to us in his word and then answering, we pray.

There are an infinite variety of approaches to private prayer. No doubt you've tried many of them and left them behind as impractical or dissatisfying. Everyone needs a disciplined approach to prayer.

That may sound like bad news, but it's actually good news; the trick is to find a discipline that suits you. In case you haven't noticed, God didn't use a cookie cutter when he created us. He makes each human in his own image and likeness, it's true, yet each person has their unique aptitudes and imagination. Some of us are more visual, others more verbal. Some are highly theoretical, others concrete. So while I'm going to provide broad parameters for the ingredients in a rich life of personal prayer and devotion, it'll be up to you to take those parameters and design an approach that works best for your own temperament and situation.

Essentially, there are two components in the care of your own soul: God's word and prayer. The first is the means of the Holy Spirit to sanctify your soul and body. The second is your response; the result of your sanctification, you could say. Paul urged Timothy to teach this theology of sanctification to his people: "For everything created by God is good, and nothing is to be rejected if it is received with thanksgiving, for it is made holy by the word of God and prayer" (1 Tim 4:4–5). Thus your life of mediation and prayer really constitute your personal sanctification. Your holiness is not your own; it's not self-generated, but borrowed from God and received in proximity to his presence. God is present in his word. Drawing near to him at his invitation, you speak to him as you are spoken to. All prayer, then, is responsive.

So a good pastoral *habitus* entails a rich life of personal meditation and prayer. The word of God is the hub of both. This is what distinguishes Christian mediation from all other versions. Research shows that people who meditate to silence the constant chatter of inner turmoil in their minds and achieve inner calm and stability will achieve demonstrably greater resilience and productivity. Eastern religions, of course, have famously practiced meditation for centuries. More recently, secular psychologists have touted the benefits of "mindfulness," strategies to quiet racing inner thoughts and bring tranquility and peace to the mind. Brain science research documents demonstrable mental and physiological improvement among people who practice meditation strategies of whatever sort. This only stands to reason, of course; it's a matter of wellness. The simple fact is that we humans were not designed by our Creator to have our brains in high gear 24/7. So certainly there will be a noticeable benefit when people get in touch with themselves through meditation and mindfulness techniques. There is indeed a bit of overlap with biblical meditation in that all meditation involves the human mind. But that's where the similarity stops. For Christian meditation is not getting in touch with the self, but getting in touch with God.

PRAYING OUT LOUD

Many years ago one of the leaders in our church published a two-volume daily guide for prayer for pastors.[1] It languished in my library, but one day I picked it up and began using it. The next time I saw the author I expressed my appreciation for his work. Before even saying, "Thank you," he responded: "I hope you're praying out loud." As a matter of fact, I wasn't. But since then I've learned the wisdom behind his response. Now almost all my private prayer is spoken aloud, or at least whispered loud enough for my own ears to hear it.

If you're not accustomed to doing this, it might seem strange to you at first. Like me, you may have assumed that spoken prayers are for little kids, but silent prayer is the norm for adults. Perhaps you fear embarrassment if someone suddenly comes within earshot; they might think you're talking to yourself. But there should be no more embarrassment in speaking to your heavenly Father privately than when praying aloud corporately in church. And spoken prayer in private is not just for children. In fact, it's the norm in the history of the church and the longer experience of Christ's people. I've discovered that speaking my prayers keeps me on target so I'm not distracted by my wandering mind. What at first seemed novel and contrived soon became normal and enriching.

God hears not only the words of our mouth, but the meditation of our hearts as well. Silent prayer is just as valid as spoken prayer. Yet prayer, after all, is talking with God. And I think we can agree that speech is the default mode of communication for us humans. If you've ever tried communicating with your spouse by mental telepathy, you know what I mean. We don't transfer the thoughts in our head and the meditation of our hearts to other people by brain waves,

1. See Robert C. Sauer, *Daily Prayer*, 2 vols. (St. Louis: Concordia, 1986).

but by *speaking* them. Therefore the best way to pray to our Father in heaven is to pray aloud even when we're alone. Begin the practice if it's not yet your habit. I believe it will grow on you as it has on me.

It's clear from the New Testament record that our Lord Jesus customarily prayed out loud in private. We learn in Luke 5:15 that it was his habit to withdraw to isolated places to pray to his Father in heaven. Matthew records that during the bitter night of Jesus' betrayal and arrest in Gethsemane, he withdrew from his disciples to pray, taking with him his inner circle of friends: Peter, James and John (Matt 26:36–38). Asking them to keep prayerful watch with him, he withdrew even farther and prayed aloud: "My Father, if it be possible, let this cup pass from me; nevertheless, not as I will, but as you will" (Matt 26:39). If the Son of God incarnate in human flesh prayed out loud, I guess we can too. He, after all, was one with the Father from all eternity. Yet if he in his flesh prayed aloud to his Father who sees in secret, so can we.

Such prayer doesn't come naturally; it must be taught. And, thank God, it can be learned.

DEVELOPING A PRAYER *HABITUS*

Most people have the impression that all Christians should automatically know how to pray. That's why they are intimidated by folks who seem comfortable praying in the presence of others. Many are threatened by the ease with which others pray freely in their own words, wondering secretly if perhaps there's something missing in their own faith. Yet a moment's reflection will set us straight. Prayer, after all, is talking to God. And though you likely don't remember learning to talk, you've all seen children acquire speech. Perhaps some of you have raised your own children from infancy. Babies begin to speak by listening to their parents and mimicking what they hear.

Linguists tell us that no matter how complexly different one language is from another, the first words babies learn are the words for father and mother. And, remarkably, no matter how vastly different the vocal and grammatical structure of almost seven thousand different living languages on the planet, universally the words for mother and father are nearly the same. They are variations of "Ba," "Da," "Ta," "Baba," "Dada" or "Tata" for father and "Ma," "Na," or "Mama" and "Nana" for mother. Infant mouths can easily form these early vocalizations, and so these simple words are the basis of all linguistic development. Chemists, brain surgeons, rocket scientists, computer programmers, theologians, and philosophers as well as plumbers, carpenters, farmers, and factory workers—all these diverse people erect the colossal superstructure of their distinct and elaborate vocabularies on a very rudimentary foundation. All language rests on the treasured words we all learned as infants by which we magically invoked the presence of the most important people in our private universe: "mommy" and "daddy."

So learning human speech begins with listening to our parents. We speak as we were spoken to. It's the same way with prayer; we have to first listen to God before we can speak to him. Take, for example, the familiar Lord's Prayer. A careful reading of the New Testament shows us that it's not so much a prayer in itself as it is a way of prayer or pattern for prayer. In Matthew's Gospel, Jesus introduces the prayer by teaching his disciples: "Pray, then, like this" (Matt 6:9). Luke records that he provided the prayer in response to a request: "Lord, teach us to pray, as John taught his disciples" (Luke 11:1).

Notice that in both instances Jesus teaches prayer by praying "Our Father." We're accustomed to thinking of that first person plural in terms of all the fellow believers who are praying with us. Yet when you consider the setting of his teaching, that "our" includes Jesus himself; Jesus invites us to pray to his Father in heaven in solidarity with him. Just as he existed in perfect union with God the Father from all eternity as his well-beloved Son, so he invites us to approach the almighty Maker of heaven and earth as dearly beloved children approach their dearly beloved father—with all boldness and confidence.

In effect, he's telling his disciples "any Father of mine is your Father too." No holding back. Whatever joy or sorrow that is on your heart is fair game for your prayers. So whatever you do, don't launder your prayers; keep the pain and frustration in them. Remember, a good share of the psalms are prayers of lament. Whenever you're up against it, you can file a complaint with God. Name your enemies, what they've done to you, then ask him for vindication. Call to him in your distress, just as Jesus did when he cried out in agony from his cross: "My God, my God, why have you abandoned me?" (Ps 22:1;

Matthew 27:46). After all, when your little toddler hurts, you want to hear his distress so you can comfort him. So don't deprive your Father in heaven of the joy of hearing your lament; it's not whining, but an exercise in faith.

SPIRITUAL EXERCISE: *ASKĒSIS*

The ancient Greeks had a word for exercise: *askēsis*. They were of course great believers in fitness of all sorts. A sound mind in a sound body was their classic ideal. The cultivation of moral virtue, physical strength and intellectual knowledge was for them the epitome of the human ideal. For the moral philosophers, the only way to achieve these ideals was through conscious suppression of the appetites and passions. This involved exercise (*askēsis*) of the will. Hence the origins of the word "ascetic." Moral, mental, and physical perfection entailed a constant battle against the baser instincts of the human spirit.

So let me level with you. When you set about to care for your own soul by meditation and prayer it's going to take some discipline on your part. Meditation and prayer rooted in God's word are richly rewarding, but they don't come naturally. Just like physical exercise, you will need to establish a plan and set a routine for your spiritual exercise. You'll need to go into training mode. Outwardly physical training and spiritual training are the same: Both demand discipline. Inwardly, however, spiritual training is more comprehensive than physical: "Train yourself for godliness; for while bodily training is of some value, godliness is of value in every way, as it holds promise for the present life and also for the life to come." (1 Tim 4:7-8)

Ultimately it's up to you to set aside the time and develop a structure and strategy that works for you. What I've found is that my discipline has morphed over the years to fit my circumstances.

EARLY TO RISE

When our children were young, Jane handled morning household routines. I supervised after school hours, giving me time with the kids before the onset of evening duties that frequently took me away from home. So during those years the early morning hours were wonderfully conducive for my personal prayer.

The best time and place for private prayer and meditation at that point in my life was around 6:00 or 6:30 a.m. in my study at church. Though we had a large staff in our church and school, relative peace and quiet reigned supreme until 7:00 or so. I was blessed to have a hand-crafted wall altar and a prie-dieu (a padded kneeler). After lighting candles and kneeling before the image of the crucified Lord, I found this to be a wonderful place to immerse myself in the word and prayer. Many blissful cumulative hours were spent there in spoken prayer and meditation, weaving together the words of Scripture, the words of my lips and the meditation of my heart. Most mornings I had at least a solid half hour before the bustle of the day began outside my closed study door. Though I was not trying to show off my piety, some parishioners mentioned that on their way to work they were encouraged to glimpse me through my study window, kneeling at prayer. One said: "It's comforting to know our pastor is praying for us."

Another pastor I know practices a variation on this morning discipline. Like me, he serves a large and busy parish. The church sanctuary is set apart from the parish school and the administrative offices, yet the altar committee and other volunteers are frequently active in the church at the start of the day. This pastor requests that there be no foot traffic in the church for the first half hour of the day because he has reserved the sanctuary for his private devotion. Sometimes he sits quietly in the pew meditating, sometimes kneeling at the altar rail. Frequently he prays the order of Matins aloud.

Yet another pastor uses a small crucifix to focus his attention as he reads Scripture aloud and prays. He burns incense in a small censor, thus wrapping his prayerful meditation in sensory stimulation (Rev 5:8). The incense provides the rich aroma of holiness and a visual depiction of the prayers of the faithful rising to the throne of God.

PARK BENCH

Recently I've taken to using my morning walks as a time for prayer. I strive for a vigorous pace to exercise my heart, but at the same time I rest my soul with the great music of the church's choral tradition using my smartphone and ear buds. After about a mile of vigorous hiking, I stop at an isolated park bench, unplug my ear buds, and spend time in

God's word and spoken prayer. First I recite a psalm and then weave my wreath of prayer around that psalm and my thanksgivings, fears, confessions and intercessions of the day. That quiet park bench at the top of a knoll in a serene little park in my neighborhood has become almost as precious to me as my prie-dieu and candles.

My wife, despite chronic pain and increasing physical limitations, is a veritable prayer athlete. Jane puts her whole heart and mind to work in prayer for me, for our children and grandchildren, for our friends and their families, and everyone in need. In the prime of her life as a full-time mom with a full-time job as an English teacher, she had to snatch time for prayer whenever she could: In the car on her daily thirty minute commutes was one opportunity. But I admired her swimming prayers most. Three days a week she stopped at the health club to swim laps before coming home to start the evening routine: laundry, cooking, homework supervision, and teaching prep. Depending on her energy level, she would swim either a mile or a half mile. With each lap she would review the events of a different year of our marriage and family, giving thanks and interceding for events and people called to mind and heart for that particular year. That wouldn't work for me, since I can just barely swim. But it served Jane well and combined the *askesis* of both body and soul.

All disciplines are not the same. What works at one stage of life may not work in the next. What works for me may not work for you, and what enriches my mind and heart may leave you cold. Our Father in heaven has made all of us humans distinct and different from one another. Not only do our fingerprints vary, but our minds and imaginations are vastly different as well. It's up to each of us to find a discipline of prayer that best fits our unique personality and circumstance.

Which discipline will work for you? Try a variety of approaches and see what works best. Experiment and see. Be ready for sporadic fits and starts. Some ups and downs are to be expected. Every worthwhile regimen takes effort. Changing personal habits of eating and physical exercise doesn't come without challenge; spiritual exercise requires deliberate effort too. Pick a discipline and give it a go. Modify as necessary. If you fail, begin again. That's the way spiritual self-care works. When the habits of prayer come more and more naturally, you'll notice something isn't quite right if you have to go without for a day or two. When that begins to happen, you'll know that the care of your own soul is part and parcel of your pastoral *habitus*.

LUTHER'S PRAYER WREATH

The doctrinal legacy of Martin Luther's work is much better known than his pastoral and devotional writings. Yet in a very real way the Reformation was more pastoral than doctrinal. The quest for a clean conscience before God was uppermost in Luther's personal spiritual struggle. That quest led him to become a vigorous champion of justification by grace through faith in Christ's saving work on his cross. We regard this teaching of justification to be the central article of the faith once delivered to the saints. Yet our confession is not sectarian or parochial; it belongs to the church catholic. Our goal is to teach nothing other than what has been believed always, everywhere and by all. So also Lutheran piety can inform any Christian's life of meditation and prayer.

Expanding upon the *lectio divina* tradition of the medieval church, Martin Luther practiced a method of devotion by which prayer and meditation were woven together, wreath-like, in which God's word and prayer are combined into a seamless whole. Far from an intellectual exercise, for Luther this was an experience of the Holy Spirit's blessing. First the Spirit instructs us by his word and then he calls forth our reflection, thanksgiving, confession, and intercession in answer to that word.

I've already demonstrated how the "wreath prayer" can be used in the course of pastoral care, but do think seriously about using this model for your own private spoken meditation and prayer. With practice you will find, as I have, that you can use any text of Scripture as the starting point. As a little child learns to speak by mimicking its parents, begin your prayer by simply mirroring that text. The first step in this approach is to read God's word aloud and then begin echoing back to God in your words what you have heard in his word. Precept, then, becomes the first strand in the wreath. Then comes thanksgiving, where you give God thanks for what he has given, promised, or taught in this scriptural word. After that, confess your sins of omission or commission against this word. Finally, ask him for what he has commanded or promised in that particular scriptural text.

Here's how Luther himself explained his personal practice in the little tract *To Master Peter, On Prayer* he wrote for his barber, Peter Beskendorf:

If I have had time and opportunity to go through the Lord's Prayer, I do the same with the Ten Commandments. I take one part after another and free myself as much as possible from distractions in order to pray. I divide each commandment into four parts, thereby fashioning a garland of four strands. That is, I think of each commandment as, first, instruction, which is really what it is intended to be, and consider what the Lord God demands of me so earnestly. Second, I turn it into a thanksgiving; third, a confession; and fourth, a prayer.[2]

EXERCISE VS. BEING EXERCISED

Note that this model prayer doesn't really originate internally. Rather, the word of God generates such prayer in the Christian. In this approach word and prayer are woven together so tightly that it's hard to separate them. Word informs prayer; then prayer reflects on that word and responds. It's a task, a discipline, to be sure. And yet at the same time it's a discipline that bestows the gift of God's Spirit, who always comes by means of his word.

Thus the close affinity between physical and spiritual exercise that the apostle Paul mentioned to Timothy. Both entail effort. Yet any exertion is far outweighed by the benefit: "promise for the present life and also for the life to come" (1 Tim 4:8). As verbal reflection on God's word and ensuing prayer come more and more naturally to you, it requires less and less conscious effort on your part. Or perhaps more correctly, prayer is more and more prayed in you than it is prayed by you. As the psalmist puts it: "O Lord, open my lips, and my mouth will declare your praise" (Ps 51:15). When this kind of meditation and prayer become your regular habit, not only are you habituated in a life of prayer, but it becomes a central element in your pastoral *habitus*.

2. Martin Luther, *A Simple Way to Pray* (1535), LW 43:200.

TEACHING AN OLD DOG NEW TRICKS

I've never been much for physical exercise. Growing up, I wasn't into sports. I used to say that the only thing athletic about me was my athlete's foot. So throughout my ministry I've been a consistent couch potato—exercising my mind, but not my body. Let's face it: This is an all too common problem in our profession. Sadly, obesity and its complications are rampant among clergy. You would do well to address this early in your career; I had to learn good habits of physical exercise in my old age the hard way.

I really had no choice. Suffering from shortness of breath, I was diagnosed with four blocked coronary arteries. When angioplasty didn't work, I found myself in a hospital undergoing triple bypass surgery. I joke that now I've been given another lap around the track in the relay race of the ministry. But it really was no laughing matter. I could have died, to be sure, but now my cardiologist tells me I'm in good physical condition, for an old man. Since undergoing cardio rehab I've learned the importance of weight control and regular exercise.

But I have to credit my closest friend—he's an athlete and fitness enthusiast—for helping me learn the importance of regular exercise even before my surgeon held a knife to my chest. My friend had come to visit and we were both enjoying some relaxation and the invigorating theological arm wrestling that has come to be a treasured hallmark of our friendship. At the end of the evening, out of the blue, he asked: "So what time are we going to the health club in the morning?" I did have a club membership at the time, but let's just say I was an infrequent patron.

We went that next morning. And I stuck with it. Over the years my friend has been both an inspiration and a coach, providing pointers on technique and encouraging healthy exercise habits. His cheerleading plus occasional nudging have been a good combination keeping me on this regimen. Because of him I can frankly say now that I'm an old man, it's my goal is to earn and keep the adjective "spry." Today I'm not by any means a fitness fanatic, but I've learned that regular exercise is beneficial to physical health. Now that exercise is habitual it's become part of my *habitus*, you could say.

Not that exercise is always fun, mind you. There's a lot of truth in the old mantra, "No pain, no gain." I'm no physiologist, but my understanding is that muscles need to be exerted beyond their comfort level to grow stronger. So the pain of exercise is an indication that muscles are gaining strength. I've certainly found that to be true, but I can tell you that left to myself I would not have exercised. That took discipline, discipline first instigated by my friend's question and then fueled by his interest ever since.

EXERCISE PARTNERS

Of course, my exercise would never have gotten off the ground as it has without my friend's intervention and likely wouldn't be what it is today without his encouragement. Just so, remember that your private prayer life is not really a solo enterprise. It's aided and abetted by the public prayers of the church. In her liturgy, the church teaches every baptized soul how to pray. And she can teach her pastors, too. Draw upon the rich treasury of the church's heritage of prayer to fashion your own private life of prayer.

And above all, for your encouragement remember that the Lord Jesus prays for you just as he prays in and with you to his Father in heaven. The "our" in the Our Father includes the Son of God himself, you know, together with all your brothers and sisters in the family of Christ's church. This in itself is a great balm for the aching loneliness that perpetually plagues pastors. Most importantly, it's the reason you can be confident that God the almighty Maker of heaven and earth is truly your dear Father and thus for Jesus' sake will hear your prayer. Luther reminded his barber that his private prayers were never truly private: "Never think that you are kneeling or standing alone, rather think that the whole of Christendom, all devout Christians, are standing there beside you and you are standing among them in a common, united petition which God cannot disdain."[3]

---

3. Luther, *A Simple Way to Pray* (1535), LW 43:198. In Luther's usage, "Christendom" simply means church or all Christians.

As a sheepdog for the Great Shepherd you're occupied with following his directions. Your goal is the same as his: that the sheep and lambs already within his flock are given tender, faithful care—and that those other sheep who do not yet know him are safely gathered in to find their life and sustenance in him before he returns to judge the living and the dead. But while giving your full attention to the physical dimension where these people live and work, you need to be alert to attacks on the spiritual front as well.

Since in the care of souls you're daily working in the realm of sanctification you automatically come under demonic scrutiny. Satan and his horde are strangely drawn to holiness; wherever the Holy Spirit calls, gathers, enlightens and sanctifies by means of his word and sacraments, Satan goes to work to dismantle and destroy God's kingdom. And that means that he has targeted you and yours. That's good reason not to venture out in ministry without putting on the armor supplied by Christ, our hero who fights for us. Clothed in his blood and righteousness, you have the shield of faith, the helmet of salvation, the breastplate of righteousness, the shoes of the gospel. And you take up the sword of the Spirit, the word of God, to defend yourself and your flock. But the best defense against the devil is not just quoting the Bible. Rather, the apostle urges that the Scripture be used in prayer: "praying at all times in the Spirit, with all prayer and supplication. To that end, keep alert with all perseverance, making supplication for all the saints" (Eph 6:18).

Meditation on the word of God and prayer go hand in hand. You don't need just one or the other; you need both. When you come under spiritual attack in ministry, turn to the sword of the Spirit, the word of God, by which the Spirit comes. As that word repels the enemy, so it strengthens and equips us for battle, placing us in proximity to our God and Savior. But then we use that same word of God as the threads by which we weave our wreath of prayer to our Father in Heaven, asking that he would lead us not into temptation but deliver us from the Evil One. Prayer itself then is a weapon forged and shaped by the living and abiding word of God.

MY SPIRITUAL BATTLES

I've had my share of skirmishes with the devil. Some of them came as a result of faithful ministry, standing for the truth of God's word in the interests of the care and cure of souls. But many of them were simply my own fault. Though my spirit is usually willing, my flesh is frequently weak. My misbelief, despair, and other great shame and vice provided a toehold for the devil, who went to work to undermine my faith and love in Christ. I've discovered that, left to my own resources, I'm no match for the devil. Just like I learned the necessity of physical exercise the hard way, so it's taken numerous firefights with Satan to impress on me my need for the spiritual exercise of meditation and prayer. Meditation and prayer are not a convenient way of escape, but a vital lifeline to God himself when you come under fire.

And spiritual warfare is not a one-time skirmish. When you were baptized into Christ, you were conscripted into battle for the rest of your life. And when you are ordained into office, you are enlisted for the duration of your ministry. Remember, all things are sanctified by word and prayer. By these means God the Holy Spirit continues to make you holy, yet that very holiness targets you for further attack. In his high priestly prayer Jesus prayed not just for his disciples, but for "all those who will believe in me through their word" (John 17:20). He prayed for *you*. He asked that the Father would protect you from the Evil One, knowing full well that all those called to proclaim the holy word he received from his heavenly Father would draw Satan's fire.

THE TOUCHSTONE OF AFFLICTION

That's the bad news. Just by meditating on God's word you draw the devil's ire. But when you preach that word in Christ's church and console his sheep and lambs with it, there's no escaping attack. It's sure to come. Yet all is not lost. That very assault serves a positive purpose. Paradoxically it draws you closer and closer to God.

Martin Luther was no stranger to demonic assault. Plagued by chronic melancholy, as he called what we would today label depression, he was often on the brink of despair. Coming under frequent attack by political, theological, and ecclesiastical authorities, he lived frequently on the edge. Yet he considered these attacks both human and demonic to be a spiritual blessing. For him the devil was always God's devil. Unwittingly and unwillingly Satan does the will of God. The devil is God's fool. For whenever he attacks the people of God, they are driven to find their refuge in him and depend more exclusively on his word alone by which they live now and eternally.

So important was this principle that Luther considered this kind of demonic affliction to be the usual result of meditating on God's word. *Anfechtungen*, or attacks, as he called them, were the last in a natural progression. First comes prayer, by which the Christian invokes the enlightenment of God's word. Second comes meditation, through which the Holy Spirit enlightens the Christian by his word. "Thirdly, there is *tentatio, Anfechtung*. This is the touchstone which teaches you not only to know and understand, but also to experience how right, how true, how sweet, how lovely, how mighty, how comforting God's word is, wisdom beyond all wisdom."[4]

Note the sweet irony: Spiritual assault serves as the touchstone of faith. As gold and silver can be tested for purity by the mark it leaves when pressed against a touchstone, so faith is proven genuine when brought up against the attacks and assaults of the devil. What Satan intends for evil, God uses for good. By these assaults we move from mere intellectual comprehension of his grace to very personal and experiential enjoyment of the multifaceted dimensions of God's comforting mercy and love.

Prayer and meditation do not occur in blissful peace in some sweet never-never land or beautiful isle somewhere, but in the throes of real life. Prayer, meditation, and spiritual warfare are a package deal. The struggle goes with the territory in God's economy. Pain, distress of body and soul, emotional struggle and spiritual assault come to all of God's people. And you can be sure that they will come to you—if they haven't already. Don't be alarmed if the battle gets fierce or the warfare long. This too shall pass; the cross comes first, but afterward the crown. Like a good soldier get ready for the fight, knowing that

4. Martin Luther, "Preface to the Wittenberg Edition of Luther's Writings" (1539), LW 34:286–87.

he who has begun a good work in you will bring it to completion on the Day of Jesus Christ. As Dr. Luther discovered before you, when the devil attacks you the worst he can do will only teach you to know and love God's word all the more. "For as soon as God's word takes root and grows in you, the devil will harry you, and will make a real doctor of you, and by his assaults will teach you to seek and love God's word."[5]

PRAYER UNDER FIRE

In this chapter my goal has been to open new vistas in the cure of your own soul. Together we've reviewed the importance of seeking out care for yourself. I hope I've drilled this into you. Repeat after me: "Every pastor needs a pastor."

Yet you also need to tend your own soul. The nature of our office is such that much of pastoral work is done solo. Being privy to the deepest secrets and yearnings of people's private lives, we are not at liberty to divulge these to our wife, our closest friend, or any fellow pastor. The confidential nature of the care of souls means that we not only guard the confessional seal, but keep confidences entrusted to us. Yet there is One to whom we may (and must) continually turn. Christ Jesus bids us unburden our worn and weary hearts to Him: "Come to me, all who labor and are heavy laden, and I will give you rest" (Matt 11:28). Remember that despite all their busy exertion, when sheepdogs are at rest they are usually found together with their shepherd. Make it happen, won't you?

Jesus is your Sabbath rest; so take your rest in him. By prayer and meditation find refreshment for your soul, healing for your wounds, and strength for your service. Your calendar is your friend: Use it to make sure your days and weeks are sanctified by God's word and prayer. This will see you through seasons of both joy and sorrow, heartache and jubilation.

Yet never be surprised when you come under fire. Look beyond the usual suspects like flesh and blood people who make your life and ministry so difficult at times. They are not the enemy. The struggle is against a much more formidable foe. Satan works overtime to

| Chapter Eleven

---

5. Luther, "Preface to the Wittenberg Edition of Luther's Writings" (1539), LW 34:286–87.

interrupt your prayer and so seduce you into misbelief and drive you to despair. That's what makes prayer, as simple as it is, so hard. One fourth-century desert father who devoted his life to solitary prayer and meditation wrote of this struggle:

> The brethren also asked him, 'Amongst all good works, which is the virtue which requires the greatest effort?' He answered, 'Forgive me, but I think there is no labour greater than that of prayer to God. For every time a man wants to pray, his enemies, the demons, want to prevent him, for they know that it is only by turning him from prayer that they can hinder his journey. Whatever good work a man undertakes, if he perseveres in it, he will attain rest. But prayer is warfare to the last breath.[6]

But don't listen to Satan; he's already judged. He can harm you none. Tell him to get lost and go back to hell where he belongs. You've got more important things to do than listen to his twisted lies and accusations. Instead, your Lord Jesus invites you to come to him in prayer to find rest for your soul.

Try it; you'll like it.

The Care of Souls

6. *The Sayings of the Desert Fathers*, trans. Benedicta Ward (London and Oxford: Mowbray, 1975), 21–22.

CHAPTER TWELVE

Always Be Steady

Equilibrium in Ministry

You probably picked up from all the tales of my childhood and adolescence growing up on the farm in the 1950s and '60s that I'm a bit nostalgic. That picture in my mind's eye of those days is most likely not one hundred percent accurate. Once as I bragged up my mom's cooking to my new bride (a practice I wouldn't recommend, by the way) she told Jane: "He forgets all the nights when I just opened a can of soup." Likewise, my sentimental depiction of farm life in those days leaves out the brutal biting winds of sub-zero winter mornings or the fierce unrelenting sun on unbearably hot summer days. It wasn't a lot of fun making hay in weather like that. And it was quite a feat to milk our twenty-four cows when a winter storm knocked out rural power lines. My dad jerry-rigged one of our three milking machines using a vacuum hose hooked to the decompression petcocks of our two-cylinder John Deere, but milking time still took three times as long. Memories are like that; they make the heart grow fonder and you forget the nasty details.

Likewise there's a tendency, for old timers like me to look fondly at the church of twenty, thirty—or fifty—years ago through rose-colored glasses. We forget that the human heart was just as recalcitrant in sin back in those days as it is today. We magnify the dynamic numerical growth of the post-war years, but ignore the superficial, perfunctory faith that too often resulted when people joined a church because of social pressures. We fail to remember that there were really no "glory days" for the church. Every age has its unique challenges, and devil, world, and flesh guarantee that it's tough going for the gospel no matter what era you're talking about. Christians who embrace a classically biblical world view and pastors who uphold the tenets of creedal Christianity as confessed in *The Book of Concord*—or for that matter, any other classically confessional tradition—will be seen as hopelessly outdated and irrelevant in a world that has passed them by.

Sometimes we come across as nostalgia freaks, yearning for the golden days of yore when life was simpler and Christianity and culture were in synch. But Jesus did not say: "Go therefore and change your culture," but "make disciples of every nation." We are not called to turn the clock back to the 1950s, the robust missionary era of the eighteenth century or the lively doctrinal vibrancy of the sixteenth and seventeenth centuries. Rather, the church in each succeeding era must give a clear and vigorous defense and confession of its timeless faith to the complexities and chaos of its own generation.

WE'RE NOT IN KANSAS ANYMORE

True, things have changed dramatically in the last six decades. Social structures and moral values have radically imploded. The proverbial *Father Knows Best* world of the 1950s, reprised twenty years later in the popular *Happy Days* television series, is now long gone. Streaming TV services pipe into your family room (or your handheld device) any combination of blood, gore, and decadence your mind can imagine— or your heart desires—all under the guise of entertainment. Having grown up in the 1950s, I can tell you those were indeed far simpler days, with a place for everything and everything in its place sociologically speaking. That world seems hopelessly naïve and antiquated now, as far removed from us today as an ancient civilization or a distant galaxy. Yet our mission is to confess the gospel today, not to retrofit society to yesteryear. One of my friends, describing contemporary mission challenges, once remarked: "Remember, the Eisenhower administration isn't coming back any time soon."

So stay current with the world around you. Remain a student of your culture as well as the Bible. Note the trends of your time and its widely accepted values. As a faithful sheepdog for the Great

Shepherd your task is to bring his gifts to the people in the present, not the past. In his pastoral letter to Titus, Paul calls a pastor "God's steward" (Titus 1:7). That means you should be faithful with what's been entrusted to you. Faithful confession in the era you live in means you'll need to be thoroughly familiar with the beliefs and assumptions of your contemporaries.

Besides being a man of integrity, fidelity and moral uprightness, Paul writes that a pastor must not only distinguish truth from error, but confess the former and refute the latter. "He must hold firm to the trustworthy word as taught, so that he may be able to give instruction in sound doctrine and also to rebuke those who contradict it" (Titus 1:9). So in order to faithfully teach the truth, you also need to deny the error. The problem is that people are too easily blinded by their culture; often they can't sort truth from error. By just going with the flow, they unknowingly embrace cultural assumptions inimical to the faith. So you'll need a backbone in ministry; to teach correctly you'll need to also refute error in all its forms. It's the loving thing to do; truth and love go hand in glove in pastoral work. Having compassion on Christ's sheep also means having the courage to speak the truth. That's especially true in an age of syncretism and compromise.

JACK'S CHALLENGE

Sometimes seemingly chance meetings turn out to be blessings in disguise. At a pastors' conference I met a man I'll call Jack. A handsome young man, Jack was the epitome of the fresh, eager seminary graduate—just into his second year of ministry. Yet his earnest and insightful questions betrayed a maturity beyond his years. After my talk he told me he was taken by the compassion with which I approach pastoral care.

I wanted to know more, so I sought him out for a bit of extended cross-generational dialogue on pastoral work. It turns out that Jack and his peers have observed a tendency among us older pastors to become calloused and hardened—not, as I assumed, when it comes to concern and empathy for people, but in terms of maintaining the connection between right doctrine and right practice. "When I use the word compassion," Jack said, "I include right doctrine." Like a knife gradually loses its edge after repeated sharpening, he has noticed that many older pastors tend to become less and less sensitive to the intimate link between teaching and practice with every passing year.

"The younger pastors that I'm around are beginning to see the absolute connection between right doctrine and right practice," he said. "But many of the older pastors are saying: 'you're just out of the seminary and you don't understand yet; I used to be like that, but that'll change once you're more out in the ministry.'"

It's unfortunate, don't you think, when seasoned pastors squelch young men's enthusiasm like that? How tragic to use experience as a trump card over against faithfulness to God's word. "What I respected about your presentation," Jack continued, "is that it stemmed from the correct understanding of the word and then from that—no matter how difficult it may be—comes the proper care for souls."

Still, for him proper discernment and tact are important as well: "I do believe that there are good ways to say things and there are appropriate ways and appropriate places," Jack contends. "I don't advocate speaking in a way that is insensitive to people." Yet for him and his young colleagues, truth and love are a winning combination: "You can't lie when it comes to the truth."

I was moved by this young man's zeal for adherence to the truth of God's word coupled with his love for souls, and told him so: "It's very encouraging to me to see your intelligence, your eagerness, your competence, your desire to be of service in the Lord's church," I said. "Sometimes from my end of the spectrum it gets discouraging wondering what the future will bring." I should have known better. The Lord Jesus promised that the gates of hell will not prevail against his church, so it's no wonder that in every generation he provides new servants like Jack to take up the mantle of ministry in turn.

Jack's generation is certainly eager to take things on for Christ and his kingdom: "As I'm talking to my brother pastors my age," he said, "we're all like: 'Let's go; we're ready, we meet the challenges.'" Jack is persuaded that the Holy Spirit will encourage his generation through the difficult days ahead, conforming to his word. And he's not alone, apparently. "I'm encouraged by my brother pastors," he continued. "My generation is a generation that appreciates what was handed down. We may not (completely) understand it (and) we may have to grow into it." One thing's for certain: Jack and his age group are determined to grow into faithful confession of the word of God, not grow out of it. And that's thrilling to hear–for a codger like me.

In these final years of my own ministry it's thrilling to see younger generations growing into the *habitus* of pastoral work, faithfully clinging to right teaching, yet at the same time eagerly embracing right practice for the sake of the souls for whom Jesus gave his life. Jack's final words to me bode well for the future of Christ's church: "Stay strong and firm in the Lord and he will give you the strength."

Right on, Jack; may your number increase. But I also have a word for those of you who—like me—are in the twilight years of ministry: Don't neglect these youngest colleagues in office; come alongside and encourage them by your godly example, your prayers and personal counsel.

THE SEXUAL DEBACLE

The first task of any evangelist/pastor is to evaluate current popular lifestyles and values in light of the baptismal life to which Christians have been called. Here's just one example. As I write, the sexual revolution project launched in the 1960s to separate sex from procreation has gained rapid momentum with every passing decade, spilling over into widespread endorsement of abortion, infanticide, and all kinds of sexual aberrations. In the name of liberty and human rights a full spectrum of sexual liaisons now enjoy not merely tolerance but wide approval and promotion. Marriage "equality" has successfully ripped sex out of its natural setting within conjugal matrimony and the family. However the stage was set for this aberration long ago, when marriage between a man and woman was successfully redefined as consisting primarily of romantic attraction plus orgasm—the more spectacular, the better.

A "brave new world" of sexual promiscuity and decadence has dawned. As a result people are alienated not just from other people, but from their own bodies as well. The new orthodoxy of "gender fluidity" insists that sexual identity is rooted in feelings rather than anatomy; and so bodies are modified chemically and surgically to an approximation of the desired sex. Binary sexual distinction is viewed as an oppressive invention of patriarchal hierarchy designed to suppress innate human dignity. Thus as a matter of personal freedom, people are applauded when they project masculine or feminine persona and appearances in flagrant rejection of the actual female or male bodies with which they were born.

The stolid dad portrayed by Robert Young in *Father Knows Best*—and even bad boy "Fonzi" Fonzarelli in *Happy Days*—would be not only shocked by these developments; they would be stunned speechless. Assumptions governing public morality and social taboos commonly held for millennia lie everywhere in ruin. Evidence is that the sexual revolution has not only successfully stormed the barricades protecting marriage and the family, but also breached the very walls of logic. When biologically male humans become self-declared women and females masquerade as men, we've collectively entered the world of social lunacy. This is uncharted territory in the history of humanity.

On another level, though, this is nothing new. The Christian church has faced antagonistic cultures throughout history. And she has certainly known pagan environments before; in that respect the pre-Christian experience of early Christians is instructive to us modern-day Christians who face a post-Christian world. Yet in certain critical aspects our situation is unique. Although missionaries in previous centuries certainly encountered opposition, they always dealt with people who thought and lived in human categories. Pagans operated in a world with classifications for truth and error, right and wrong; instinctively they grasped what it meant to be male and female, mother and father. But in our world where expressive individualism holds sway, all that's up for grabs now. Life for contemporary pagans is like trying to navigate by dead reckoning when you've lost sight of the North Star.

I have a friend who describes the challenge before Christians today as mission work in the suburbs of humanity. Using the imagery of Augustine's classic work *The City of God*, he writes that while obviously we don't live in the city of God any longer, we don't even live in the city of man. Rather, he contends, we live in the suburbs of the city of man. I think he's right. The twisted assumptions embraced increasingly in current culture constitute an inhuman—you might even say subhuman—world.

FAITHFUL CONFESSION

So fasten your seatbelts; it's going to be a rough ride. Anyone who thinks and lives biblically will be constantly out of step with his contemporaries, as foreign as an alien from outer space. When the world is upside down, anyone right-side up is automatically the odd man out—and quite likely to be branded a bigot or hater. Thus the perennial temptation for God's people and their pastors is to go along to get along and not make waves by contradicting the trends of the day. But we are collectively called to faithfulness in a faithless world. That means the church is always countercultural to the mainstream. In a world fixated on building its own idols there will always be a price to pay for faithful confession of Christ's gospel in every era. That's the bad news.

Yet there's good news too. "In the world you will have tribulation," says Jesus. "But take heart; I have overcome the world" (John 16:33). That's the thing about Jesus; He's a realist. He never promised us a rose garden—just the opposite, in fact. he told the men he had commissioned that he was sending them out like sheep among wolves (Matt 10:16). They were bound to come under attack. No soldier under orders is surprised to come under enemy fire, and it should be no shock when those who do Christ's work face the same opposition he did. If people scorn the teacher they will scorn his pupils. And if they reject the master they will reject his servants.

"A disciple is not above his teacher, nor a servant above his master. It is enough for the disciple to be like his teacher, and the servant like his master. If they have called the master of the house Beelzebul, how much more will they malign those of his household" (Matt 10:24–25).

When you're with Jesus there'll be hell to pay. Not only do you come under demonic attack; the ungodly world will also resist you at every turn. But when you come under attack, you're in good company. He came, he said, "not to be served but to serve, and to give his life as a ransom for many" (Matt 20:28). Yet by his cross he snatched victory from the apparent jaws of defeat. Ironically, then, the misery and degradation of the cross signals triumph for all of Christ's own.

FIRST THE CROSS, THEN THE CROWN

And that's the way it is for you too. To know Christ and the power of his resurrection means to also share in the fellowship of his sufferings (Phil 3:10). The most effective way to learn to be like Jesus is to take up his cross. Though that path leads to glory, it's often painful along the way. Over the years I've known scores of faithful Christians who have taught me much about suffering.

L et's call her Mary. When I came to serve as her pastor, she and her husband Fred were every Sunday churchgoers, exemplary "pillars of the church," you might say. Fred was a WWII navy vet, and exhibited many of the characteristics common among those we now call "the greatest generation." He was a hard worker, and they lived on an acreage with an apple orchard they had planted themselves around the sturdy little house Fred had built with his own hands after coming home from the war.

When Mary's health began to fail, Fred was her rock. Degenerative arthritis began to rob her of mobility, and he was constantly at her side. I can still see them making their way up the side aisle from their weekly pew about four rows back, a modern day princess escorted by the gallant prince at her side. The bread of heaven sustained them both; at first they knelt together to receive the Lord's body and blood. Then when Mary's arthritic knees could no longer bend, she would bend her heart to receive humbly with her mouth the food that endures to eternal life. Gradually the arthritis took over; inflammation imperiled her joints and made walking harder and harder.

When Fred landed in the hospital with serious heart complications, Mary bravely made the trip every day and waited with him while his condition worsened day by day. I can still see her shrunken figure sitting stoically by his side in the tiny confines of his intensive care cubicle, instruments beeping and whirring, measuring out his waning life.

When the end finally came, Mary carried heroically on without her gallant prince consort, shrinking in stature, but growing in simple child-like faith in the Lord. She was a true heroine in her determination, driving herself to church and to lunch with friends. It was an inspiration to see her fend off her disability as best she could, bravely making do without the man who for more than five decades had been her stalwart strength and protection.

As the years wore on, her gentle spirit and quiet faith inspired friends and acquaintances alike. She touched our lives in particular because Mary became my wife's "other mom." Since Jane had lost her own mother as a young bride, they grew quite close, sharing laughter, joys, and sorrows as well. But then Mary's health declined still more. Her disease-riddled bones grew frail and brittle; her spine could no longer support her body and she had to be fitted with a special brace to encapsulate her torso, lobster-like. She loved to break out of the confines of her house and especially enjoyed treating us to dinner at some of the fine restaurants she and Fred used to frequent. With her body collapsing on itself, there was little room in her stomach for a full size meal, but she relished the tastes and company anyway. No meal was complete without a round of chocolate desserts; somehow she managed to down hers entirely every time.

Shortly after she moved into an assisted living complex, Mary fell, breaking her already broken back. At her hospital room, I found a pitiful scene. This brave woman had endured so many atrocities already; now this? I turned to the words of Paul to the Corinthians: "So we do not lose heart. Though our outer self is wasting away, our inner self is being renewed day by day. For this light momentary affliction is preparing for us an eternal weight of glory beyond all comparison, as we look not to the things that are seen but to the things that are unseen. For the things that are seen are transient, but the things that are unseen are eternal" (2 Cor 4:16–18).

Mid-sentence my voice cracked and my eyes brimmed with tears. I apologized when I had finished, but Mary said: "No, don't be sorry for crying; it's comforting to know you care." That's the way it is among Christ's people. There is a time to laugh and a time for tears; a time to rejoice and a time to mourn. When both tears and laughter are shared, sorrows are divided and joys are multiplied.

Mary lived for many more years. Her flesh was undeniably weak, but her spirit was extraordinarily strong. The day of her funeral, I preached to her family and friends—and Jane and myself—these words based upon Jesus' stilling of the storm:

> You will recall that Jesus gently called his disciples out of their distress: "Why are you afraid, O you of little faith?" Those of us who had the privilege to minister to Mary over the years of her illness found great encouragement in her consistent faith. In the face of things that would make strong men weep, she showed a consistent confidence that the God who had claimed her when she was but a baby would not let her go; not ever, no never. It was shortly after she was born 88 years ago next week Monday that Mary was baptized in the name of the Father and of the Son and of the Holy Spirit. And by that bath of regeneration she was joined to Jesus in his death and resurrection. And those whom Jesus has claimed as his own he will never leave. Not death nor life nor things present nor things to come can ever separate them from the love of God in Christ.

Many of you have already known other Marys and Freds in your ministry. God willing, all of you will meet people like them one day. You will find, as I have, that the suffering saints of God will teach you how to bear your own crosses with patience and grace. You will learn that when you are weak, then you are strong. You will learn (sometimes the hard way) that God's grace is made perfect in your weakness. You will learn that along with Jesus comes his cross and you come to know him best in the fellowship of his sufferings.

STEADFASTNESS

But don't go looking for trouble. I've met some pastors who are proud of the problems they've run into. They claim they're being persecuted because of their faithfulness, when actually they themselves are the problem. Long ago Peter warned pastors against domineering over their flock (1 Peter 5:3). Always make sure that Jesus and his cross are the offense, not you and your obnoxiousness.

Still, the sober truth is that no matter how tactfully and humbly you speak as a pastor, you're bound to get flack. Cultures come and go over the centuries, but faithful Christian teaching has never been fashionable. The world has things upside down, Jesus reminds us. False prophets are praised while faithful prophets are persecuted. Therefore the world's reaction to your teaching is a pretty accurate indicator of where you stand with him. "Blessed are you when people hate you and when they exclude you and revile you and spurn your name as evil, on account of the Son of Man! … Woe to you, when all people speak well of you, for so their fathers did to the false prophets" (Luke 6:22, 26).

The secret to steady ministry in a chaotic world of flux is to be a sheepdog for the Great Shepherd. If your attention is fixed on Jesus and carrying out his will for his sheep and lambs, you will be less bothered by the inevitable distractions. Sheepdogs look to their shepherd for approval, not his sheep. Yet their whole being is centered on the care and protection of those sheep. Likewise, as Christ's faithful servant, you can confidently devote all your energy to the faithful care of his people no matter what the apparent result.

Paul advised a novice pastor to preach the word "in season and out of season" (2 Tim 4:2). That's the best way to begin your ministry and continue in it all life long. Keep one eye on the sheep, but the other on your Shepherd by means of his word. Faithful preaching and teaching is always governed by the text, not the context. If your finger is always in the air, testing the direction the wind is blowing in the culture around you, you will not be a faithful emissary of the crucified and risen Lord. His divine word is designed to fit the needs of people of every land and tongue and time, and when you stick to the text of his word you know that you are always on target to the needs of your contemporaries. This will keep you on an even keel even in those times when chaos reigns supreme all around. This even-tempered calm governed by the word is one of the chief characteristics of a genuinely pastoral *habitus*. Centering on Jesus and his will for the sheep will sustain you in times of turmoil because it is part and parcel of who you are, not merely what you do.

Humor me; I have yet one more farming analogy for you—this one about sticking to your craft no matter what.

My dad had his faults and would be the first to admit his failures and shortcomings, but one of his characteristics was an even-tempered devotion to his work. This was his *habitus*; his whole being was wrapped up in farming because above all else he was a farmer. That sustained him through some very tough times on his farm—like the dust storms of the "dirty thirties." Extended drought combined with poor farming methods led to tons of the rich topsoil of the Midwest being carried aloft by the winds. During the worst storms, ferocious winds blew the blinding dust high into the air and sandblasted everything in its path. Cattle huddled together, their backs to the wind, as outbuildings shivered and shook. Meanwhile in the farmhouse my dad and his family held pillows against windowpanes facing the brunt of the wind—to keep the glass from breaking in. The driving dust and sand shredded any surviving vegetation and filtered relentlessly through every crack in window, door, and siding—leaving a thin residue of grit everywhere inside the house.

Many a farmer went under in those catastrophic years, and indeed my grandfather lost the deed to the property he had homesteaded some twenty-five years earlier. Truth be told, dad spent most of the rest of his life buying back his own family farm. Some would call this foolhardy, others heroic, but my dad farmed because he was a farmer at heart. Through thick and thin, dry and wet years, crops bountiful and scarce, he and my mom kept to the task of planting, cultivating, harvesting, animal husbandry—and raising their kids. Why? Farming, you could say, was in their blood. It was their true calling. It was their *habitus*.

Keep on keeping on. If you are already a pastor—or contemplating becoming one—I pray that you will by God's grace develop a pastoral *habitus*. Remember, in a very real way this is not something you achieve on your own. It is a charisma—a gift worked in you. In a real way, you learn the ministry by doing ministry. You acquire this "practical *habitus* of the soul," as C. F. W. Walther called it, by steadily keeping on task no matter what, just as my dad kept on farming through the lean and hard years and for the rest of his life.

In a very real way a *habitus* for ministry is not your work, but is worked in you through a lifelong process of receiving for yourself the gifts of Christ, and then handing them on to others as he sends you to do, daily tending his beloved sheep and lambs. No matter how hard the task or heavy the burden you keep steadily on doing what he gives you to do because you know his loving purpose and will: He will stop at nothing until he has safely gathered his flock into his eternal fold. This unswerving devotion is really not your doing. It too is worked in you by the overwhelming love of him who gave his life and shed his blood not just for those you serve, but for you as well. The love of Christ constrains you; you cannot but speak of the things you have seen and heard.

So steady, then, come what may. You and I don't know what the future holds, but we do know who holds the future. I've told you of some of the challenges facing Christians and their pastors as of this writing, but I can't possibly predict what's coming down the pike. As my dad faced bounty and scarcity, overwhelming joys and deepest sorrow doing his work, you will too, most certainly. Keeping one eye fixed on the Great Shepherd; he will sustain you come what may. The apostle Paul forecast difficulty for his young protégé: false teachers, rebellious hearers, apostasy within the church and persecution from an unbelieving world. Yet he urged him to stick with the *habitus* given him by divine commission: "As for you, always be sober-minded, endure suffering, do the work of an evangelist, fulfill your ministry" (2 Tim 4:5).

HOPE FOR THE DURATION

These are the times that try men's souls. Uncertainty is everywhere around and fear is often the result, giving rise to all kinds of mischief as church leaders scramble to find the magic pill to connect with a world that seems to have come unglued. But we need not fear. We know the last chapter of this world's history. Our Lord promises that the very gates of hell will not prevail against his church, and that he will be with us always, to the very end of the age.

Besides, the church has been in situations like ours before. Take Augustine for example. As the Roman Empire was tottering toward extinction, there were many who blamed the new state religion, Christianity, for its failure. The comfortable world that had provided ease and security for a thousand years was coming unraveled. The city of Rome, which many had believed would stand forever, had been sacked by barbarian invaders in the year 410, and her classic monuments lay in ruin. The adherents of the old pagan gods were looking for a scapegoat, and Christians provided an easy target.

In many ways our world is much like theirs. Things familiar and comfortable have vanished, replaced by radically different lifestyles and values. I joked about the Eisenhower administration, but even younger generations today know the tug of nostalgia. We all long for something simpler and more predictable; surroundings less threatening and tumultuous, more comfortable and secure. But such is not our lot. We are not nostalgia freaks, trying to retreat to a more comfortable past. We move confidently into an uncertain future emboldened by our Lord who gives us his word of hope and life to preach to a world lost in despair and death.

We live in an era of change now between the age of reason and whatever comes after it. It is much like that world of late antiquity—when the classic age was collapsing and the early Middle Ages were just beginning to dawn. But those threatening years turned out to be the church's moment in the sun, one of its best periods of vigorous mission and growth. It wouldn't be too many centuries before those Germanic hordes that had sacked and looted the city of Rome would themselves become Christians.

Church historians tell us that these eras between the collapse of one worldview and the dawn of another are frequently epochs of great opportunity. So rather than shrinking with fear for what is coming on the world in this post Christian era, it's time to rise to the challenge. We can learn a great deal from the example of Aurelius Augustine, Bishop of Hippo in North Africa. Over a period of thirteen years he drafted an apologetic for Christianity that still stands as a classic: his monumental *City of God*.

In this classic work Augustine tells a tale of two cities: the city of man, transient and passing, and the city of God, transcendent and lasting. Here is an important lesson for us as each generation in turn struggles to discover how to respond to contemporary challenges. Especially when they, like the citizens of the ancient Roman Empire, get too comfortable and attached to their own culture. We need a more objective vantage point. Like Augustine, we need to step back from our culture to sort out what belongs to the city of man and what belongs to the city of God.

THINGS UNSHAKEN

Here amid the kingdoms of this world we have no continuing city. That's why we dare not become attached to the values and passing fancies of any human culture. We await a city with foundations, whose maker and builder is God. Even though the comfortable world all around us is shaken, the city of God remains secure; his eternal kingdom is built squarely on the person and work of his Son. Thanks be to God, his kingdom comes all by itself without our prayer, but we pray that it may come among us also as our heavenly Father gives us his Holy Spirit so that by his grace we believe his holy word and lead godly lives both here in time and there in eternity.

Whenever threatened by conflicted times and cultures, Christians can learn much from our ancient cousins in late antiquity. Things comfortable and familiar can vanish seemingly overnight, never to return, leaving chaos and confusion in their wake. Yet the church perpetually looks beyond dark shadows of uncertainty and disorder to glimpse the dawning light of eternity. She has the promise of her living Lord to sustain her: "I will never leave you nor forsake you." In Christ Jesus her Lord the church in every age has a hope and a future.

Steady, my friend. The burden may seem overwhelming and the labor unbearably hard and long, but in the Lord your labor is never in vain. You have his word and promise and he will see you through. In the closing words of his epic *City of God* Bishop Augustine encouraged the fainting hearts of the faithful by pointing them on ahead to their glorious future, to an end without ending; to that time yet to come when they would know God's eternal kingdom no longer by faith but by sight:

> The seventh (day) shall be our Sabbath, which shall be brought to a close, not by an evening, but by the Lord's day, as an eighth and eternal day, consecrated by the resurrection of Christ, and prefiguring the eternal repose not only of the spirit, but also

of the body. There we shall rest and see, see and love, love and praise. This is what shall be in the end without end. For what other end do we propose to ourselves than to attain to the kingdom of which there is no end?[1]

Take courage, then, for the task before you. A pastoral *habitus* brings enduring joy. The work may seem exhausting, but repose awaits: rest eternal, sight unending, love undying, praise eternally resounding.

1. Augustine, *The City of God*, trans. Marcus Dods (New York: The Modern Library, 1950), 867.

CONCLUSION

Joy in Office

I have used memories from my childhood and youth to illustrate the idea of *habitus*, and I hope the concept has grown on you. That's exactly what is meant by *habitus*, after all—it's not something you *achieve*, but something you *acquire*. It's not something you set out to develop, but a disposition that is developed in you in the regular course of pastoral work. As that process continues, you discover increasingly that you have a "nose" for the care of souls. You begin to think more and more diagnostically. You begin to notice you have less and less inclination to impetuously jump in to tackle the symptoms of dysfunction, but first you take the time to attentively assess underlying idolatries and misbeliefs before intentionally treating them with the gifts God has provided in his word and sacrament. When you discover this approach is coming more and more instinctively to you—as I pray it will—then you can be confident that you're growing into a *habitus* of ministry for the cure of souls.

Likewise I've provided a few episodes from my nearly five decades of ministry not because I consider myself an exemplary pastor, but simply to let you into my head and heart so you can see from the inside what utter joy it is to serve as a spiritual physician. I'm not some kind of snake oil salesman. I didn't want to peddle yet another latest and greatest surefire method to enhance your ministry and take your church to the next level. I've tried to level with you; my frank goal throughout has been simply to enthrall you with this classic model for the cure of souls. I'd like you to be as infatuated with soul care as I've become—and as generations of faithful pastors have been before us. Let me tell you, there's great joy in this work—if we just have the eyes to see it.

A nd that's what I want to leave you with as I bring our dialogue to a close: joy—but not in the usual sense of the word. You and I tend to think of joy negatively, namely as the absence of anything difficult or unpleasant. But Jesus teaches joy positively, as love in action: "As the Father has loved me, so have I loved you. Abide in my love. If you keep my commandments, you will abide in my love, just as I have kept my Father's commandments and abide in his love. These things I have spoken to you, that my joy may be in you, and that your joy may be full" (John 15:9–11).

Jesus found his joy in doing his Father's will because it was love in action. God the Father loved the world so that he gave his Son the lost to save. So the Father's love meant excruciating agony in body and soul for Jesus, climaxing in a tortuous death. Yet Scripture teaches that it was for the joy set before him that he endured the cross, scorning its shame, and is now seated at the right hand of the Father in glory (Heb 12:2). Love and joy are inseparably bound together in the inscrutable will of God. The Father's love in action sent Jesus through first suffering and shame, and only then to glory. The Father's love brought him pain and death, but both were joy for Jesus because he confidently knew he was doing the Father's loving will. First the cross and then the crown; that's the way it works in God's economy. And that's the way it will work for you. Your joy will come as you see God's love in action through you, even in the tight spots of ministry.

G enerations of German Lutheran pastors spoke frequently about *Freudigkeit im Amt*, "joy in office." I can remember in my early years of ministry hearing vestiges of German phrases like *Freudigkeit* and *Seelsorger*, even though by then several generations had ministered exclusively in English. But those forebears in ministry were on to something. They saw that the work of the cure of souls (*Seelsorge*) brought joy (*Freudigkeit*) despite the burdens of office. When God's love is in motion, there is joy even in the midst of sorrow. And never forget it: Your ministry is God's love in motion.

When you love Jesus, you tend and feed his lambs and sheep. Then Jesus loves his flock through you as you faithfully bring them to him—and his gifts to them. From start to finish, ministry is a ministry of love in action. Always remember you're a sheepdog under the Great Shepherd's direction. Your continuing delight is to do Christ's will, just as his delight was to do his Father's will.

I've tried not to paint a Pollyanna picture of ministry; I can tell you firsthand the work of pastoring isn't always fun. It involves long hours, difficult people, and sorrows galore as you are privy to some of the deepest heartaches and miseries imaginable. But at the same time I assure you there is nothing else I can imagine doing that could have brought me such abiding joy. Don't misunderstand me; I haven't always been happy in ministry. You can ask Jane; she'll tell you I've had bouts of loneliness and unhappiness, episodes of sadness and discontent. Sometimes I wasn't much fun to live with, I'm sure.

No, I haven't always been happy in ministry. But why settle for mere happiness when you can have deep and lasting joy instead? Happiness is a passing thing here this side of eternity anyway. It's forever slipping away; it remains always elusive. Just when you think you're happy, something happens to snatch that happiness away from you. But joy is an entirely different matter. Jesus told his disciples that although happiness is fleeting, joy is eternal: "So also you have sorrow now, but I will see you again, and your hearts will rejoice, and no one will take your joy from you" (John 16:22).

You and I both know faithful ministry isn't always fun, especially these days. Those who live according to the precepts of God's word rather than the trends of the day face increasing opposition and persecutions, both subtle and overt. Ministry, quite frankly, is hard. And sometimes it will break your heart. But since Jesus has commissioned you in his service, there's joy in doing his will—even when happiness is scarce.

So remain faithful, then, even during those stretches when ministry isn't fun. Keep on keeping on in Jesus' name. That's where you'll find your joy—in the gifts he gives by means of your hands and mouth: the washing of regeneration and renewing of the Holy Spirit, the

Lord's Supper of forgiveness, life and salvation in his body and blood, in his word of transforming life and hope which you proclaim to dying and despairing souls. Take your delight in being the Savior's untiring sheepdog, knowing that when the chief Shepherd appears you will hear with your own ears: "Well done, good and faithful servant. You have been faithful over a little; I will set you over much. Enter into the joy of your master" (Matt 25:23).

I can't resist sharing one last scene with my father; this one toward the very end of his life. When he was first diagnosed he told me (and these were his exact words): "I have cancer. I've lived a long life, and I know that my Redeemer lives." And so he died as he had lived, in unflinching faith. Of course, he didn't die right away. It was about two years from his diagnosis to his death. We made the long journey to my parents' home as often as we could, and it was evident with each visit that he was failing. Any of you who have seen this in family members or parishioners know the telling indicators: emaciation and growing weakness as cancerous cells gradually overcome healthy cells in the body.

But Dad's soul was as healthy as ever. At the end of what turned out to be our last visit, he insisted on driving us to the local airport, though it was difficult for him to get in and out of a car any longer. I could see his heart was full as he said goodbye to Jane and me in that little airport lobby. We leaned in for our final farewells, and as he wrapped his arms around me he said into my ear: "The Holy Spirit bless you."

I've never forgotten that blessing. As you know, blessings are no small thing. They do what they say: God's own presence is bestowed by blessing. His holy word and name sanctify his people for his service. In the waters of baptism the Holy Spirit sanctifies our body to be his temple. And that day in that modest little airport my father invoked the Spirit's blessing just as on the day of my ordination the Spirit's blessing was conferred on me along with the pastorate to which I was called and in which I've served all these long years since.

So I can think of no more fitting way to close this book than to give my blessing to all who pick up these pages in years to come. Whether you're already engaged in pastoral work, thinking of entering into

Conclusion

preparation, or simply one who loves Christ and his church, I want to extend you the blessing the apostle Paul gave the pastors from Ephesus assembled for his final farewell:

> And now I commend you to God and to the word of his grace, which is able to build you up and to give you the inheritance among all those who are sanctified. (Acts 20:32)

> And the blessing of God:
> the Father, the Son—and yes, God the Holy Spirit—
> be with you now and forevermore. Amen.

Works Cited

Augustine. *The City of God*. Translated by Marcus Dods. New York: The Modern Library, 1950.

Gregory the Great. *Pastoral Care*. Translated by Henry David. Ancient Christian Writers 11. New York: Newman Press, 1950.

Gregory Nazianzus. "In Defense of His Flight to Pontus." *Oration* 2. In *Nicene and Post-Nicene Fathers*, 28 vols. in two series, edited by Philip Schaff, series two 7:205–527. Buffalo, NY: Christian Literature, 1887–1894.

John Chrysostom. *On the Priesthood*. Popular Patristics Series 1. Crestwood, NY: Vladimir's Seminary Press, 1964.

Kleinig, John. "Pastoring by Blessing." Accessed http://www.doxology.us/wp-content/uploads/2015/03/28_blessing.pdf.

Kolb, Robert and Timothy J. Wengert, eds. *The Book of Concord: The Confessions of the Evangelical Lutheran Church*. Translated by Charles Arand et al. Minneapolis: Fortress Press, 2000.

Luther, Martin. *Luther's Small Catechism*. St. Louis: Concordia, 1986.

Luther, Martin. *A Simple Way to Pray* (1535). In *Luther's Works* 43:193–211. 82 vols. projected. St. Louis: Concordia; Philadelphia: Fortress, 1955–1986, 2009–.

———. *Fourteen Consolations* (1520). In *Luther's Works* 42:121–66. 82 vols. projected. St. Louis: Concordia; Philadelphia: Fortress, 1955–1986, 2009–.

———. "Preface to the Wittenberg Edition of Luther's Writings" (1539). In *Luther's Works* 34:283–88. 82 vols. projected. St. Louis: Concordia; Philadelphia: Fortress, 1955–1986, 2009–.

Pruyser, Paul. *The Minister as Diagnostician: Personal Problems in Pastoral Perspective* (Philadelphia, Westminster Press, 1976.

Sauer, Robert C. *Daily Prayer.* 2 vols. St. Louis: Concordia, 1986.

Tappert, Theodore G. *The Book of Concord: The Confessions of the Evangelical Lutheran Church.* Philadelphia: Fortress, 1959.

The Sayings of the Desert Fathers. Translated by Benedicta Ward. London: Mowbray, 1975.

Underhill, Evelyn. "The Teacher's Vocation." In *The Mount of Purification.* New York: Longmans, Gen and Co., 1946.

Walther, C. F. W. *Amerikanisch-Lutherische Pastoraltheologie.* St. Louis: Druckerei der Synode von Missouri, Ohio u. a. Staaten, 1872.

———. *Pastoral Theology.* Translated by Christian C. Tiews. St. Louis: Concordia, 2017.

———. *Law and Gospel.* Translated by Herbert J. A. Bouman. Selected Writings of C. F. W. Walther. St. Louis: Concordia, 1981.

Subject Index

Scripture Index

Old Testament

New Testament